Drunk Japan

Drunk Japan

Law and Alcohol in Japanese Society

MARK D. WEST

OXFORD
UNIVERSITY PRESS

OXFORD
UNIVERSITY PRESS

Oxford University Press is a department of the University of Oxford. It furthers the University's objective of excellence in research, scholarship, and education by publishing worldwide. Oxford is a registered trade mark of Oxford University Press in the UK and certain other countries.

Published in the United States of America by Oxford University Press
198 Madison Avenue, New York, NY 10016, United States of America.

Library of Congress Cataloging-in-Publication Data
Names: West, Mark D., 1968– author.
Title: Drunk Japan : law and alcohol in Japanese society / Mark D. West.
Description: New York, NY : Oxford University Press, [2020] |
Includes bibliographical references and index.
Identifiers: LCCN 2019038103 (print) | LCCN 2019038104 (ebook) |
ISBN 9780190070847 (hardback) | ISBN 9780190070854 |
ISBN 9780190070861 (epub) | ISBN 9780190070878
Subjects: LCSH: Alcoholism—Social aspects—Japan. | Drinking of alcoholic beverages—Social aspects—Japan. | Liquor laws—Japan.
Classification: LCC HV5613 .W48 2019 (print) | LCC HV5613 (ebook) |
DDC 362.2920952—dc23
LC record available at https://lccn.loc.gov/2019038103
LC ebook record available at https://lccn.loc.gov/2019038104

1 3 5 7 9 8 6 4 2

Printed by Integrated Books International, United States of America

For Amber

CONTENTS

PREFACE

When a stranger in Japan tries to strike up a conversation with me in Japanese, there is a nontrivial chance that the subject of alcohol will arise. Sometimes I'm asked if I like sake or Japanese beer, and occasionally I receive an alleged compliment like "You look like someone who can drink a lot." I don't, really, at least not in the U.S. But some people in Japan think non-Japanese people can hold their liquor relatively well, so to them, I might, in fact, look like a person who can drink a lot.

I actually can't drink a lot, and even if I could, I doubt I would. But since I began living, traveling, studying, and working in various capacities in Japan in the 1980s, I have drunk every drink and visited almost every type of drinking establishment mentioned in the judicial opinions that form the basis for this book. I take no pride in that whatsoever, but you should know it.

Perhaps more significant, I have shared drinks in Japan with carpenters, baseball players, sushi chefs, schoolteachers, mechanics, farmers, sumo wrestlers, salarymen, CEOs, artists, engineers, actors, mobsters, and priests (Buddhist, Shinto, and Catholic), as well as legislators, bureaucrats, lawyers, law professors, prosecutors, and police officers. And yes, I've shared drinks with some of the judges who authored the court opinions that are the core of this book. I'm glad I had these varied experiences with wonderful people, and I learned a lot from them. (I can't say the same for them; the combination of my inability and unwillingness to keep pace, at least for the past twenty-five years or so, makes me a bit of a buzzkill.) But there is nothing unusual about these experiences for someone who has spent as much time in Japan as I; they simply reflect life in Japan, or at least segments of it, and they happen to correlate with the stories that are the subject of the book. Still, I won't litter the book with personal anecdotes, as they would merely reflect my singular perspective.

That perspective (and yours) necessarily is informed by observations of other drinking cultures. In fact, it was only after I became thoroughly ensconced in this project that I realized my curiosity about drinking culture is chronic. I spent most of my early childhood in the rural South, with no alcohol in my home, ever, but surrounded by it in ways I did not fully grasp until I was an adult. An hour and a half by car but effectively a world away from New Orleans, I heard rumors of beer on fishing boats, found puzzling the fact that some people apparently used the 70-percent alcohol concoction known as Dr. Tichenor's antiseptic for things other than mosquito bites, and speculated about the mystery that lurked inside the dark building in Sun, Louisiana, with the lighted sign advertising Jax beer; it was the only bar I knew. (The bar burned down and the brewery is now defunct.) I wanted to know more, and apparently I still do.

Fortunately, the court opinions allow us to focus largely on the judges' perspectives, lessening, but not eliminating, biases that I might introduce as a narrator. For readers with experience in Japan, I hope you will both gain new insights and catch glimpses of the familiar through the judicial lens. For readers for whom this is new territory, I hope you'll be equally intrigued by the unfamiliar evidence the law provides about what lurks not only inside in the dark buildings but also across the especially well-lit landscape of drunk Japan.

ACKNOWLEDGMENTS

I owe a tremendous debt to the University of Michigan Law School, my academic home since 1998. The idea for this book grew directly out of conversations with Michigan Law students in my Japanese Law and Criminal Law classes. My colleagues on the Michigan Law faculty have shaped my work in enormous ways: by scholarly example, with critical comments, and through discussions that help define our community values. Financial support was provided in part through the endowments of the Nippon Life Insurance Company and the Sumitomo Bank, Ltd., at the Law School, as well as contributions to the school from Mori Hamada & Matsumoto.

I worked on this book while serving as dean. The book is a reflection of my belief that deans who maintain the intellectual curiosity that led them to higher education are more effective leaders. In most cases they should look for opportunities to do at least one thing they did before becoming dean: teaching, research, service. It's impossible to do any of those things without significant support from many people who care about the institution's success. I'm especially grateful to Robyn Grimes, Rachel Perrell, Shelley Rodgers, Gil Seinfeld, Michele Frasier Wing, and Sarah Zearfoss.

I am thankful for the helpful comments on the manuscript that I received from Allison Alexy, Paul Christensen, Don Herzog (twice!), John Hudson, Lisa Liu, Kyle Logue, Curtis Milhaupt, Bill Miller, Markus Nornes, Bill Novak, Mark Ramseyer, and Kiyoteru Tsutsui. Atsushi Kinami read the manuscript and generously sent me source materials that I would have missed without him.

This book is dedicated to my wife, Amber, whose support was essential and whose feedback was vital despite the fact that, or perhaps because, she is allergic to alcohol.

EXPLANATORY NOTES

Case reporters often use pseudonyms for party names for privacy reasons. Unless otherwise stated, if the case reporter uses the real name of a party, or if I can determine the name from press accounts, I use it. If not, to keep the players straight and to preserve some humanity in the opinions, I occasionally choose different pseudonyms for the parties. Following the convention in Asian studies, Japanese names in the text are presented in the conventional Japanese order, with family names first. Also following convention, I reverse the rule in endnote citations and when Japanese people living outside Japan choose to follow the opposite order.

All translations are mine, and all case facts come from court opinions unless I say otherwise. I use a modified Hepburn system for transliteration, with long vowels doubled (uu, oo, and so on) instead of using macrons. For words that commonly appear in English, I do not further transliterate (including names of cities, like Tokyo instead of Toukyou and Osaka instead of Oosaka; personal names, like Ichiro and Taro instead of Ichirou and Tarou; and words that are increasingly common in English, like shochu instead of shouchuu).

Several measures and terms appear frequently throughout the book:

Money: All yen amounts are converted to dollars at the rate of $1 = 100 yen. The actual average closing prices were 145 in 1990, 108 in 2000, 88 in 2010, 121 in 2015, and 109 in 2019. For purposes of this book, however, the differences won't matter.

Courts: Court cases in Japan begin in one of three places: summary court (438 courts, for civil cases with damages claimed of less than $14,000 and petty criminal cases), family court (fifty courts, with 203 branches and seventy-seven local offices, for domestic relations and personal status cases), or district court (fifty courts and 203 branches, for everything else). District courts hear appeals from summary courts. Eight high courts hear appeals from district courts and family courts. The Supreme Court is the court of last resort. Most cases in this book are from district courts, high courts, or the Supreme Court.

Japanese alcohol units: One *gou* of sake is equal to 180 milliliters, or about six ounces (a small can). One *shou* is equal to 1.8 liters, or about half a gallon (a little more than two bottles, or one magnum, of wine).

1

Drinker's Paradise?

According to the opinion written by the Kyoto District Court, the defendant had worked in water construction for Osaka City since 1954. He did not get along with his boss, the court tells us. On June 16, 1955, he decided to quit his job and look for another. The following day, around noon, he went to work to return documents and submit his resignation. Along the way he stopped at a bar, where he began drinking sake. Around 2 p.m., his friend Tatsuo, a tofu delivery man, stopped by. The defendant began to drink "more than a usual amount," beginning with two or three mugs of *uwazumi* (the top layer of home-brewed sake that remains after everything settles) of an unrefined sake called *doburoku*. Each mug held two *gou* of *doburoku*, for a total of more than a liter.

That the defendant and Tatsuo drank *doburoku*, a drink far more common in the nineteenth century than today, has significance. As Penelope Francks reports, "[T]he unrefined home-brewed version [of sake] known as doburoku was widely produced and consumed in the Tokugawa countryside: villages brewed large quantities for mass drinking at festivals, weddings and other celebrations, but households also made their own and consumed it regularly throughout the day as a kind of food, just as rural Europeans drank weak forms of wine, beer and cider."[1]

Doburoku has virtually vanished from modern case law. In all of the postwar Japanese court opinions that form the database for this book, *doburoku* appears 102 times before 1960 (spelled with various combinations of Japanese characters) but only eleven times thereafter (and one of those mentions is of the Korean version). It appears most prominently in a case popularly known as the "*Doburoku* Case" (*doburoku saiban*) from the 1980s. In that case, the defendant, Maeda Toshihiro, the author of *Let's Make* Doburoku (*Doburoku o Tsukurou*), brewed his own. He was prosecuted for violating liquor laws that prevented unlicensed brewing. He argued that his prosecution violated his constitutional (art. 31) right to life and liberty, claiming that "making one's own liquor in one's own home from one's own ingredients and enjoying drinking is, like cooking and eating one's own food, a completely private act." The court

Drunk Japan. Mark D. West, Oxford University Press (2020) © Oxford University Press.
DOI: 10.1093/oso/9780190070847.001.0001

did not comment on his enjoyment; it focused instead on the government's discretion to tax, and fined him $300.[2] The Tokyo High Court and the Supreme Court agreed.[3]

As that case suggests, *doburoku* is an inexpensive, easily made drink somewhat comparable to moonshine. And that's what our protagonist defendant and Tatsuo chose to drink at the bar. At 3 p.m. they left the bar and went to a pawn shop, where the defendant sold his briefcase for $3. He bought a beer at a liquor and cigarette shop and returned to the bar, where he drank two more mugs. At 5 p.m. he returned home, where he pocketed a dagger.

The defendant went to the park to sumo wrestle with Tatsuo, but it began to drizzle, so they returned to the bar for a third time. At a nearby table three men were drinking shochu (another common Japanese drink; more on that later). One of the three men fell down, and the defendant tried to help him up. The man said, "I'm no woman; stop it." The defendant said, "What the hell is wrong with you?" (*omae nanja*) and threw a cup at him. The man, one of his friends, and the defendant began throwing chairs and fighting.

The owner of the establishment kicked them all out. The fighting stopped. And then the defendant used the dagger to stab one of the men in the chest.

Let us stop here to examine some of the facts. Some of them clearly will inform the court's ruling, as they show mental state, level of intoxication, potential defenses, and other legally relevant matters. Some of them push the narrative—when the dagger is pocketed, we can guess why. But the role of some other facts isn't entirely clear. Why does it matter that Tatsuo is a tofu delivery man? How does the amount received at a pawn shop for a briefcase affect the outcome? As this book will show, the court is getting at something particular to the individuals, giving us information that turns random bits of information into a *doburoku*-soaked story with recognizable characters that fit neatly into specific socioeconomic spaces.

Prosecutors charged the defendant with attempted murder. He argued that he was of unsound mind at the time due to intoxication and therefore could not be criminally liable. That's an amazing and, as we will see, common defense.

The court then analyzed the facts it had just laid out. It hardly discussed the details of the crime: the type of knife, the angle of the blade's entry, the precise injuries it caused. Instead it jumped right to the drinking defense. The court confirmed that the amount of alcohol the defendant drank "exceeded a reasonable amount"; that amount of liquor "usually will put one to sleep." But the defendant sumo wrestled with his friend, even as he fell all over himself, singing and dancing. The court concluded that he was unable to distinguish between right and wrong and was therefore of unsound mind. Accordingly, the defendant was found not guilty.

The court should now stop. There is no need for more words. And yet the court continued, beginning with a discussion of a law that is not directly relevant to the facts of the case:

> Through the Law to Prevent Underage Drinking, our country has prohibited alcohol consumption by minors, and with [the implementation of laws and regulations pertaining to drunk driving, drunk driving is punished], but in all other cases, drinking is permitted. It would be difficult for anyone but a legal expert to understand how, in a case like this, in which the defendant, at lunch, on his way to work, drinks an unacceptably large amount of *uwazumi*, becomes incapable of distinguishing right from wrong, and causes injury, could be declared innocent by this court. Lately there have been many such crimes that disturb social order and violate the rights of others. In order to avoid unease in society, the court, pursuant to the request of the prosecutor regarding the defendant's mental condition, ordered a psychiatric reevaluation, but under our Penal Code, when a person commits a crime without the ability to distinguish right from wrong [he may not be punished], and unless intoxication is made an exception to this rule, this court has no choice but to issue a not guilty verdict. This country is a drinker's paradise [*sake o tashinamu hito no tame ni wa tengoku*]. Among developed countries, it must be quite rare for the law to allow a criminal to be able to overdrink voluntarily, lose capacity, and inflict bodily injury upon another person.

The court then examined the laws of some of those other countries, an issue that was not remotely before it. Australia and Germany, it said, put such people in facilities. The Soviet Union, it noted, also had laws in place to protect the public from such persons. And Anglo-American law, it stated, had long held that intoxication is not a defense to a crime. The Japanese law, the court found, "has been in place since 1908, for roughly a half-century, but if it fails to maintain order, there is no reason to hesitate to revise it." The court then issued its not guilty verdict concurrently with a request that the legislature revise this "imperfection" in the law.[4]

History elucidates the tone of the 1956 opinion. The Allied Occupation, in which consumption of cheap alcohol was widespread and dangerous,[5] ended a mere two years before the events of the case. Japan was struggling with legal and moral issues that remained in the Occupation's wake, as new forms of bars, tea shops, and "late-night coffeehouses" began to proliferate in cities.[6] A methamphetamine epidemic gripped the country.[7] Alcohol consumption patterns changed; from 1948 to 1953 consumption of beer, then considered a foreign beverage, more than quadrupled.[8] Journalistic accounts of crimes by intoxicated people surged briefly in the 1950s.[9] Japan was also lurching toward status as an advanced nation, hence the references to the laws of other countries and the hint that perhaps Japanese law needed modernization.

Japanese law journals often introduce court cases with commentary provided by scholars (and sometimes by the judges themselves; because the commentaries are unsigned, authorship is unknown). The contemporaneous commentary to this case offered some perspective:

> There is nothing particularly unique about this court opinion, which concerns a case of attempted murder under the influence of alcohol in which the defendant was determined to be not guilty as a result of lack of capacity. But the text of the opinion reflects the recent increase in incidents of people drinking themselves into mental incapacity and harming others, disrupting society, and intruding on the rights of individuals. . . . Scholars and practitioners should think seriously about these matters.[10]

They did. Two years later, the Judicial Affairs Committee of the House of Councillors discussed the case, along with the court's "drinker's paradise" (*sakenomi no tengoku*) moniker. It left the law intact.[11] A year after that, as the legal and legislative communities were preparing a public intoxication law, the well-known legal scholar Nishimura Katsuhiko wrote that the court's description of Japan as a "drinker's paradise" "caused quite a sensation." He added, "I understand the court's dilemma."[12] The court, of course, was delivering a sort of lecture on decency, focusing on the dangers not only of alcohol but also of allowing the law to continue as is. It was a statement about both the law and the state of the country.[13]

In this book I use court opinions like this one to examine the role of alcohol in Japan. I examine the laws that the court interprets, its rulings, and its social commentary, but I'm also interested in parsing the facts to tease out details, incongruities, and unspoken assumptions that courts convey, intentionally or otherwise, about Japanese drinking life. I examine the opinions to ask: Out of all the ways that the judges could have framed and described the facts, why did they choose *these* words, or begin and end the narrative at *these* points in time, and what do those choices mean? The fact that the men went to the park and time passed might have been necessary to tell our opening story coherently, but the particular act of sumo wrestling was not. And yet there it was. That the parties' drinks contained a certain percentage of alcohol mattered; that it was bottom-of-the-barrel alcohol did not. Or did it? Why is it there, if it didn't matter?

It's not that U.S. courts don't do this. They just do it differently. And it's not that Japanese drinking life is so utterly bizarre; my exploration of it in this book is certainly not intended to be a tale that ends in "and that's how odd Japan is," a pervasive and troubling news-reporting style. For a bit of comparison, then, here's a case from the United States. The legal rule at issue is not relevant here; it is the facts—which take virtually the same form here that they would in a Japanese opinion—that matter:

> Prior to the accident, plaintiff had been out on a first date with Keith Young, with whom she had developed an online relationship. The couple started their date at Chili's, located on Route 9 in Freehold sometime after 8:00 p.m. Before being seated for dinner, plaintiff ordered one Appletini, and during the course of the dinner, consumed two or three more Appletinis. After dinner, she and Young decided to continue their evening at another establishment. They left Chili's around 11:15 p.m. in one car, with plaintiff driving, and headed towards Club Abyss, where they arrived approximately thirty minutes later. At Club Abyss, plaintiff recalls that she and Young danced and she continued to drink alcoholic beverages. After she drank a second beer, plaintiff recalled that she "continued dancing" but "lost track from there." According to plaintiff, she did not fall or spill any beer while dancing and was "never loud" or "obnoxious."
>
> In his deposition testimony, Young confirmed that plaintiff's demeanor was never loud at anytime during the course of their evening together. He described plaintiff as engaging in a "normal" conversation with him at Chili's, where she talked about real estate. He believed that he could have had "up to three" beers and believed that plaintiff had a "couple of drinks" which he described as possibly being "reddish," "blue," or "pink." When they left Chili's, they walked to her car and plaintiff suggested that she drive to Club Abyss, since she knew where she was going. Nothing in her demeanor led Young, at that point, to believe that plaintiff was intoxicated. Plaintiff obeyed all traffic signals and "wasn't . . . speeding or going crazy on the road" as they traveled to Club Abyss. Once they arrived, he recalled they had a shot together and she may have had another shot, but he did not know. He testified that plaintiff did "loosen[] up a little bit as far as the dancing around[.]"[14]

Welcome to New Jersey. Some of the facts might sound familiar, but they would be peculiar in a Japanese court opinion. The drinker is a woman (and the case states her real name, which would rarely occur in Japan). Only two people are drinking—not one, and not a group, as is more often the Japanese norm. They are at a Chili's restaurant, and although there are in fact Chili's restaurants in Japan, they are all on U.S. military bases. The woman is drinking an Appletini—you can order that at some bars in Japan, but at most you'll have to explain what it is, and then they won't have the ingredients. She drank beer after the liquor, not before—the reverse of the Japanese order. They danced at Club Abyss, where they drank shots as a dating couple. Not in Japan—and that's among the details I want to use law to explore.

I reviewed over five thousand Japanese court opinions for this book. My research relies heavily on RELX Group's continuously updated online database, Lexis AS ONE, which contains over a quarter-million Japanese court opinions, including every official and unofficially published case since July 1944. I began by retrieving and examining every case in the database in which a court was required to adjudicate an intoxication defense, the primary issue in which I initially was interested. Next I expanded the search to all cases connected to those cases, and I soon began to accumulate many additional cases through my regular reading of Japanese law journals and case reporters. I then probed systematically and thoroughly, conducting hundreds of searches for various Japanese legal and alcohol-related terms or other concepts that might provide insight into the role of alcohol in Japan. A sampling of those searches includes words commonly associated with drinking and law in both languages (drinking: "beer," "drunk," "teetotaler"; law: "intoxication," "drunk driving," "blood alcohol level") as well as the Japanese translations of culturally loaded words and phrases like "whisky and water," "alcohol habit," "medium mug," "drinking party," "coming-of-age day," "bottle keep," and so on. (A comparatively culturally loaded U.S. list might have included terms like "pregame," "bachelor party," and lots of wine-related words, such as "oenophile," "wine tasting," and "wine country.") I also read many cases in search of the *absence* of alcohol, such as cases in which a wedding is mentioned but alcohol is not, as well as non-alcohol-related cases that might provide parallels to drinking, such as cases of people who suffer seizures while driving. I began this chapter with the "drinker's paradise" case to provide historical context for the cases that lie ahead, but I rely more heavily on more recent cases, and most that I have chosen for inclusion in this book are from after 2000.

Some readers might prefer a more tightly defined construction of the evidence. In a few areas I provide it by limiting the field of cases by statute, area of law, or concept. But given the choice of a strictly defined data set or a rich account of the subject beyond legal rules, I chose the latter and simply read everything I thought might be useful.

Equipped with these cases, my goal is to use law to illuminate the complexity of alcohol in Japanese society and to use alcohol to illuminate the complexity of Japanese law. As for the former, although the "drinker's paradise" language had vanished from court opinions by the 1970s, Japan continues to be seen as such by many people both in and out of Japan: The leading guidebook in English on drinking in Japan calls Japan the "best place to drink alcohol in the world" (in a chapter entitled "Japan: A Drinker's Paradise").[15] Japan's drinking culture includes elements and tropes of permissiveness that are familiar (such as drunken salarymen and a *kanpai* ["cheers"] exclaimed over a beer) and some that are not (such as railway cameras that use technology to detect those drunken salarymen before they fall on the tracks[16] or widely available fake beer made for children to enable them to join in their beer-drinking parents' *kanpai*[17]). Etiquette guides for foreigners abound with tips to help navigate the world of Japanese drinking (e.g., "If you got drunk and don't remember anything from the night before, don't worry. The Japanese forgive easily, and as long as no harm was done, no one will ever mention it!"[18]). Even the Basic Law on Measures against Alcohol-Related Health Problems begins (art. 1), "Alcoholic beverages enrich our lives and alcohol traditions and culture are deeply engrained in our lives."[19] The Ministry of Justice agrees, noting that drinking "plays an important cultural role, as it encourages human relations, relieves stress, and revitalizes, and society is relatively tolerant even of people who 'completely let go' while intoxicated."[20]

At least a kernel of truth lurks behind each element of this vision, but the role of alcohol in Japanese society cannot be so easily expressed. The law—under which even a simple word like "drunk" has multiple expressions and meanings—provides rich descriptions of four broad areas of drinking in Japan. First, the who (and with whom), what, where, when, and why of drinking emerges largely from the facts of the cases (particularly in chapter 2). Second, Japanese law provides descriptions, sometimes concrete, sometimes not, of how drunk is too drunk (particularly in chapters 3 and 4). Third, the law, broadly defined, creates an uneven picture regarding when drunk people and those around them are responsible—or not—for behavior (chapter 5). Finally, the cases in particular show how at least one group of people—the bureaucrats who form the Japanese judiciary—think about all of these issues, whether they intended to express those opinions ("drinker's paradise") or not (throughout, but particularly in chapters 6 and 7). By exploring the role of alcohol in many different cases and contexts, I aim to make drunk Japan, with all its richness and complexity, understandable, and perhaps even familiar.

The second part of this book's goal is also important: Just as law can teach us about alcohol, so too can alcohol teach us about law. The traditional view of the legal system in Japan goes something like this: Japan is a civil law country that relies primarily on a legislated code (like most of Europe), not judicial precedent (like the United Kingdom and the United States). As such, judges are uniformly trained to view problems similarly and write consistent court opinions, with little role for judicial activism.[21] Like judges in other centralized bureaucratic judiciaries, Japanese judges usually enter the judiciary for life, so their decision-making and writing styles lend themselves to routine.

In the particular case of Japan, an even stronger notion of uniformity, consistency, and predictability has become conventional wisdom in the comparative law field. University of Tokyo Law Professor Dan Foote argues that "nameless, faceless" judges in Japan are seen as "ideal," as "no matter who sits in the judge's chair, the court opinions that are produced will be similar."[22] Harvard Law's Mark Ramseyer makes the case along a different dimension, arguing that Japanese judges "do not pretend to offer the level of particularized inquiry that we expect in American courts."[23] Instead they "relentlessly systematize and routinize" and employ "bureaucratized courts" in which "fewer of those individualized [American] circumstances matter."[24] Kyoto University Professor Emeritus Tanase Takao expresses a similar view, finding merit in "standardized compensation" in Japanese courts that leads to "simplicity and accessibility to the wider public."[25]

These accounts ring true in some areas of the law, such as auto accidents, products liability, and medical malpractice, in which young Japanese assistant judges in fact spend considerable time at their desks looking at grids and spreadsheets. But in this book I take a deep dive into the Japanese case law, focusing not only on outcomes but also on the words the judges use in their narratives, to present a different Japanese legal system—a system that is highly particularized, often contradictory and unpredictable, and not remotely routine.

In short, I aim to show—through alcohol—that the conventional wisdom about the Japanese legal system is, not to put too fine a point on things, wrong. And not just a little wrong; as a characterization of the entirety of Japanese law, it utterly fails. Japanese justice in the cases in this book is personal and real. At its most extreme, law in Japanese courts as it relates to drinking is hyperindividualized: Among other things, situation-specific facts can trump blood alcohol content standards, a defendant's individually measured tolerance for alcohol can determine guilt, and individual judges disagree broadly about what kinds of alcohol-related behavior are acceptable. The facts, then, are particularly significant in these cases because judges tell us what traits, conditions, and circumstances, some of which are quite specific to the case, matter.

Some of these details can be chalked up to good storytelling. Japanese judges tell stories in more detail than judges in many other civil law countries, and one of the hallmarks of a good storyteller is an ability to instill in the reader a sense of inevitability so that when the end of the story arrives, it feels right.[26] Japanese judicial stories usually feature interesting characters and rarely have plot holes or missing dialogue. The stories are complete, and when Japanese judges drop clues in their narratives, they often do so as a way of leading the reader toward a predetermined conclusion. If a Chekhovian gun is on the wall in a Japanese court opinion, it might not necessarily go off, but it will still tell us something—something about the gun, the wall, the room, or, more likely, the owner.

Still, it's not entirely clear who is decorating these gun-covered walls. Cases, of course, begin as actual events. Those events are then distilled by people—parties, witnesses, experts, with all their flaws and biases—into stories that are then retold by attorneys, whether in the courtroom or in the briefs they file with the court. Japanese judges are busy, and they can save time by cutting and pasting facts from the briefs and into their opinions with minimal editing. They often do so strategically, but it is of course possible that at least a few of the facts that I deem relevant made their way into the opinion by judicial accident, in which case they might tell us more about lawyers, or about parties, procedure, or legal argument, than they do the judges' actual thought process.

Moreover, the cases are not a random slice of jurisprudence. Perhaps issues of intoxication are necessarily tangled and therefore lead to more elaborate, more interesting, or more humanizing storytelling. (As a recent uncredited meme puts it, "Alcohol . . . because no great story ever got started with a glass of milk.") But alcohol-related cases aren't the sole outliers; there are other large swaths of the law, particularly those that deal with relationships, in which a similar case can be made.[27]

The fact that these cases *are* about alcohol, a beverage with many variations, each of which has cultural significance, and the way it is consumed, with all its taboos and rituals, means that the facts often reveal much beyond the bottle, especially the importance of class and social status in Japan. Purposely or otherwise, courts often let readers know directly or indirectly whether the characters in the stories are rich or poor, male or female, young or old, educated or uneducated, members of organized crime syndicates—and as such, likely both poor and members of an ethnic or social minority[28]—or civilians. Some class-related specific correlations emerge: If a defendant frequents a certain kind of club, he probably will drive drunk; if he drinks a certain kind of alcohol, he probably will kill someone; if he plays a certain drinking game, he will be found not guilty of sexual assault of the woman with whom he played. And if we change "he" to "she," in many cases the storytelling, and sometimes the outcomes, differ. The calculus is not always exact, but the cases show clear correlations nonetheless because the judges create them.[29]

One aim of this book, as I use law to illuminate the role of alcohol in Japanese society, is to connect the status- and situation-laden cultural dots, even when judges do not do so explicitly, to make sense of both the outcomes of cases and the processes through which those outcomes are reached. As for outcomes, if upon first read the outcome of a particular case doesn't make sense, a likely explanation often can be found in individual characteristics at which the facts hint. As for processes, if judges occasionally seem to be random in their choices of whether to use evidence-based, scientific approaches to intoxication or their own discretion to determine whether a defendant was drunk, clues as to why can often be seen in the way they talk about the individuals involved.

These cases of hyperindividualized justice often make interesting stories, but they have broader significance beyond my primary claims about law and alcohol. Japan is the third largest economy in the world (behind the United States and China), and alcohol plays a significant role in daily lives and business culture. Knowing how people drink there, then, is a useful step to understanding social practices and business norms. Japan can also potentially be a useful schoolhouse for other developed democracies, as it seems to have figured out, for instance, how to have plenty of drunks but relatively little drunk driving. Finally, the cases help contextualize seeming contradictions often observed in everyday Japan, including this one described by Amy Borovoy: "It is not unusual to see men in suits passed out on train platforms or street corners in after-hours commercial districts of Tokyo, or to see pools of vomit on train platforms and street corners, sights that strike many visitors as incongruous with the general level of safety and decorum in public spaces in Japan."[30]

Although that particular sight is common in both real life and the case law, the cases are not necessarily representative of real Japanese drinking life. I've (mostly) chosen cases that mention drinking, and I'm using those cases to create a picture of drinking—excluding all the times when people in Japan drink and don't wind up in court opinions, which often occurs because drinking goes awry. Among the real-life phenomena that do not appear in the cases are *toso* (a medicinal New Year's drink made with sake), meticulous ice carving with knives and mallets at upscale cocktail bars, and the Toyama prefecture ritual in which people pour sake into the mouths of live fish to ward off the bad luck that is said to accompany certain years of people's lives (especially year thirty-three for women and year forty-two for men).[31] Those elements are fundamental in some corners of Japanese society but do not lead to the tragic events about which judges often opine.

Still, three factors give me some confidence that the opinions have more than a passing correlation to real Japanese drinking culture. First, the way people drink is often unrelated to the tragedy that is the subject of the opinion. Although *intoxication* plays a large role in many of the cases, the *act* of drinking alcohol and the rituals that accompany it sometimes are sideshows. The descriptions of drinking, then, often reach beyond the confrontational or tragic nature of the cases to provide glimpses of more everyday situations. In other words, not all people who drink in the cases get behind the wheel or punch someone; sometimes they just drink.

Second, others have studied aspects of Japanese drinking life from other angles, and their descriptions often correlate nicely with the picture that court accounts provide. Stephen Smith's 1988 dissertation, "Drinking and Sobriety in Japan," describes Japanese drinking practices and the treatment of alcoholism.[32] More recently, Amy Borovoy's *The Too-Good Wife* studies Japanese women who manage male alcoholism so that it does not disrupt society,[33] and Paul Christensen's *Japan, Alcoholism, and Masculinity* looks particularly at alcoholism in Japanese men.[34] Literature abounds in Japanese, much of it on what is called "the alcoholism society."[35] The English-language media contains thousands of human interest stories that depict aspects of Japanese attitudes toward alcohol, many of them focusing on the public presence or absence of drunken salarymen or the rituals of workplace drinking. I rely on these nonjudicial accounts throughout the book to complement, and only occasionally to counterpoint, the Japan the judges depict in their opinions.

Third, judges drink. That they do so means that the insights in the cases come not from outside spectators of real Japanese drinking life but from a subset of its participants.

Before we turn to the cases, let's briefly discuss these judges. The fact that they drink would surprise many people in Japan. As one legal journalist explains in a book written for a general audience, "Judges are always getting asked questions like, 'Have you ever drunk at a red lantern [a particular kind of drinking establishment that serves food]?'" The journalist's response: "When I was working as a reporter in the press club for the Tokyo High Court, I shared drinks many times with the judges, and we even played mahjong all night."[36] In a more academic work, two Osaka District Court judges explain that judges self-categorize their "hobbies" for "reducing stress" as "playing tennis, golfing, playing baseball, climbing mountains, drinking, singing karaoke, and others."[37] In a similar vein, novelist Mishima Yukio lists the hobbies of judges of a fictional Osaka High Court in *Runaway Horses*: "[S]ome read novels, others took up the changes and No plays of the Kanzé School, and still others gathered to write haiku and make sketches illustrating the poems. Most of these diversions, however, served as pretexts for getting together to do some drinking."[38]

That a judge might have a drinking hobby would be surprising to some because the Japanese judiciary has a well-defined image of decorum and seriousness. The Supreme Court bureaucracy chooses young assistant judges from the best of the best minds in the country. They study at a handful of universities, excel at the bar exam, prove themselves in their final stages of training, and work extraordinarily hard. The court opinions they write are usually very carefully crafted—in part because judges want to succeed within the institutional hierarchy, and in part because careful people self-select for the job. Japan has only one court system, not a hodgepodge of systems as in the United States, which has elected and appointed officials of varying backgrounds on its benches. Judicial training in Japan is similarly unified; final legal training and certification occurs at one institution, not one of over two hundred law schools and more than fifty state bar systems. Judges often socialize with other judges—sometimes exclusively. If a young male judge is about to marry and you get one guess as to the identity of his bride-to-be, "daughter of a senior judge" is a safe choice.

In fact, a frequent criticism of Japanese judges is that their hard work, selection process, and lifestyle mold them into elite bureaucrats who are isolated from the rest of society. Judges, it is often said, know little about the lives of ordinary people. They work separately and often live separately—together. A 2010 speech to assistant judges by Monguchi Masahito, chief judge of the Nagoya High Court, printed in a leading Japanese law journal, laments the criticism:

> Judges are heavily criticized for not knowing the ways of the world. Of course, it is shameful to be asked whether one knows the ways of the world, and the only response is to bow one's head frankly. Even so, a categorical expression like "judges don't know the way of the world" is not very lawyerly.
>
> Now, the author La Bruyère, along with Montaigne and La Rochefoucauld, was a prominent French moralist. He was born in 1645 in Paris, studied law, became a member of the Paris bar, and then bought a post in the revenue department at Caen.[39]

Judge Monguchi went on to discuss La Bruyère's novel *Caractères* and its lessons for the Japanese judiciary. Of course, Judge Monguchi was addressing an educated legal audience, both in person and in print, and he chose his words accordingly. But for those who raise the criticism that the judge discusses, the fact that he stakes his position on references to seventeenth-century French literature proves the point: Judges seem to inhabit a world very different from that of ordinary people in Japan.

The elite status of Japanese judges comes from their position and not necessarily their compensation. According to the most recent Ministry of Health, Labor, and Welfare survey (2016 data), average household income in Japan is roughly $50,000, and median household income is roughly $40,000.[40] Japanese assistant judges earn roughly $27,000 annually. Assistant judges may be promoted to judge after ten years; their starting salary at that position is about $50,000. The most highly ranked ordinary judge earns $110,000; a Supreme Court justice earns $145,000; and the chief judge of the Supreme Court earns $200,000.[41] By comparison, every U.S. district court judge earns more ($210,900) than the chief of Japan's Supreme Court.[42] Over the course of a career, Japanese judicial compensation is quite good, but judges don't actually rise above middle class until midcareer.[43] Still, in terms of social standing, Japanese judges are definitively the upper echelon.

The world in which Japanese judges function encourages conformity. The Japanese codes of civil and criminal procedure set forth the basics of what must be included in a judge's work product, the judicial opinion.[44] The Legal Training and Research Institute, at which all judges complete their training, goes further. Since the late 1950s, for instance, judges-in-training are taught, according to a judge and University of Tokyo lecturer, that an opinion in a civil suit takes the following form: "(1) case number, case name, date of oral argument, title, parties, their representatives, and so on, (2) the order of the court [*shubun*], (3) the facts, including (a) the parties' requests to the court and (b) the parties' arguments, (4) the reasons for the decision, and (5) the seal of the court or judge."[45] The Institute publishes textbooks on how to write both civil and criminal opinions (supplemented by forms created by courts[46]),[47] and potential recruits who do not conform to the style cannot enter the judiciary (they become lawyers).

The drafting process also discourages originality. At the district court level, judges may not rule on a case alone until they have five years' experience on the bench.[48] Until then, they sit on three-judge panels with more senior judges. The junior judge generally writes the first draft of the opinion, which is approved by the midcareer judge on the panel, and finally the senior, presiding judge signs off.[49] Only at the Supreme Court may a judge issue a dissenting or concurring opinion, and even then, the form is relatively consistent. Any personality in an opinion, then, must occur within a relatively constricted genre—and again, as in any civil law system, we should thus expect to find predictable, general opinions.

For readers of Japanese opinions, this devotion to form is convenient. U.S. court opinions are more likely than Japanese opinions to stray from the core of a case. Although older Japanese cases tend to use more legal jargon than U.S. cases, since 1990, under the motto "Judicial opinions that parties can read" (*toujisha ga yonde wakaru hanketsubun*), opinions have become more accessible.[50] The 2009 establishment of a lay judge system in which ordinary citizens sit on panels with judges in certain criminal cases further encourages a simple, patterned form of opinion. (I will point out the few cases in this book in which the system was used.) If I want to read an opinion that explores all issues thoroughly, I prefer the U.S. style; if I want an opinion that gets to the facts and resolves the case systematically, I prefer the Japanese.

The fact that I have a preference prompts a caveat to this book: I use the cases in a way they were not intended. Judges write opinions primarily to settle disputes, and in Japan judges state that their audience is the litigants, and occasionally the public.[51] Their opinions are not meant to form a database for examination of social constructs and individual details, especially not by a non-Japanese scholar (which arguably gives me an advantage at certain kinds of interpretation, as my assumptions often differ from the ones shared by the judges and their predominantly Japanese readership). Judges, lawyers, and legal academics need to decide which facts matter to determine the *ratio decidendi* of the precedent case—the basis for the court's decision. They make distinctions between material facts and immaterial facts; only the material facts matter as precedent. Significant ink has been spilled in both the English[52] and the Japanese literature (the Japanese often cites the English[53]) on the topic, which one of the primary author-participants later called "a somewhat tedious controversy,"[54] and I will not add to that debate. I assume that when judges write things like "drinker's paradise," they are inviting, or at least not discouraging, a different sort of interpretation of their words.

A final point on judges that contrasts with the "drinker's paradise" language: Although I have known several Japanese judges who had drinking problems, I can find only one published case of a drinking judge. In a 1986 case, on a 10 a.m. investigative site visit in a civil case, a judge and a litigant had the following conversation, as described by the court:

> The plaintiff criticized the judge's decision not to issue a temporary injunction. The judge said, "It's my decision whether to issue a temporary injunction, and I don't take orders from you," and "Shut up. If you keep talking like that I'll reject your claim," to which the plaintiff replied, "Please reject it. Reject it, and I'll appeal to the high court." The two continued to bicker, and as the plaintiff tried to get his point across, the judge told him in a loud voice, "Are you stupid?" [*bakaka*]. (There is no debate regarding the fact that the judge used the word "stupid.")
>
> Upon hearing this, the plaintiff said to the judge, "Stupid? Is it okay for a judge to speak in such a way?" [*osshatte iindesuka*, a formal expression], and "You've been drinking, haven't you. Are you ranting like this because you've been drinking or because you haven't had enough to drink?"

That's a great line, and we can thank the court for its inclusion. The plaintiff sued, claiming defamation and a denial of his constitutional right to access to the courts (art. 32). The court denied the defamation claim, stating that although being called stupid was "inappropriate," it was insufficient for such an action because it did not lower his social standing (more on that standard in chapter 7).

The court then evaluated the claim of judicial drunkenness to determine whether the plaintiff was deprived of access to the courts:

> According to the evidence, on the day of the site visit, the judge drank at dawn, and when he arrived at the site, there is some suspicion that he still carried the faint smell of alcohol, but the plaintiff was the only person who noticed it.

> The judge smelled slightly of alcohol, and the fact that he conducted a site inspection in a situation in which the smell still lingered can only be called an unscrupulous [*fukinshin*; also "imprudent" or "shameless"] act, but the judge did not lose his decision-making ability as a result of the alcohol.

That's all. The court found the act shameless and the "stupid" comment inappropriate, but it commented no further. It offered no comment on the judge's statement that although he did not drink in the courthouse, and he did not drink *every* day, he did, on occasion, "drink a cup or two of sake when he woke up early in the morning around three or four, leaving the smell of alcohol on his breath when he arrived at the courthouse."[55]

A couple of takeaways lie in that sentence. First, note what is absent: Unlike the "drinker's paradise" case, the court didn't scold. Second, why would the judge admit to starting his day with a couple of drinks, and how could the court repeat it with the literary equivalent of a straight face? To answer such questions, throughout this book I follow Thomas Kuhn's suggestion, "[L]ook first for the apparent absurdities in the text and ask yourself how a sensible person could have written them."[56] Developing an understanding of how sensible people can write such words requires more information about how people drink in Japan.

2

How to Drink in Japan

In a court opinion, the phrase "_______ while drinking" (*sake o nominagara*)—drinking in combination with some other verb—is often a harbinger of bad behavior. The words appear across a broad range of legal contexts. From a murder case: "The defendant returned home around 5:30, and after he went to his room on the second floor, where he *used dangerous drugs while drinking,* his mother called him downstairs to eat." Drinking alone in one's room, in combination with the "dangerous" drugs, signals trouble: He stabbed his parents to death.[1] From an assault case: "In the back room, the three of them *talked while drinking,* and the mood soured between victim and the victim's sister, but after an argument, things returned to normal." The drinking and talking in a "back room," as emotions flare, is Steinbeck-level foreshadowing: The defendant stabbed the victim in the gut with a sashimi knife.[2] From a tort case: "Beginning around 10 a.m. on April 9, 2000, the victim began fishing near the Yatsurugi Bridge on the Shinnaka River. His friend B showed up around 11:30, and his friend C joined around 1:30 in the afternoon, and they began *fishing while drinking.*" Fishing while drinking might sound relaxing, but it signals danger: A drinking party developed, an argument started, and the defendant pushed the victim, severing his spinal cord. He died.[3] From a sexual harassment case (these are frequent): "On the bullet train from Shin-Yokohama to Kyoto, for a period of about two hours, the defendant requested sexual intercourse with the plaintiff, *saying, while drinking,* 'If you're not going to have sex, I wouldn't have hired you in the first place,' 'If you weren't going to have sex with me, why did you go on this trip with me in the green [first-class] car? This costs me, you know.' "[4] The phrase "while drinking" was unnecessary to establish culpability given the things that the defendant was saying, but the court threw it in just the same.

Bad acts also occur in the "drinking seats" (*shuseki* or, less commonly, *sake no seki*), a phrase that can mean trouble or minimize the seriousness of events that occur there. The phrase might simply be translated as "drinking party," but it's a party that can be held with very few attendees. A defendant attempts to discount his serious threats by arguing that they were merely "jokes from the

Drunk Japan. Mark D. West, Oxford University Press (2020) © Oxford University Press.
DOI: 10.1093/oso/9780190070847.001.0001

drinking seats."[5] Murder-for-insurance-money schemes are hatched "in the drinking seats."[6] Customers "begin arguing in the drinking seats."[7] Sexual harassment is frequently located in the drinking seats: Alleged sexual harassers "force cheek dances" in the drinking seats[8] or say "I want to rape you" in the drinking seats[9] or coerce victims to drink one-on-one because "people can express their true feelings more easily" in the drinking seats.[10] Tabloids defame professors who falsely are said to "commit lewd acts with women in the drinking seats."[11] A defendant attempts to minimize the evidentiary impact of a surreptitious peek at a cell phone by claiming that she "only did so once, in the drinking seats."[12] Employees receive advice from bosses in the drinking seats[13] and criticize executives in the drinking seats.[14] And when an employee confiding to his boss in the drinking seats declares his intent to retire, courts find that the statement was not an actual resignation; because it occurred in the drinking seats, it must not have been serious.[15]

And so on. By telling us that actions occurred while drinking or in the drinking seats, courts make clear that those actions occurred in a setting in which the strictures of ordinary life do not necessarily apply. But other rules might apply: the rituals of Japanese drinking life. The opinions provide an unintentional guidebook to those rituals. Consider, for instance, the Japanese version of "cheers," *kanpai,* which appears in a wide range of cases. Sometimes the word easily translates to "cheers" (but not in the British "thank you" or Hawaiian "aloha" sense; its usage is confined to the alcohol setting). From a 2010 rape case: "[A]fter A entered the karaoke box, and after she drank with the opening *kanpai,* she had little to drink."[16] We learn not only that a party starts with *kanpai* but that one can have a party in a karaoke box (a private room or, in rural areas, a trailer, with a karaoke machine). Sometimes the word conveys something more akin to a formal toast, as in a 2010 case that adjudicated the applicability of the Constitution's freedom of religion clause to a mayor's congratulatory speech delivered at a shrine: "The order of the inauguration ceremony was as follows: opening words, president's greetings, congratulations to attendees, introduction to officers, introduction to guests, explanation of plans, words of thanks from the priest, *kanpai,* greetings, and, finally, closing words. There were 120 attendees and the ceremony was forty minutes long."[17] From this language it is clear that the *kanpai* can function as a significant, stand-alone element in a ceremony.

It is these kinds of insights that I want to explore in this chapter. Before burrowing through legal rules in later chapters, I want to set the stage here, using the facts of the cases to explore the broad contours of alcohol in Japanese society: the what, where, and why of drinking in Japan.

But first, a preliminary question to which the cases offer no easy answer: How much? In an international comparison, Japanese alcohol consumption is neither particularly high nor particularly low. According to the World Health Organization, recorded per capita consumption in Japan averages 6.9 liters of alcohol annually, just below the United States (8.8) and far below Estonia (15.8) and Lithuania (13.8), which lead the world. If unrecorded alcohol consumption is included, Moldova, Hungary, and Russia bolt to the top of the list. Most of Japan's alcohol consumption is recorded.[18]

Japanese alcohol consumption differs in two significant ways from that of the United States. First, the United States has a higher prevalence of diagnosed health consequences, including alcohol use disorders (13.9 percent in the United States compared to 3.4 in Japan) and alcohol dependence (7.7 percent compared to 1.1). But Japan has a slightly higher percentage than the United States of "heavy episodic" or "binge" male drinkers, those who drank more than 60 grams of pure alcohol on at least one occasion in the previous month, an amount roughly equal to four or five beers, glasses of wine, or 1.5-ounce shots. Fifty-three percent of Japanese male drinkers fall in that category, while 50 percent reach that mark in the United States.[19] In Japan, 12.7 percent of men and 3.4 percent of women report that they drink that much *every day*.[20]

Japan differs from other countries in its attitudes toward alcohol. In a 2017 Pew Research Center study, residents of forty countries were asked whether certain practices and customs were "morally acceptable." Japan was relatively permissive on most issues (especially when compared to predominantly Muslim countries), including divorce and gambling, suggesting that there might be differences in the interpretation of "moral" that are of such significance that we should discount the comparative findings. But the issue on which Japan differs most markedly, perhaps enough to overcome the discount, is alcohol consumption. At the bottom of the chart, only 1 percent of Pakistani respondents said that drinking alcohol was morally acceptable; 32 percent of U.S. respondents agreed. And at the other end of the spectrum, Japan, which has no major religion that significantly discourages alcohol consumption, the percentage of respondents who said that drinking was morally *unacceptable* was the lowest of all countries, at 6 percent.[21] Other cross-cultural studies concur: One finds that "[o]nly in Japan did the response 'getting drunk is all right' ever receive a relatively high endorsement";[22] another finds that the "major differences in attitudes" between Japanese and Japanese Americans "are that the Japanese associated spending time with small children with a situation appropriate for drinking," while "Japanese Americans associate spending time with small children with a situation inappropriate for drinking."[23]

The Japanese government often presents the data on drinking as cause for alarm. The Ministry of Health, Labor, and Welfare as well as the National Cabinet Office publicize that 8.6 million Japanese are binge drinkers, 4.4 million are suspected alcoholics, and 800,000 are alcoholic patients who require medical care.[24] Those numbers come from a Ministry-supported academic study that describes the situation as a serious social problem that requires government action.[25] Men in particular are a concern; the Ministry of Justice compiled nine government studies, each with a different methodology and in a different time period. Across those studies the percentage of male drinkers ranges from 66.6 to 90.8, and the percentage of men who drank every day varies from 29.7 to 44.5.[26]

The Ministry of Health, Labor, and Welfare embarked on a campaign in 2000 to reduce the number of binge drinkers, those daily 60-gram imbibers. The Ministry's data differed from the World Health Organization data. The Ministry's baseline in the campaign was 1996, when, according to their data, 4.1 percent of men and 0.3 percent of women drank that amount. The stated goal was to reduce those numbers to 3.2 percent and 0.2 percent. But at the end of the campaign, in 2009, the numbers had actually *risen* to 4.7 and 0.4.[27]

What

What are they drinking? The three most common kinds of alcohol drunk in Japan are:

Sake

Made from fermented rice, sake has been a staple in Japan for well over one thousand years.[28] It is usually served in a *gou* of 180 milliliters. Ten *gou* constitute one 1,800-milliliter *shou,* a little more than twice the size of a bottle of wine, a little less than a magnum. Sake is generally 15 to 20 percent alcohol. A *gou* of sake can be found for $5 to $10, but luxury brands are priced much higher. Sake varies in type and quality—connoisseurs can break down sake into several types (*junmai, honjozo, ginjo, daiginjo*)—but the case law does not reflect the differences.

In Japanese, "sake" refers to alcohol in general, and the drink that is referred to in English as "sake" is *nihonshu* ("Japanese liquor," frequently used in cases) or *seishu* ("clear liquor," used in tax law). I use "sake" in this book because of its common English usage.

Shochu

Shochu is Japan's indigenous distilled beverage, usually made from sweet potatoes, rice, barley, or buckwheat. It is served in the same measures as sake but is considerably more potent. Regular shochu most often is 25 percent alcohol, but high-end shochu can surpass 40 percent, a strength equal to vodka. A regular

720-milliliter bottle of the cheap stuff might cost $7, while $50 bottles are available for more expensive tastes.

Shochu is not even a close cousin of sake. As the leading English book on shochu explains, "[L]et's get one thing straight—shochu should never be confused with nihonshu. This is something that countless people from the shochu and nihonshu industries in Japan have asked me to stress. . . . Nihonshu, which is known as saké outside of Japan and sometimes called *seishu* domestically, is a drink brewed from polished rice. Quite simply, shochu is distilled, but nihonshu is not."[29]

Sake held a "near monopoly" in Japan until the middle of the twentieth century. Shochu was historically a drink of last resort in rural areas, and it "took on an image as the means for the poor to get drunk quickly that was not really lost until *shochu* was reinvented as a fashionable cocktail ingredient in the 1980s."[30]

Shochu consumption is now ubiquitous, and while not a direct indicator of any particular social status, it certainly does not suggest upper class. Consider a review in the *Journal of Japanese Studies* of the leading book on male alcoholism in Japan: "[T]here are in my opinion many problems with this book, beginning with the cover photograph. This photo is of a grey-haired man sitting on a sidewalk next to two vending machines and fingering the opening of an overturned bottle of Suntory Nanko *shochu*. This is exactly the type of problematic image that reproduces stereotypes of alcoholism as associated with the failed masculinities of day laborers and homeless men." [31] Note the detail in that comment: The reviewer took care to identify the brand. (It's not very expensive; $8 or so for a 720-milliliter bottle of 25 percent alcohol.) Of course, the image of a man sitting on a sidewalk with a bottle by vending machines does not suggest success; Edward Fowler's 1996 study of Tokyo's poor day laborers likewise prominently features alcohol in both the narrative and the accompanying photographs.[32] But note here the reviewer's ability to make the correlation between the label and class. (Judges can do the same.)

Beginning in the early 2000s, however, shochu became increasingly untethered from class, sex, and age. Once associated largely with older middle-class men, shochu expanded its audience to younger people, becoming a symbol of cool largely for men in their twenties and thirties during the "shochu boom."[33] Specialty bars emerged, and new tastes proliferated, including a 43 percent alcohol-by-volume vodka-substitute shochu marketed exclusively outside of Japan, made "specifically for mixology."[34]

Shochu is produced at distilleries throughout Japan, but primarily on the southern island of Kyushu, which has the highest per capita consumption of the drink[35] and among the highest levels of alcohol consumption generally.[36]

Beer

Beer is a relative newcomer in Japan. Although imported beer was available soon after Japan opened to the West in the 1850s, it was an American who opened the first brewery in 1869 or 1870 and produced what later would become Kirin Beer.[37] Still, beer was said to have, as the scholar and statesman Fukuzawa Yukichi put it, an "extremely bitter taste" and was not immediately popular.[38] But by the late nineteenth century, beer, like many Western things, was seen as modern and progressive, leading it eventually to replace sake—first in the cities and then in rural areas—as the everyday drink of choice.[39]

Beer is sold in cans of either 350 or 500 milliliters, roughly the same as 12- and 16-ounce cans in the United States. A small can bought in a store is roughly $2, and a large is roughly $3; premium and craft brews cost a little more. Mugs of beer served at bars are generally 350 to 500 milliliters for medium, and 700 to 800 for large. Japanese beer is usually about 5 percent alcohol.

In the United States 47 percent of alcohol consumed is beer, 35 percent is spirits, and 18 percent is wine. Japan consumes most of its alcohol, 40 percent, as spirits, such as whisky, vodka, and shochu; 36 percent as "other," including sake; and only 18 percent as beer. Wine, at 6 percent, hardly counts. (But Japanese bookstores stock far more books about wine than about any other type of alcohol, perhaps a reflection of overlap in the markets for wine and books.) Like South Korea (69 percent other, 22 percent beer, 2 percent wine) and China (67 percent spirits, 30 percent beer, and 3 percent wine), most of Japan's alcohol is consumed in the form of drinks with higher alcohol content.[40]

By liquid volume, however, the clear winner in Japan is beer and its lesser relatives. Convenience stores often offer a broad array of choices, and each of the large breweries regularly issues special editions for seasons, events, and test marketing. Beer coupons are popular gifts. (But as one mayoral candidate learned the hard way, gifting a total of $3,000 of them to all ninety-two city hall employees upon one's retirement as deputy mayor violates the Public Office Election Law.)[41] Craft beers have begun to proliferate. And in the summer, when beer is considered a thirst quencher, advertising abounds, and with good reason. As one drunk-driving defendant explained when asked why he drank beer before driving, "It was hot."[42]

* * *

These three drinks—sake, shochu, and beer—appear frequently in this book, but court opinions also tell us much about what to drink in Japan beyond those three primary libations. The case law contains 1,027 cases in which intoxication is specifically raised (whether as an inculpatory concept, as in drunk driving, or an exculpatory concept, such as for a capacity defense), and the court specifies the type of alcohol consumed to be sake, shochu, beer, whisky, wine, brandy, or plum wine. Of these 1,027 cases, 249 concern sake, 215 concern shochu, 401 concern beer, 109 concern whisky, 31 concern wine, 20 concern brandy, and 2 concern plum wine. (Plum wine is largely popular with women, who less commonly appear in the cases.)

These drinks and others carry cultural meaning. The same is of course true in the United States; consider the different reactions and contexts that accompany, for instance, a flute of champagne, a Pabst Blue Ribbon beer, a cognac, and breakfast beverages like mimosas and Bloody Marys. But in the context of official case law, the correlations in Japan are particularly revealing.

Let's begin to explore these correlations with a simple drink: water. The seemingly innocuous term *mizuwari* ("mixed with water") refers to alcohol mixed with cold water. It appears frequently in the case law (313 cases, including152 that mention intoxication). *Mizuwari* can refer to any kind of alcohol, but usually either shochu or whisky, the choice of which predicts the location at which it is likely to be drunk. Whisky and water is the drink of choice at a snack (*sunakku*, a small pub with a counter, usually with karaoke and usually staffed by an older *mama* and younger women; more on them soon). (Though some might cringe at the idea of watering down an aged single malt, it is not unusual to see expensive whisky being mixed with ice and water; the theory in Japan—as in Scotland, among other places—is that water enhances the flavor.) The case law contains 92 cases that include both shochu and snack, and 161 that include both *mizuwari* and snack. Shochu is more likely to be consumed in *izakaya* (which serve food; more on them to come as well), which shares 109 opinions with the drink but only 78 with *mizuwari*.

Near the bottom of the alcohol prestige list is "One Cup sake." One Cup is a 180-millileter (about 6 ounces), one-*gou* serving available in convenience stores for about $2. It is sold in a clear glass container that resembles a hospital specimen jar with a metal ring-pull top. The best-selling and inexpensive Oozeki brand, with its familiar blue and white label, was first sold at the 1964 Tokyo Olympic Games and has a reputation as "a drink of old men" (*ojisan*, literally, "uncles").[43]

One Cup has a particular cultural meaning. It is no coincidence that Tom Gill's essay on homelessness in Japan is accompanied by a photo of the author and a homeless man toasting with One Cup.[44] Nor is it surprising that when the Ministry of Health, Labor, and Welfare created a campaign poster for the 2017 Alcohol Awareness Week featuring seven faceless people, each representing a problem and holding an item, the following items were linked with the following problems: underage drinking = canned citrus drink, overconsumption = large mug of beer, pregnant drinking = large red wine goblet, domestic violence = large sake bottle, drunk driving = steering wheel, health problems = bandage on liver, and, finally, alcoholism = One Cup sake.[45] And it seems only fitting that the origin story of Yoshi Ikuzou's 1988 hit traditional song "Liquor" ("Sakeyo"), a karaoke staple about love, drinking, and regret, begins with this encounter by its composer: "On my way home from eating ramen, I came across a completely drunk dad type, with his blazer hung on a mailbox, saying 'I won't go hoooooooome!' (*kaeranee-yo*) and drinking One Cup Oozeki."[46]

One Cup sake appears in thirty-four cases (a couple of which are based on the same facts). That number is relatively small, but the cases show a consistent pattern. Twenty-three are criminal cases in which the following acts occur: nine murders,[47] two cases of negligent driving causing death[48] and two causing injury (in one of them, the driver drank standing up at the convenience store[49]; in the other, the driver downed six One Cups at once[50]), five robberies,[51] two arsons,[52] two assaults (including one of a police officer[53]),[54] and one each of theft,[55] intimidation with a knife,[56] and groping on a train.[57] The remaining eleven civil cases are also dark: three cases of drunk driving (two of which involved death),[58] three workers' compensation deaths,[59] one case of medical malpractice resulting in death,[60] two iterations of the same case in which a blind man falls on the train tracks and breaks both of his legs,[61] and one anticompetition injunction case in which the Osaka High Court ruled that the Hakutsuru Corporation's labeling of their "Sake Cup" in English was sufficiently different from the Oozeki corporation's labeling of their drink as "One Cup" in English.[62]

With the exception of that last case, the inclusion of One Cup in the opinions sends a clear message about the defendant, especially when it plays no causal role in the facts. In one of the robberies, for instance, the court needed to decide whether the defendant was of unsound mind, and thus not liable, due to schizophrenia. The defendant had attempted to steal a bottle of whisky and assaulted a worker at a convenience store. The court concluded that the defendant had not entered the store for the purpose of obtaining alcohol and instead was delusional because he did not opt for his "usual" beverage (according to a worker's testimony), One Cup.[63] The court could have made that point in many different ways without mentioning One Cup; perhaps it was easy to mention because it was in the court record. But the fact remains that the court made a choice to do so. Still, this case is a rhetorical exception: One Cup usually does not arise as part of the narrative, as does wine or beer; rather One Cup sake means trouble, and it is trotted out by litigants and repeated by judges to trace a clearly defined causal path from inexpensive alcohol to tragedy.

Some correlations between alcohol-related factors and individual characteristics are clear: Researchers have found, for instance, that lower educational background in Japan is associated with a higher risk for hazardous drinking for both men and women, while binge drinking is associated not with education but with higher socioeconomic status for men and working women.[64] No one in Japan would think that One Cup consumption correlates with higher education or socioeconomic status. But the linkage in the case law between a type of alcohol (with relatively low alcohol content) and this degree of tragedy is surprising.

At a completely different price point, the same dangerous correlation is true—oddly—for port wine. Port wine appears a paltry sixteen times in the case law, and none of those cases has anything to do with intoxication: Two use "port wine" merely to describe the color of a person's urine, one lists it as a product sold at an agricultural co-op, and one cites it as an entry on a list of products in the cargo of a ship—showing again that the mere mention of alcohol does not always mean trouble. But eight of those cases concern murder, a correlation that is skewed by a single incident. In 1961 in the small town of Nabari, near Nara, in western Japan, Okunishi Masaru killed his wife, his mistress, and three other women with port wine poisoned with agricultural chemicals. Okunishi confessed at the time and was sentenced to death. He spent over forty years on death row as he appealed his sentence (he won once at the district court, but the ruling was overturned) and requested retrials multiple times based on new evidence and a claim that his confession was coerced.[65] The fact that port wine equals murder, then, is representative of the spiked wine in the so-called Nabari Poisoned Wine Incident—without it, port wine would never be consumed in the case law.

When spirits with higher alcohol content appear in the case law, danger lurks. Take vodka. Vodka appears in only sixteen cases, and only seven criminal cases, the earliest from 1985. Vodka is often used in the cases to cause a victim to lose consciousness; it was the weapon of choice in the highly publicized case of Obara Jouji, who was accused of raping and killing multiple women, including a twenty-one-year-old British bar hostess, Lucie Blackman.[66] In fact, although vodka could conceivably appear in a case that adjudicates any kind of dispute, in 75 percent of the cases in which vodka appears, someone dies. And one of the four nonlethal exceptions, from 1985, is far from innocuous: the defendant hostess bar manager and her male bartender friend conspired to serve customers vodka with orange juice, telling them it was an energy drink. When the customers passed out, the duo stole their cash.[67]

In one vodka case concerning events that took place in 2000, several family members conspired to kill the family's patriarch, a sixty-seven-year-old company president named Kuriyama Hiroshi. Kuriyama suffered from hepatic cirrhosis, a condition that rendered him unable to drink alcohol. The family hired a contract killer, hoping for a large insurance payout. The killer's weapon: vodka. Kuriyama drank and died, and prosecutors brought murder charges. The court sentenced the killer to life imprisonment. That incident accounts for three of the cases that mention vodka.[68] But it's not the only murder-for-insurance case. In a 2002 case the defendant stated, "[V]odka is clear, so we can mix it in with shochu and he won't know." The victim drank the vodka as though it were shochu, which has a lower alcohol content.[69]

The only type of alcohol more dangerous than vodka that appears in the case law is the 192- to 196-proof (96 to 98 percent alcohol) Polish rectified spirit Spirytus Stawski (*supiritasu*), which appears five times. The first three cases are related to the 2000 Kuriyama murder-for-insurance case.[70] In the fourth, three female workers at a snack conspired to rob a male patron who later died of alcohol poisoning; their weapon was Spirytus mixed with shochu and oolong tea.[71] In the fifth, a leader of an Aum Supreme Truth religious splinter group helped beat a member to death with a bamboo sword; the defendant argued (unsuccessfully) in effect that she was not a co-conspirator because the fact that one of the other beaters forced another member to drink Spirytus suggested that that member acted independently.[72] Finally, in a case in which the court did *not* specify the type of alcohol, the spirit was used by male university students to get female university students drunk. They then gang-raped the women. The opinion merely mentions "liquor with a high alcohol content," but the type, Spirytus, was widely reported.[73] (It is unclear why the court in this case wasn't more specific, but perhaps it did not wish to write an opinion that could be used as an instruction manual.)

At the other end of the danger spectrum is *mirin*, a rice-based product similar to sake but with a lower alcohol content, usually around 14 percent, similar to wine. *Mirin* is sweet and used almost exclusively for cooking, but it is drinkable if one gets the urge. Mixing *mirin* with shochu makes a somewhat uncommon drink called *yanagikage*.[74] *Mirin* appears forty-seven times in the case law; each time, nothing bad happens, with one exception: a well-known 2002 case in which a woman poisoned a communal pot of curry with arsenic, killing four. In that case the court listed *mirin* as one among several ingredients; along with sugar and soy sauce, it was part of a recipe, and it foretold nothing in particular.[75] The other cases are mundane: a copyright dispute, a violation of tax laws, a food labeling issue. No one in the case law has ever been drunk on *mirin*. Accordingly *mirin* won't appear in this book again; it tells us nothing about the defendant, the victim, or anyone else in the cases, and as such courts have little use for it in their narratives. It might as well be nonalcoholic beer, which appears twelve times in the case law, and in only one case does anything of consequence occur. In that case the court explains that the defendants *planned* to drink it at the golf clubhouse, but instead they actually got drunk on real beer, after which they hijacked a golf cart, flipped it, and caused $850,000 in damages.[76] Had they actually drunk nonalcoholic beer as planned, there presumably would have been no case.

One final determinant of what to drink in Japan remains: the role of government regulation. In Japan regulation of alcohol comes mostly in the form of licensing and taxation. The government requires licenses for the production and sales of all types of alcohol, but not in bars or restaurants, where it is sold easily alongside nonalcoholic beverages. Japan does not restrict hours, days, or places of sale; advertising (but a health warning is required); or public consumption.[77] The minimum drinking age is twenty.

Alcohol is heavily taxed. The taxation system is complex and evolving, but in general, sake is effectively taxed at around 18 percent, shochu at 32 to 38 percent depending on alcohol content, and whisky at 22 percent. Beer is more complicated. It must contain 67 percent malt content to be classified and labeled as beer, and is taxed at 40 to 47 percent.[78] The Brewers Association of Japan points out that Japanese beer is the highest priced in the world due to the tax, which is said to be nine times that of the U.S. tax, four times France's, and nineteen times Germany's.[79] To circumvent the tax, brewers introduced in 1994 (beginning with Suntory's Hop's Nama) a beer-like drink called *happoushu,* which had too little malt to be taxed as beer but was less expensive and tasted enough like beer to be an acceptable substitute. A beverage with the malt content of *happoushu* was taxed at 34 percent. Brewers then invented so-called third beers such as Sapporo's Draft One, which use malt alternatives like caramel and pea protein so that they are taxed at the still lower rate of 25 percent.[80]

The three-tiered market that resulted from tax-reducing innovations arguably leads to greater consumer choice.[81] Still, some consider the newer types of beverages substandard. For instance, one beer authority describes *happoushu* as "sweet yellow stuff" or "Frankenbeer" and points out the obvious: "The only reason for their low malt is price."[82]

The places at which people buy alcohol are determined in part by regulation. In 1995 liquor stores accounted for more than 66 percent of alcohol sellers, while convenience stores represented 11.8 percent and supermarkets 4.7.[83] By 2015 convenience stores dominated, with 33.8 percent of licenses, followed by liquor stores (28.4 percent) and supermarkets (12.6 percent).[84] Liquor stores, which historically have been small, struggle to compete with convenience stores, which are always open. (In 1985 there were 7,419 convenience stores in Japan. In 1995 there were 29,144, and by 2019 there were 55,979.)[85] Small regulatory changes can have widespread effects: A 2017 revision to the Liquor Tax Law designed to prevent price wars between large retailers (thereby protecting smaller liquor stores) by prohibiting "unfairly low" prices caused increases in beer prices within months, first at those retailers, and then at other distributors.[86]

The *absence* of regulation has given rise to another place to buy alcohol: vending machines, which are said to be unique to Japan.[87] The machines, which usually sell beer and sake and flourished with beer sales in the 1970s,[88] were once ubiquitous. (Especially in rural Japan they were a frequent fixture in front of mom-and-pop liquor stores to ensure availability after mom and pop close the shop in the evening.) In 1996 there were 185,829 such machines in operation. In 2018 there were only 2,753, many of which are equipped with identification readers to mitigate underage drinking.[89] The decline comes as a result of a voluntary regulation (to prevent involuntary regulation) and subsequent self-enforcement by the All-Japan Liquor Merchants Association.

Where

In a nationwide 2018 survey, 35 percent of respondents in Japan stated that they drank at home every day. The older one becomes, the more likely one is to drink at home (more than half of men in their fifties and sixties do so daily), though frequency is influenced by one's sex as well (only a quarter of women in their fifties and sixties, the age category with the highest percentage, do so daily). Most at-home drinkers usually drink beer or beer-like products. (Only about 3 percent of "nonbeer beer" is sold in drinking establishments; the remaining 97 percent is consumed at home.)[90] About half of the drinking is done alone, and about half occurs with a spouse.[91]

Much of the drinking at home occurs at night, a practice so prevalent there is a word for it: *banshaku* (literally, "night serving of alcohol"). Drinking with dinner is normal, a lesson the Supreme Court teaches by implication. In a case in which an older man suffering from dementia was hit by a train, the Court noted that as his symptoms worsened, the man "would forget that he had already *banshaku* and continue to drink many times."[92] Multiple *banshaku*, then, is not normal; a single-sitting *banshaku* is.

Many people enjoy *banshaku* in the same way that some people enjoy a glass of wine with dinner; a team of Japanese social psychologists explains that "*ban-shaku*, as the first half of the meal, plays an important part in enriching, enhancing, and perfecting one's dinner."[93] But sometimes *banshaku* is a euphemism, as Keiko Kato learned in her interviews of Japanese alcoholics' wives: "[I]t was in the later part of the interviews that I noticed a pattern where wives claim that their husbands are drinking in the name of *banshaku* but their *banshaku* did not mean genuine *banshaku* (e.g. they were not having meals at all, drinking on an empty stomach and eating a little bit afterwards, or drinking *sake* as a substitute of eating rice)."[94] One of the wives, Akiko, explained her husband's pattern of drinking at home: "During the Japanese economical boom, he often drank outside. But that was still only once or twice per week. . . . Most of the drinking, which he did in a relaxed manner, was done at home. He was doing *banshaku* every day. In our house we have a kit called *kan-petto* [Japanese sake bottle heater] which warms the *sake* to the right temperature. [Akiko laughed.] Using that, he drank two bottles every day. No *kyuukanbi*."[95]

That word, *kyuukanbi*, consists of three characters: "rest," "liver," and "day." The theory behind the word is that abstaining from alcohol for at least one day a week will slow the ravages of alcoholism upon one's liver. Recent Japanese research in English confirms that the practice, which the researchers call "liver holidays," works; based on a large-scale study, they recommend that "persons, especially male heavy drinkers, abstain from drinking alcohol for more than 2 days per week."[96] The case law often notes the lack of a *kyuukanbi* as a sign of problems with alcohol,[97] and defendants often promise to increase their *kyuukanbi* in order to receive favorable treatment from courts.[98]

After *banshaku* comes the nightcap, which in Japanese is literally "sleep alcohol" (*nezake*). The concepts of *banshanku* and *nezake* are distinct; in one case, for instance, a litigant claimed in a suit against her deceased husband's employer that he "stopped having *banshaku* with his father-in-law every evening and simply had a nightcap in order to sleep."[99] Nightcaps frequently appear in the cases as one of the following: two drinks of whisky mixed with water,[100] plum wine on the rocks,[101] a can of beer and two *gou* of sake,[102] a beer,[103] or a beer and a small bottle of sake.[104] As those examples suggest, nightcap amounts should be small: In one case, the defendant's bus company employer "allowed him to drink at the nightcap level";[105] in another, the fact that the defendant drank too much as a nightcap was a factor in a successful divorce suit (along with the defendant's financial mismanagement, physical abuse, and excessive playing of pachinko—a mechanical gambling game that resembles an upright pinball machine with many small metal balls).[106] In the absence of excess, courts do not find nightcaps problematic, though as a health matter some see nightcaps as a cause for concern, as nearly 50 percent of all men and 18 percent of women report using alcohol as a sleep aid more than once per week.[107] A multinational survey reveals that Japan has the lowest rate of sleep medication use, but that alcohol is far more likely to be used as a sleep aid in Japan than elsewhere.[108]

Concurrent with these at-home drinking patterns, much drinking, as the label "drinking seats" suggests, occurs in drinking establishments. Drinking establishments vary, but in that variety often lies uniformity. Take Shinjuku's Golden Gai district, home to roughly three hundred bars, glorified holes-in-the-wall crammed into six narrow alleys and numerous narrow side alleys.[109] It is known as a place where journalists and artsy types drink—not the working corporate men or the poor that populate many of the cases. Most of the tiny, often *very* tiny bars (some seat as few as six) have a unique theme: world music, video games, pornography, the Red Army, biology. But while each is different in character, they all have a similar style, format, and hope for differentiation. Though Golden Gai is a very small place, it occasionally lends itself to case law, as when a defendant in a murder case stated that he became upset while intoxicated after he "got into an argument after bumping into a person of Chinese ancestry in

Shinjuku's Golden Gai."[110] Naming the specific place prepares the reader for individual treatment of the subject of the case narrative.

The case law is dominated by bars, especially certain types of bars, as those places tend to lend themselves to the kind of drinking that leads to court cases. A good example of a drinking establishment that is underrepresented in the case law relative to its role in real life is the *ryoutei*: a high-end restaurant that serves Japanese food, usually with sake, in a private setting, at a high price.[111] Many require a referral for a reservation. The *New York Times* calls them "magnificent and often exclusive,"[112] and they are a frequent entertainment venue of choice of celebrities and politicians. They usually appear in the case law not because of outrageous drinking or conduct but because the bills are too high or certain customers shouldn't be there. As for the former, the most common theme in the *ryoutei*-related case law is a suit by citizens against a public official who charges expenses incurred there to the government. In a 2001 case, for instance, the mayor of Kitakyushu and seventy other city officials were ordered to reimburse money that they spent primarily hosting national bureaucrats. At one event they drank eleven bottles of beer, twenty-four bottles of Isami-brand shochu, and two bottles of whisky. No one got hurt and no one even was rowdy, because this is a *ryoutei*.[113]

Now for the people who arguably should not visit *ryoutei*. In a 2014 case a company president's wife brought an alienation of affections action against a bar hostess, claiming that she was entitled to damages because the hostess had a seven-year sexual relationship with her husband. Such affairs are not uncommon; although sex is not necessarily part of a hostess's duties, dates with clients (called *dohan*; literally, "companion") are commonplace (and they occur frequently at high-end establishments near hostess bars), and sometimes they lead to more. Nor is the legal action itself unusual; it's grounded firmly in Japanese tort law, and hostesses are frequent defendants.[114]

What's unusual here is the result: The court found that the hostess did not owe the wife compensation, as she slept with the husband only as what literally translates to a "pillow sales tactic" (*makura eigyou*) to keep him as a customer. As such, she was more akin to a sex worker than a lover, and therefore the relationship shouldn't "damage the peace of the marriage." The opinion made clear that the hostess drank with the husband at *ryoutei*, but of course that was not the focus of the case, as the alcohol did not lead directly to anything objectionable.[115]

That outcome is surprising. Although no court had ruled directly on the point, the Supreme Court had held that a hostess could be liable for damages in an alienation of affections action if the marital "peace" was not already destroyed.[116] The district court in this case did not cite that ruling, but it appears to be saying that sex for business reasons is per se *not* destructive of peace.[117]

The location of drinking in a *ryoutei* matters in this case in part because it strongly suggests that the hostess-patron relationship was neither headed toward something more permanent (such as marriage, which would by definition destroy the first marriage) nor an emotional fling based solely on lust (in which case the parties might have had a purely sexual arrangement that did not involve *ryoutei* visits). To the court, *ryoutei* suggested business.

Those are the kinds of cases in which *ryoutei* appear. Employees sue to get their jobs back when they run up expenses in *ryoutei*;[118] sellers of expensive kimono target consumers unfairly when they entertain them at *ryoutei*;[119] and politicians bring defamation actions over claims that they have geisha-led orgies at *ryoutei*.[120] Alcohol might appear briefly (it doesn't in those three cases), but it doesn't seem to affect the outcome of the case.

Far more frequently mentioned in the case law are *izakaya*, which are abundant and include several prominent national franchises. New York and London each has more than twenty, and the word is sufficiently prominent in English now that from this point forward I will not treat it as foreign by italicizing it. Izakaya, which are usually easily identified by the red lanterns that hang in front, appear in roughly one of every two hundred published legal opinions. Some of those opinions are not necessarily informative; in a 2012 Intellectual Property High Court case, for instance, the court equated izakaya with "tavern,"[121] a translation that is not altogether incorrect (and it came from both litigants' briefs) but misses the Japaneseness of the izakaya as a place for after-work meetings, for group blind dates, for eating izakaya-esque foods like *yakitori* (chicken skewers), *karaage* (Japanese fried chicken), and edamame soybeans (rice and noodles, which do not usually go with liquor, might be ordered at the end of the drinking), and of course for drinking beer and shochu-based drinks. The leading English-language book on izakaya explains their particular social meaning:

> Neither restaurant nor bar, the izakaya is more than a place where you can share delicious food and relaxing drink—though it is certainly that. In many neighborhoods, it is a community hub with a cast of characters and ongoing narratives. The customers will range from locals and regulars to office workers, academics or day-laborers. They will order small-dish delicacies throughout the evening, perhaps in the beginning sharing just a couple of items. . . . And as the evening progresses and energy levels rise, you will hear straight talk and the uttering of hard truths that won't ordinarily be spoken. In short, at the izakaya, people are more themselves.[122]

Izakaya dining involves routine. When asked to order before looking at a menu, for instance, the socially correct response is "For starters, beer" (*toriaezu/*

mazu biiru/nama). Data show that 64.1 percent of work-related drinking begins with beer; the number is nearly 80 percent for men. For women, who are said to prefer sweet carbonated sho*chu high*balls (the combination of the two underlined syllables in Japanese yields *chuuhai*, with an alcohol content of 8 or 9 percent), the figure is 49.2 percent.[123]

Some izakaya, as well as some other drinking establishments, offer a set-price all-you-can-drink (*nomihoudai*) service, a relatively inexpensive drinking method that also allows the bill to be split equally among partygoers. (This service usually is not offered to patrons drinking alone.) All-you-can-drink is so pervasive that one might expect it to lead to all sorts of problems in the case law. It doesn't. Thirty-three cases mention all-you-can-drink, but only four of those are criminal matters. The most egregious of those four is a drunk-driving case in which the defendant drank five or six beers and two or three glasses of shochu before running into a bicyclist, severely injuring him. He received a sentence of three years and eight months in prison.[124] But the other matters are comparatively trifling: a nuisance case that resulted in a not guilty verdict,[125] a drug case in which the defendant received a suspended sentence,[126] and another not guilty verdict in a case of a violation of nightlife industry regulations.[127]

It is possible that courts simply don't mention the system, but other factors might better account for its absence. Japanese research unsurprisingly shows a correlation between all-you-can-drink availability and alcohol consumption (especially among college students),[128] but at least three factors mitigate the ability to actually drink all one can. First, such plans often are time-limited by minutes or hours. Second, many establishments require customers to ask servers for a new glass for each new drink, which reduces the ability to drink quickly. Finally, all-you-can-drink is often offered with all-you-can-eat, which creates speed bumps to both consumption and metabolism. Each factor seems to have the effect of mitigating malfeasance, at least in the case law.

Much drinking also occurs in snacks, the small bars in which female companionship is offered, usually with karaoke and whisky and water. They are virtually everywhere; one study estimates that there are over 100,000 in Japan, compared with 80,000 izakaya. (For further comparison, there are roughly 62,000 bars in the United States,[129] and only 22,519 Starbucks and 36,000 McDonald's in the entire world, including 1,415 and 2,208 in Japan).[130] That's one izakaya or snack for every 705 people, more than twice the number of bars per capita in the U.S. state with the highest per capita figure, North Dakota.[131] Snacks are mentioned in one way or another in roughly one of every 150 published legal opinions. A Japanese judge writing a legal opinion has no need to describe or define a snack or an izakaya—those simply are places of everyday life, the way that a wine bar or a college dive needs little explanation in the United States. The setting requires no exposition, as in this 2011 murder case: "From four in the afternoon, the defendant drank one bottle of beer (middle-size bottles) per hour, for a total of seven beers, and at half past midnight he was told by the *mama* 'it's about time to go home,' and at 12:40 p.m. he returned home."[132] That scene is repeated night after night at snacks across Japan.

For readers not familiar with Japan, the snack needs elaboration. A snack always has a counter bar, a *mama*, and alcohol, and sometimes a few tables. The customers are almost always male. The *mama*, often with younger female workers—hostesses—serve drinks, sing karaoke, and attempt to make customers feel more masculine.

Snacks might sound a little seedy. Workers there usually do not have high social status, and surely many regrettable acts have occurred at snacks. But snacks have only a hint of unsavory connotation in Japan, and none at all in many, or perhaps most, social circles. One Japanese researcher has even found that snacks are *negatively* correlated with crime: An increase of ten snacks in an area leads to a decrease of forty-six crime reports. Of course, there are other possible explanations here—perhaps crimes simply aren't reported in areas with snacks, for instance—but the fact that libraries showed a similar correlation to reported crimes at least is encouraging for snacks.[133]

Snacks are easily identifiable across Japan, but some differentiation occurs. For instance, the Tokyo District Court described in a 2011 immigration case a Philippine woman who, "after immigrating, worked at snacks and pubs [*pabu*] to send money to her parents."[134] The sentence is loaded; snacks and pubs can be categorized together as drinking establishments, but pubs are a broader class and do not usually offer female companionship. However, although the court does not specify, it is likely that it is referring not to a regular pub (which resembles a U.S. bar) but to a "Philippine pub," which does in fact offer female companionship and whose workers are from that country.[135] Then again, when the Tokyo High Court described another pub in a robbery-murder case nine months earlier, and with a different panel of judges in yet another murder case a year earlier, it specified both times that the drinking establishment was a "so-called Philippine club," so the lack of specificity is not always conclusive.[136]

Back to "regular" snacks. At a snack, drinking is often done not by the glass but over time, by the bottle. Customers often purchase their own bottles of whisky (or generally less expensive shochu or sake), which sit on a shelf on the wall behind the bar, each bearing a tag with a customer's name around its neck. Bottles, row after row, await their keepers' return. Many people keep bottles—and that is what the practice is called, *botoru kiipu*—at more than one snack, and in some cases those bottles can be used for favors (as in "He can drink from my bottle"). The bottle occasionally serves as a status symbol, as everyone can see the names on the tags, but more often it represents a sort of loyalty program, as customers who return to drink from their bottle develop close ties with servers and other customers. Customers generally pay one time for the bottle and each time thereafter for the privilege of visiting and receiving pours, perhaps with light snacks.

Keeping a bottle can be expensive. In a 2014 murder case, the court raised "bottle keep" as a natural element of the night's narrative, but also to suggest that bottle keep was above the financial means of the defendant's live-in boyfriend. The court introduced the boyfriend, whom it names "A," by saying that after he moved in with the defendant in the summer of 2011, he received all his money from the defendant's pension and her business, a hair salon at which she also sold specialty scissors. He spent the money on pachinko and visits to snacks. (The court does not state their ages, but the pension and the business are sufficient to signal a couple who are roughly in their sixties, and in fact press accounts name the boyfriend as fifty-nine-year-old Yamamura Osamu and the defendant as sixty-four-year old Nagamine Hideko.)[137] He was so physically and verbally abusive that the police were occasionally called, and the defendant had told her sister and her friends that she feared for her life. With that background loaded in the first paragraph, the court turned to the events of the evening:

> On June 14, 2013, at 9 p.m., the defendant and "A" visited a nearby snack, where they ate, but because the defendant had to work the next morning, she left the snack around 9:30. On her way home, she stopped at a convenience store and picked up some fried chicken for A to eat after he returned home. After she arrived home, she went to bed to rest for work the next day. Her boyfriend, on the other hand, was still at the snack, where he was drinking from a very expensive kept bottle, and when he left after drinking until 1:05 in the morning, he paid only $70 of the $350 bill in cash and put the remainder on his tab.

It is unclear precisely why the bill was so high, but because the snack is in the city of Seki, a town of fewer than 90,000 people about an hour's drive north of Nagoya, I suspect that the only thing that expensive at the snack is the bottle. Presumably he bought it that night with the intention of keeping it to drink from later. But that night's sip was his last:

> At 1:15, as the defendant was sleeping in their bedroom to prepare to wake up early for work in the morning, A returned from drinking at the snack, woke her up, and told her to hurry and pay the remainder of the tab immediately, ignoring her pleas to let her sleep. Moreover, A told the defendant to take the salt-flavored fried chicken back to the store and immediately exchange it for the soy-sauce-flavored variety. The defendant, upon hearing these unreasonable demands, and taking them together with the accumulated stress and pressure that characterized

> the last two years of her suppressed lifestyle, exploded with anger toward A.

She stabbed him to death four times in the kitchen with a seven-inch blade. He died. The court found her guilty.[138] The court later returned in the opinion to the defendant's lifestyle issues as it sentenced her to only five years and six months in prison. But it need not have lingered, as the facts communicated precisely both the socioeconomic level of the couple and their internal dynamics. Readers can tell why the bottle keep might have been out of financial range (even before the court specifically said "expensive") and why that factor, along with a host of others, including the fried chicken, led to the defendant's actions.

It's unusual that the pair visited the snack as a couple, though it's not unheard of, especially in rural settings such as this one. On that score, the cases do not detail every aspect of female drinking life in Japan. When cases do involve women drinking, it is often because they have become victims of crime.[139]

Perhaps because of this element of victimhood, courts sometimes seem to treat women who drink outside the home differently than they treat men who do. Let's expand beyond snacks to examine the phenomenon. In one Tokyo civil case, the plaintiff joined a company as a new recruit one month after her university graduation—a fact the court raises, it would seem, to show her youth or perhaps even her vulnerability. She sued a man who she claimed raped her, causing posttraumatic stress disorder.

The court described the facts as follows. At a drinking party for four work colleagues held at an izakaya, the plaintiff drank "one medium mug of beer and half a bottle of wine, and because she had not been feeling well that day, she did not eat much while she drank, and after the party finished, she vomited in the women's restroom, and was in such a state of intoxication that she found it extraordinarily difficult to walk." The defendant argued that the woman was in fact not so intoxicated, as she did not have much to drink and she remembered many details from the alleged rape. The court countered with an acknowledgment of the imprecision of intoxication and an explicit recognition of individual differentiation:

> The degree of a person's intoxication varies widely depending on the speed with which one drinks, the amount of food ingested at the time, the condition of one's body at the time, and various other causes, and it is inappropriate to measure intoxication by the amount of alcohol a person normally drinks. In addition, the defendant points out that the plaintiff's concrete memory of the events is considerably high considering the level of intoxication that the plaintiff claims. *But it is said*

> *(exhibit 12) that a person's memories of the time that alcohol was ingested can be reconstructed more accurately when a person is in a condition in which she has similarly ingested alcohol than when the person is sober.* Even if she were completely drunk, the injury of rape is such an unusual, shocking, and frightening experience that her level of consciousness would surely be quite high, and it can be easily understood how those events would be engraved in her memory. Accordingly, the plaintiff's testimony does not necessarily give rise to suspicions regarding its credibility on the issue of the plaintiff's degree of intoxication or amount of alcohol consumed on the day of the incident.

The court did not delve into the details of her intoxication, in part because it found the defendant's testimony "unnatural" and "unreasonable." It simply found that a beer and half bottle of wine, coupled with the lack of food and various other intangibles, made the woman intoxicated. It awarded her $54,000 in damages.[140]

But focus on the language the court used to refute the defendant's claims that the woman was not intoxicated, particularly the sentence I have italicized. The court, citing "exhibit [*kou*] 12," states that drunken memories can be better reconstructed when one is similarly drunk than when one is sober. The phenomenon, state-dependent memory, is controversial but well-documented in the scientific literature[141] and occasionally arises in U.S. courts as well.[142] (Exhibit 12 is not attached to the case, but I suspect that it is either psychiatric testimony that might have emerged as part of the plaintiff's examination or a relevant academic article.)

The court seems to be comparing the plaintiff's actual memories of the incident as recalled later, under the influence, with those that she had when sober, and finding more validity in the drunken memories. For that comparison to be relevant, the plaintiff would have had to have become intoxicated in a way similar to the night of the incident—a feat that the court has just said is inappropriate because of all the factors that enter into intoxication—and recalled facts that would not have come to mind as easily if she were sober.

As we will see in the next chapter, such a recovery exercise would not be entirely unusual in Japan, but the opinion doesn't state that it occurred in this case. The language "it is said that" (*to mo iwareteirushi*) that precedes the claim is a very general statement of the premise that makes the claim even more opaque. Perhaps the court is simply not being careful with its words, which would be unusual, but the court at least seems comfortable skipping a rhetorical step in its argument to add a sentence of questionable necessity. Why? Maybe because the court thinks the plaintiff, the victim, should be compensated and wants one more argument in support of her memory.

Another intoxicated woman appears in a 2008 case, and again the court's language is imprecise. The female defendant visited a host club and became intoxicated. That information alone is notable for two reasons. First, she is an intoxicated woman, which is rare, and here she is a criminal defendant, which is rarer still. Second, the case takes place in a host club. Roughly speaking, a host club is the female counterpart to clubs that employ hostesses: places where women can go to drink (among other things) with young men who are paid to talk with them—and, occasionally, if the woman pays significant amounts over time, have sex with them. Hosts, says Akiko Takeyama, "respond to your stories with exaggerated bodily reactions: joyful facial expressions, merry laughter, and clapping hands. They seem to truly enjoy listening to you no matter what you say."[143] The qualifications to work at a host club, according to the Japanese sociological literature, are simple: "The prospective employee is not asked about his criminal record and needs neither education nor experience. And it is a common misperception that they must all be handsome. Of course, being good-looking helps, but good looks are not always tied to the ability to do the job." What they must do, however, is appear masculine in the eyes of their female customers by showing leadership and self-confidence.[144]

Host clubs do much of their business in the middle of the night, in part because hostesses, who often leave work when bars close at midnight (or later, depending on local law and zoning restrictions), often spend their wages at nearby host clubs. As with izakaya and snacks, the court does not need to offer the sort of explanation that I have just given—everyone in Japan knows what a host club is. The first such club opened in 1966,[145] but by the time the word appeared in its first published case in 1971, the court had no need to describe or even employ the often-used phrase "so-called" before its mention.[146]

Back to our case. The defendant, the court explains, arrived at 11 p.m. at a Kobe host club. By the time she left at 6 a.m., she had run up a tab of $560. Those facts tell us a lot about the defendant (she stayed seven hours, and she was not working at 11 p.m.), and it also tells us much about host clubs: among other things, they are expensive. As Takeyama describes in a roughly contemporaneous observation of a Tokyo club:

> A bottle of champagne, for example, costs about 40,000 yen (almost 400 US dollars). The cheapest brand of *shochu*, a potato-based liquor, available at most stores for $7, runs at about $70 at host clubs. Dishes such as spaghetti, sautéed vegetables and fruit plates cost about $50 each. Even if a female customer does not drink or eat, she is expected to pay the entire tab for the table [including the hosts' food and drink] and offer tips to the helper hosts.[147]

In our case, the woman had only $360, and she agreed to pay the remaining $200 the following night, an arrangement that apparently was acceptable to the club. She returned, as promised, the next night at midnight. She paid the $200 and stayed until 4 or 5 a.m. She paid her $230 bill for that evening. She then went to another host club and stayed until 6:30, spending another $90. Finally, at 6:45 a.m., she went to the host club that is the subject of the case, staying until 8 a.m. She paid her $50 bill. She told "host A" there that she wanted him to return with her to the first host club. He agreed (demonstrating the portability of hospitality), and along the way they stopped at a convenience store. He saw there that she had $200 to $300 in her wallet.

The woman told host A that she would like to buy a bottle of champagne for $180, and that she had bought thirty-six bottles of champagne at clubs in the past. At the time that she made the request, she had $290 in her wallet and no usable credit cards. They returned to host A's club, and she requested a champagne set that cost $230. Along with host A and five or six other hosts, they drank the bottle; she had at least a glass at a "champagne call," at which the hosts were called to gather around for a group toast. She then received ten more bottles. At this particular host club, the custom, the court explains, was to ask the customer for a deposit if the bill exceeded $1,000, but in this case no such request was made.

At 10 a.m., the woman was presented with a bill for $2,030. She asked to go to the ATM, and management acquiesced. She fled. Police were summoned and she was soon caught and arrested on theft charges.

The court first investigated whether the woman actually ordered the ten extra bottles of champagne. The answer was unclear, as the stories of host A and his assistant manager differed. Still, host A knew the woman did not have sufficient cash, yet he did not place a stop on the bill at the usual $1,000 mark. More important, the woman was intoxicated, the court said, to such an extent that she lacked capacity. As in the rape case, the court spent very little time examining the issue. It appears to have ordered no medical or psychiatric evaluation. Her blood alcohol level strongly suggested intoxication, but other physical evidence was contradictory: On the host club sofa, she was either sitting up and leaning on its backrest or completely lying down on its cushions. Those descriptions, with no evidence of other physical attributes or behavior, were sufficient for the court. Prosecutors had sought a two-year sentence, but the court found her not guilty due to her intoxication.[148]

The court seemed irked by differences in testimony and strongly suggested that she never actually ordered the ten bottles, that instead they were put on her tab to increase the size of the bill. But lurking in the opinion too was an ease with which the woman was found to have been intoxicated—to her benefit. Courts have struggled far more with less evidence to find intoxication, and perhaps there was a gender-related reason, or at least a victimhood-related reason, for their lenience here.

Or maybe courts simply find measurement of female intoxication, with which they have little experience, difficult, as only 15 percent of judges are women. Women do drink, and in fact female alcohol consumption in Japan has increased dramatically in recent years (18.1 percent of pregnant women drink),[149] but most of the cases are about men, perhaps because women are said to drink at home in the daytime as "kitchen drunks" rather than in public.[150] Anne Allison suggests, "The behavior that accompanies the drinking—throwing up, urinating in public, dancing on train platforms, falling asleep stretched out on the seat of a train, making passes at or otherwise insulting someone normally shown respect, speaking openly about things that usually go unsaid—all such behavior is for the most part excused (yet more so for males than females)."[151]

But it's not completely unusual to see women in such a state. I've avoided personal anecdotes, and will continue to do so, except to briefly mention the time when, on a Tokyo train, I saw a woman I assumed was in her twenties tell her similarly aged drinking companions that she was absolutely fine to make her way home alone and that they should get off the train before her. They did. She then appeared to have an uncontrollable urge to vomit—an act that popular surveys in Japan suggest is regarded as the worst consequence of overdrinking.[152] She was well-dressed and perhaps did not want to appear rude, so she looked feverishly for a place to throw up, realized that the doors were not opening again anytime soon, and proceeded to empty the contents of her stomach into her Hermès bag. Passengers pretended to look away while stealing glances. No one offered help or asked if she was okay. She got off the train before I did, so I don't know what happened next. It wasn't the first or the last time I've seen a woman throw up into her purse in Japan—it's just the most memorable because the bag was expensive. (Conversation of two women next to me: "That was Hermès, wasn't it?" "What a waste.")

Similar events are now recorded at a popular Instagram site called "shibuyameltdown." Named after one of Tokyo's popular nighttime neighborhoods and an activity that often occurs there, the site is a collection of photos and videos of people passed out, vomiting, or exhibiting other publicly inebriated behavior.[153] Most are men; a few are women. Some are disgusting. A few are absurd. And in most cases the only person who seems to have noticed the person lying on the ground or leaning against the fare machine or standing on the train platform is the photographer.

Although many people drink themselves into a stupor in Shibuya, it is important to note that they do so indoors, in drinking establishments. Despite the fact that Japan has no open-container laws or laws that criminalize public drunkenness in and of itself, people rarely drink on the street there. They drink outside for specific occasions and in specific places: at festivals, during fireworks displays, and, as we shall see, when viewing cherry blossoms in public parks. Beer and other drinks are sold at small shops on railway platforms, and they are frequently consumed on trains at night. Especially at night: As one court noted in a case of sexual groping on a train, it is easy to imagine a drunk person slumped over and clinging to a strap on a packed train at night, but not in the morning.[154]

This train-drunk comparison of night and day raises an aspect of Japanese drinking culture that Japanese courts simply cannot capture: the smells, especially on the trains and at train stations in urban areas. At 9 p.m. on a Friday night Shinbashi Station, the hub for Tokyo white-collar salarymen drinking in nearby pubs as well as a few professionals who walk over from the higher-end drinking spots in Ginza, is a particular sensory experience. Walking through the station at that time, passing red-faced men with their neckties in their pockets and seemingly less inebriated young women saying goodbye as each heads to her train, the fermented-birthday-cake aroma of sugar and alcohol metabolizing through bodies and wafting above the crowd, brings to mind a drunken state fair, with notes of cotton candy and kettle corn and secretionary undertones of noodles and cooked meat. It's not necessarily unpleasant, though perhaps it is an experience to which one becomes accustomed over time. The next morning is arguably less delightful, as the crowded trains of Tokyo have a different aroma, a combination of last night's alcohol (still metabolizing), breakfast cigarettes oozing out of pores, and cologne deployed in a quixotic struggle for control. The morning phenomenon is well known: Articles on the topic abound, especially in publications for men,[155] and if one conducts a search online in Japanese for the word for odorous (*kusai*) followed by the common word for middle-aged men (*ojisan*), the search engine algorithm's first autocomplete suggestion is "train" (*densha*). The trains and stations of other cities around the world have other odors of varying palatability, but none as distinctly alcohol-centric as Tokyo's.

Law doesn't attempt to control the smell, but it does attempt to mitigate the nuisances that accompany alcohol. In addition to local ordinances, Japan regulates such behavior through a national statute, the Law concerning Prevention of Acts of Nuisance by Intoxicated Persons.[156] The law was passed in part due to the emerging women's movement of the 1960s,[157] and in part as a response to the "drinker's paradise" ills identified by the Tokyo District Court in 1956 in chapter 1.[158] To be subject to the statute, a person must (a) be in public, (b) be intoxicated, and (c) engage in disorderly speech or behavior (art. 4). In the absence of (c), police may "protect" (i.e., incarcerate) the drunk for up to twenty-four hours; if (c) is present, or if drunk people refuse to comply, they can be fined. Another statute, the Police Duties Execution Act, allows police to provide "immediate protection at any appropriate place, such as a police station," to "a person who is likely to inflict injury on their own or others' lives, bodies, or property due to mental derangement or drunkenness."[159] Protected drunks are legitimately protected; they are kept in protective cells (known colloquially, but not in the formal genre of court opinions, as "tiger boxes," or *torahako,* as drunks are historically known as "big tigers," or *ootora*) and not with the general jail population (who are kept in "pig boxes," or *butabako,* which are not as nice).

Proper interpretation of the statute's terms isn't obvious. The statute defines "public," for instance, broadly to include trains, drinking establishments, streets, and ships (art. 3), but considerable ambiguity remains. Police guidelines provide more detail, instructing officers to make arrests in drinking establishments if the person is in a seat but not in the kitchen, in hospitals if the person is in a waiting room but not an examination room, and at police stations if the person is in the office but not in other sealed rooms.[160] Police are to determine intoxication by "words, appearance, walking, smell, clothes, and other physical observations"; a blood alcohol test is unnecessary.[161] Disorderly speech or behavior includes shouting to cause a fight, overturning a park bench, sitting in someone else's seat at a drinking establishment, staring, peeping, and "clinging too closely to a woman."[162]

Police data categorize the intoxicated into *meitei* (intoxicated) and *deisui* (unconsciously, completely, or blackout drunk, dead drunk, or "wasted"; I use "dead drunk" in this book). The former is said to result from drinking three to six bottles of beer, the latter from seven to ten.[163] In 2017 police nationwide protected 83,288 drunk people, including 4,673 intoxicated people and 78,615 dead drunk people.[164] It is unclear how the categories are determined for statistical purposes; in the 1990s police used only one category, drunk (*yopparai*), and they listed the number of such drunk protections in the same chart that detailed the annual number of lost children and injured people.[165] But it is unsurprising that the "dead drunk" category is the larger, as such people are more likely both to be spotted and to need protection.

Tokyo police data provide more granularity. In 2017 Tokyo police protected 14,424 drunk people, including 2,579 intoxicated people and 11,845 dead drunk people—about one-sixth of the national pool of those protected after drinking. About 15 percent of people in each category are women. About 75 percent are found outside; most are found between midnight and four in the morning; and most are held at a police station for up to eight hours. None of Tokyo's 102 police stations dominates the statistics, but the station with the most drunks is Shibuya, which accounts for about 5 percent of the total.[166] That 5 percent equates to 751 cases annually, or on average two people per night sleeping off alcohol in custody in Shibuya, though surely they do not space themselves so evenly on the calendar.

Most cases end there, as the drunk are simply released when they sober up, leaving only the persistent image in the mind of anyone who has spent much time in Japan of police helping them off the ground. In an average year, police nationwide send fewer than two hundred new cases of violations of the statute to prosecutors, and only about 10 percent of those two hundred are actually prosecuted.[167] Accordingly, case law is sparse; in fact I can find no published case of a prosecution based on the law. Public drunken nuisance, it seems, is handled at the police level. David Bayley explains how in his study of Japanese policing:

> Japanese police officers show an almost exaggerated solicitude for drunken people. They stand by impassively when teased by them, sometimes enduring a bleary baiting that would anger most American officers. Unless an individual is sodden or wild, they will allow him to go his befuddled way. Japanese drunks tend to be "happy drunks"; they are neither mean nor surly. On the street they are usually found in small groups, arms around one another's shoulder, reeling, staggering, singing, and joking. . . . The duty of a police officer is to protect them from their own excesses.[168]

This description of the police rings true, but there is no evidence that Japanese "drunks" are any "happier" than their counterparts around the globe, and there is plenty of evidence in this book that many in fact become quite "mean" and "surly." If they become so mean and surly that they are dangerous, Japanese police can use a "protective sheet" (*hogo shiito*), a blanket-like piece of plastic into which a drunk person is wrapped, not unlike a swaddled baby but perhaps better likened to a tortilla's role in a burrito. The device is not uncommon in the case law,[169] in the press,[170] or in real life.[171]

A 2014 case suggests ways the protection process can go wrong. After drinking at least three or four cups of oolong tea mixed with shochu in the afternoon, Kouno went with a friend to play pachinko. He misplaced his wallet at the pachinko parlor, and when it was returned to him, he complained—loudly—that someone had taken the cash. He kicked an employee and yelled to others that he was a gangster (implying that they had better watch out). An employee called the police.

The incident occurred in Tsu City, Mie prefecture, where many people speak in a Mie dialect that is somewhat similar to the more widespread Kansai dialect of western Japan. In the court's narrative, Kouno speaks this local dialect. The police don't, which arguably heightens their status, or at least their formality, both in the story and in real life. The first police officer asked, "Are you carrying anything with your name on it?" in standard Japanese, to which Kouno responded in dialect, "Why you gotta say that?" (*nande sonna koto iwana akan no ja*). Then, "because of the noise" of the pachinko parlor, the officer leaned toward Kouno's ear, where he was close enough to smell the strong odor of alcohol, and asked, in standard Japanese, "May I ask you one more time?," to which Kouno responded crudely, "Are you screwing with me?" (*nametonnoka*). He apparently was not; the officer took Kouno to the station, where the court found that police dragged him twenty-two meters, causing injuries and psychological trauma. The court found no evidence that the police injured him any more than that, as he had claimed. The court awarded damages of only $668.[172]

In the end, then, the plaintiff won—but not before the court had given sufficient evidence about his identity to let us know who the cops were dealing with. Sure, the cops roughed him up a bit, and for that he has to be compensated. But come on, the court seems to say: This is a man who drinks shochu in midafternoon, is abusive to pachinko parlor workers, claims to be (or might actually be) a gangster, and speaks coarsely. Wouldn't it be reasonable to assume he was looking for trouble?

Why

Surveys show that drinkers in Japan—or at least "lighter" drinkers, those who drink less than 60 grams of alcohol per day—tend to drink for four primary reasons: to cope ("I usually drink when I feel irritated or upset"), to enhance their feelings ("I like how drinking makes me feel"), to be sociable ("I like drinking with my friends and/or colleagues"), and, to a lesser extent, to pair with food ("I drink to better enjoy a delicious meal").[173] Drinking motivations are heterogeneous; men drink to cope proportionately more than women, and women drink with food proportionately more than men.[174] Drinking motivations vary even among members of an occupation that is said to be relatively homogeneous: the police. One study shows that Kyoto cops are significantly more likely to drink for "friendship" than neighboring Shiga prefecture cops, who are significantly more likely to drink for "relaxation" and "recovery from fatigue."[175] And drinking motivation even varies with the type of alcohol consumed: Sake consumption tends to correlate with winter and food, beer with thirst and stress release, and whisky with relaxation.[176]

Still, socializing, and especially workplace socializing, tends to dominate both statistics and case law as a reason for drinking. When people whose beer consumption had increased were asked why, the number one answer (12.9 percent) was "no specific reason," and the number two answer (9.8 percent) was "work."[177] In the case law, much work-based social drinking occurs at *nomikai* (literally, "drinking gatherings" that often occur after work),[178] as well as at special occasions like *shinnenkai* (beginning-of-the-year parties)[179] and *bounenkai* (end-of-the-year parties), which fill many workers' December and January calendars in order to strengthen multiple relationships.[180] Some cases contain especially blunt statements of obligation; one boss, for instance, told his employee, "[T]hese *nomikai* are very important to our company."[181]

How important? Let's explore some possible answers through a case involving Goto Yuuichi, a Tokyo University law graduate and elected member of the Tokyo Metropolitan Assembly. In 2004 Goto visited Tokyo Metropolitan Fuchuu Hospital, a public institution. His specific mission was to expose the evils of alcohol consumption in a public workplace. He had received an anonymous letter stating that the hospital kept alcohol in refrigerators in its clinical laboratory. Because the hospital was always open, Goto believed that the presence of alcohol at any time was problematic. When he visited the hospital, he announced his identity, gained access to the laboratory, and found wine bottles in a refrigerator. According to the court, the events that occurred next were as follows (Goto is the plaintiff in the case):

> In an accusatory tone, the plaintiff asked the laboratory chief when he drank the alcohol. The chief responded that the bottles were for end-of-the-year parties, retirement parties, and farewell parties. The plaintiff responded, "Those times are fine. But those aren't the only times, right? You're drinking here and there. It's easy to investigate these things." The chief responded, "Sometimes we drink after work." The plaintiff asked, "How many times a week?," to which the chief responded, "About once a week, but sometimes two or three times." The plaintiff then turned to the head of the department and scolded, "See, this is what's going on here." The department head said "But sir [*sensei*], that's for after work."
>
> The plaintiff then turned to a second refrigerator, opened it, and asked the chief, "By the way, what is this wine?" The chief was unsure of its origin but had a dim memory and answered, "I think it was a souvenir from an employee's trip to Europe . . . yes, I think that's right." The plaintiff then removed four bottles from the refrigerator, saw that all four bottles were labeled in Japanese, and said to the chief, "This isn't foreign." The chief said, "I think these are souvenirs, but I really don't know." The plaintiff put the four bottles of wine on a table and took photos. The chief said, "We will destroy this wine soon," but the department head said, "There is no reason to throw them away; just have the person who brought them take them back," and tried to put the bottles back in the refrigerator. The plaintiff told him not to put them back, and the department head put them in a cardboard box.
>
> The department head then thought he should talk with the plaintiff in the head office, and as he told the plaintiff so and headed toward the exit, box in hand, the plaintiff returned to the first two refrigerators, and found a third refrigerator on the opposite side of the room. The

> department head and the laboratory chief followed him, and the plaintiff found whisky and shochu bottles on top of the third refrigerator. He said angrily, "This is up here so openly. You're really using this a lot." He took photos. He then strongly said, "Open it." The laboratory chief didn't feel that he could refuse, and he opened the refrigerator. Inside were bottles of brandy and wine.

Following this thirty-minute investigation, Goto wrote a report on his website in which he announced that he had found twelve bottles of wine, and that the chief drank two or three times per week. The report, the fiftieth in a series that concluded, for reasons unknown, with number 138 in 2009, recounted the events and then stated that it was clear that the chief was lying when he said that the wine bottles were souvenirs from abroad because the labels on the bottles were written in Japanese.

The hospital and the Tokyo governor, through handouts distributed at press conferences, countered that Goto's report was false. One handout concluded, "The assembly member's actions cannot be called legitimate assembly investigative activity, and are highly regrettable. Accordingly, we protest vigorously, and demand an apology." Goto claimed that those statements defamed him, and he sued.

The court focused more on the differing opinions regarding alcohol than on the issue of whether the plaintiff had been defamed. The plaintiff, the court found, "takes the position that alcohol shall not be allowed at any time in the hospital, which is a 24-hour care facility, while the administrative institutions believe that if done in moderation, such as at farewell parties and after work as needed to have frank job-related discussion among employees, drinking is not entirely unacceptable." The court found that the hospital's response was reasonable under the circumstances, especially considering that the plaintiff had called the laboratory chief a liar in his report. The court ruled that the plaintiff had thus not been defamed, and he lost.[182]

The hospital's view on workplace drinking merits closer examination. According to the court, the hospital believed that alcohol is acceptable not only at events like farewell parties but, perhaps more important, also after work "as *needed* [*hitsuyou na baai*] to have *job-related* [*shigotojou*] *frank* [*zakkubaran*] discussions" among employees. Apparently the work-related drinking occasions are not simply parties, ice-breakers, or celebrations but times when work is accomplished because alcohol allows for frank discussions, perhaps especially among workers of different ranks.

That sentiment is not unusual; a plaintiff in a 2011 case assumed that because the person who had asked him to drink was a workmate, "the situation was clear that the conversation while drinking would be work-related."[183] And again

Mishima Yukio's fictional account of Judge Honda and Osaka High Court dynamics is instructive: "As for geisha parties, Honda attended only the traditional end-of-year celebration which was held at the Seikanro in the red-light district of Kita Ward. On that night superiors and underlings caroused freely together, and occasionally somebody or other, emboldened by saké, expressed himself to the Chief Justice with unwonted frankness."[184] The court in Goto's case thus seems to be stating what most readers of the opinion already know, a position with which Goto disagreed.

Given this environment, it should come as no surprise that people sometimes feel pressure at work to drink. In a 2012 case a Windsor Hotel employee sued her boss and her employer over the emotional injuries she claimed she sustained from "power harassment." Power harassment is defined in Japan in various ways, but most often as behavior that takes advantage of superiority in the workplace and that leads to physical pain, emotional distress, or "violation of personal rights." A 2012 survey by the Ministry of Health, Labor, and Welfare found that a quarter of employees had experienced such harassment.[185] The employee in the Windsor Hotel case alleged that her power harassment came in the form of, among other things, forced drinking.

According to the Tokyo District Court, the employee was hired in March 2008. Two months later she went to an izakaya with three coworkers, including her boss. (Note the parallels here to the rape case from the previous section, which began with a female employee going to an izakaya with three coworkers one month after her employment began.) Beer was ordered, *kanpai* was exclaimed, and the boss began drinking beer, followed by shochu mixed with hot water. The boss asked the plaintiff-employee to drink. She said, "I can't drink. If I drink, I throw up, so please forgive me today." The boss said, "It's okay if you just have a little," "You [*omae*, a very informal term] can drink, can't you?," and "You have such a big body [so you can take it], so just hurry up and drink." The plaintiff, who felt guilty about a mistake she had recently made in the workplace and also was aware that her boss was a fifth-degree judo wrestler, said that she felt pressured to drink. She drank, went to the restroom, and returned to her seat. When she volunteered that she had vomited, her boss responded, "Well, if you can throw it up, you can drink it," and continued to fill her cup. She drank two-thirds of a cup.

The court found that the plaintiff had suffered power harassment and ordered $7,000 in damages. But the award was based on other facts (the boss left the plaintiff a voicemail in which he threatened to kill her), not forced drinking. Among the factors that the court considered in finding that the drinking did *not* constitute harassment: the plaintiff was drinking at a public place, she returned to her seat after vomiting, and she talked to her boss about work there. Most important, the plaintiff drank only two-thirds of a cup over a three-hour period.

"Usually [*tsuujou*] in an instance of persistent and bully-like forced drinking," the court stated, "the amount of liquor drunk naturally [*touzen*] would be large." As the amount consumed was relatively small—and not "naturally" large, as in the "usual" case of harassment—the boss had not abused his power in that regard.[186]

The court's story and ruling present a confident view of workplace drinking norms in Japan. "Bully-like forced drinking," the court explained, "usually" involves more alcohol, "naturally." The court isn't saying that it doesn't find the plaintiff credible; after all, she won the case based on other claims—though perhaps it helped that she recorded a murder threat. It's simply saying that in order for forced drinking to be actionable, the amount of alcohol needs be large. Even if the plaintiff vomits, a small amount of alcohol is insufficient to fit the court's vision of drinking-related harassment.

This might be seen as an example of routinized justice—if you don't drink a certain amount, you don't have a claim no matter how poorly your body processes alcohol. But note that by the time the court reaches its ruling, it has given readers many other details about the parties that present them clearly as individuals. The plaintiff felt she needed to drink based on her guilt over a workplace mistake, and socializing was a method of atonement. She also apparently was not a small person, or at least that was her boss's opinion, a point that the court might be using to signal that a small amount of alcohol should not have had such a large effect as to induce vomiting, or might have been using to show that the boss was insulting. Finally, that the boss was a fifth-degree judo wrestler is a fact the court might have taken into account in other aspects of its ruling, but it apparently did not affect the ruling in the drinking context.

The plaintiff seems to have accepted the invitation to drink out of a combination of emotion and acquiescence to social norms. As for the latter, consider a survey of "on-the-way-home-from-the-workplace" drinking (*shigotokarei no sotonomi*). The survey found that about half of work-related drinking events begin at 7 p.m., last two (45.4 percent) to three (49.2 percent) hours, and cost about $30 per person. More important, 54.9 percent of business people say the purpose of drinking is "communication," and 58.9 percent—two-thirds of men but only half of women—think that drinking parties are "necessary" to the workplace.[187] Approximately 18 percent of workers say they cannot refuse an invitation from the boss. That figure is higher for young people; 34 percent of men in their twenties and 31 percent of women in their twenties felt they could not refuse the boss.[188] A survey sponsored indirectly by the Ministry of Economy, Trade, and Industry finds that 60 percent of *problem* drinkers are businessmen who claim that "getting drunk" is part of their job and "a mark of company loyalty."[189]

Workplace-pressured drinking is also discussed in many of the cases involving death from illness or suicide that is blamed on overwork. Death from overwork, *karoushi,* is a well-known and well-defined problem in Japan. When alcohol appears in those cases, it is sometimes raised by the defendant company to show unhealthy drinking habits (and not work) as a cause of death, and sometimes is raised by the plaintiff or the court as a tool to show the degree to which drinking is mandatory in the company setting. One family of a deceased worker successfully argued that he "did not enjoy alcohol, but had to drink with sponsor companies and the management division often."[190] In another winning case "the deceased had a strong sense of responsibility, worked hard at his job, was well regarded for his work, had a warm and quiet personality, but was occasionally high-strung, and although he drank enough to keep company with others on company trips and the like, he never drank with his friends."[191] And in another, the court matter-of-factly stated that the deceased "refused to go drinking with his co-workers even when asked" because of alcohol-induced liver disease; although alcoholism (and lost love) might have contributed to the deceased's suicide, his long working hours (eighty-two days in a row of ten-hour-plus days cooking soba and udon at an Osaka-based chain noodle shop) were, the court determined, the cause of his depression and his death.[192] And in attributing another death specifically to overwork and not drinking, a court pointed out, "The deceased was 160 centimeters tall, weighed 60 kilograms, did not smoke and was not in the habit of drinking at company banquets."[193] At 160 centimeters (just shy of five feet, three inches) and 60 kilograms (132 pounds), the teetotaling victim of overwork becomes even more deserving of our sympathy, and the company even more deserving of our opprobrium.

Outside of the work environment, emotion is often given as a reason to drink. Anger is one such emotion: In a case of multiple murders and arson on the eve of Valentine's Day, a man angrily drank home-brewed shochu after his would-be lover, who worked at a snack, jilted him.[194] Sometimes the relevant emotion is sorrow, as one defendant expressed at a beer-drenched Buddhist memorial service held forty-nine days after the death of his friend. (His drunk driving thereafter killed four and injured four.)[195] In both cases the court made clear that the drinking was a response to a specific emotion and not a causeless occurrence.

Surveys suggest that regular non-work-based drinking has complex motivations.[196] In an effort to better understand the complex relations between drinking and crime (alcoholics are more likely to commit violent crimes but less likely to commit theft),[197] the Ministry of Justice sponsored a study of prisoners and their attitudes toward alcohol. In the survey 1,440 male convicts were asked about their motivations for drinking. The results were divided by level of drinking: heavy drinkers, regular drinkers, social drinkers, and occasional drinkers. (The responses to this question did not include the 236 prisoners who did not drink.) Across every category the number one reason for drinking was "to have fun" (59.2 percent for heavy drinkers, 70.1 for regular drinkers, 67.3 for social drinkers, and 55.5 for occasional drinkers), and the number two reason was "to get close to another person" (48.8, 53.9, 54.7, and 45.8 percent, respectively).

"Fun" is of course relative. Given the rules and rituals of Japanese society, many people use drinking as an excuse to behave mildly irresponsibly. People in Japan often appear drunk after just one drink because they are allowed to "let go." Indeed "letting oneself go" is a defining feature of many court narratives. For instance, the Tokyo High Court, discussing a "habitual drunk driver" who "felt no guilt about drunk driving because everyone around him at his workplace did so as well," described his actions at a company branch office end-of-the-year party held at a boarding house (*minshuku*):

> As the end-of-the-year party began, the defendant began to drink, and he began to let himself go [*ki ga ookiku nari,* perhaps more formally "to feel uninhibited"], drinking more and more. He had a large bottle of beer and two *gou* of sake, and as he drank, he felt more lively. He realized that if he drank more, he would get drunk, and according to his testimony, he remembers that he drank two or three large bottles of beer, two or three *gou* of sake, and a cup or two of shochu mixed with warm water. But according to the testimony of B, who drank with him, the defendant drank around four large bottles of beer, had nearly ten cups of shochu mixed with warm or cold water, and it was unclear how much sake he drank. . . . He was so drunk by the middle of the end-of-the-year party that he leaned on B's back and stretched his legs out straight.[198]

After the defendant's first drink, he "let himself go," freeing himself from workplace rules. We can infer from the phrase "stretched his legs out straight" that the partygoers are kneeling or sitting with their legs crossed on tatami mats that are the typical floor of boarding houses (and the only boarding house within the court-specified two-minute walk from the station the court named is all-tatami). Stretching one's legs is a sign of complete relaxation.

So it sounds like this particular defendant's motivation was quick fun, which he seemed to have (until he drove drunk, crashed, killed two people, lost his job, and was sentenced to six years in prison). Less popular motivations—again, among prisoners—are bleak. Among heavy drinkers, 42.6 percent drink "to forget things I hate," 35.7 percent drink when they "have free time," 27.4 percent drink when they are sad, 11.6 percent drink when they are angry, and 12.8 percent drink "whenever." The third and fourth motivations, forgetting and free time, rate relatively high across all categories; even among the occasional drinkers, 23.9 percent drink to forget and 18.7 percent drink when they have free time.

The "free time" and "whenever" answers are similar to cases in which people force themselves to drink to pass the time, as if doing so is the natural thing to do when one is free. In a 2005 murder case, for instance, the defendant (and the court) made a point of saying that after the murder he "couldn't stay at home sober at home and couldn't get myself to feel like drinking." (He sniffed glue instead.)[199]

A 2011 case brought by heirs of a Self-Defense Forces air force officer, Yamakawa, presents a different reason to drink: mental health maintenance through self-medication. His heirs sued the Japanese government and a superior officer, claiming that they caused his suicide. In April 2005 Yamakawa was stopped on his moped for drunk driving as he returned from a cherry–blossom–viewing party (at which many people drink; as Jeffrey Alexander notes, one popular hangover remedy producer in the 1950s advertised that cherry blossom viewing, alcohol, and liver disease go together).[200]

Yamakawa was not convicted; he was not even arrested and was not subject to military disciplinary measures. But when his superior officer learned of the incident, he slapped Yamakawa on the head and made him swear to never drink again. Alcohol, Yamakawa's heirs claimed, was one way in which he relieved stress, and his oath of abstinence, which they described as an order from a superior officer, caused him psychological difficulties because it robbed him of a stress-relieving mechanism. A military doctor who testified agreed: Yamakawa's "opportunities for self-expression and his stress reducers were limited, as the things that relieved his stress, drinking alcohol and his passion for soccer, were limited. As these opportunities were both substantially limited, he became psychologically burdened, and in the fall of 2005, he became depressed, leading him toward suicide."

Yamakawa broke his oath in October. He drank only tea at a going-away party, a typical occasion for drinking. But at the after-party (*nijikai*, literally, the "second party") he drank alcohol. Soon thereafter his superior officer lifted the ban. The court ruled: "Considering the very long period of more than five months that Yamakawa was not able to drink in front of the defendant [superior officer], even though the officer's objective was to encourage abstinence, and even if the deceased's behavior while drinking was somewhat inappropriate, drinking is part of the deceased's private life, and the actions were illegal." Yamakawa's inability to relieve his stress with alcohol for the "very long" (*soutou choukikan*) period of five months led, the court found, to the stress that led to his suicide. It ordered the defendant Japan to pay roughly $900,000 to Yamakawa's heirs.[201]

Yamakawa's motive for drinking was stress release. That says a lot about Yamakawa, but it also says something about the court, as it quotes the doctor saying that without the release of alcohol (and Yamakawa's passion for soccer), suicide was an expected result. Given that someone in Yamakawa's life was requesting an oath that he abstain, it seems that alcohol might have played a greater role in his lifestyle than mere stress release, but the court nonetheless viewed it through that lens when it issued its ruling. It was not the presence of alcohol that mattered, but its absence.

Yamakawa's case is not the only one in which the absence of alcohol seems to make life worse. In a 2006 opinion the Aomori District Court said that the defendant, who committed arson twice and stole women's underwear off a clothesline, "was in and out of the hospital for his alcoholism, and after his hospital stint from June of 2005 until April of 2006, his siblings would not help him, and he lived alone. Even when he received welfare assistance, he spent it on alcohol, and yet he could not always drink when he wished. . . . He became lonely over the fact that he lived alone and had no one to talk to, and he became upset." Those feelings, caused in part by the absence of alcohol, led him to commit his crimes. He was sentenced to two years in prison, a year less than prosecutors had requested. The court's sympathy for this person's life seems clear.[202]

Some people claim simply to enjoy drinking. In such cases Japanese has interesting vocabulary: *suki*. *Suki* literally means "to like," but it has a wide set of connotations. One can *suki* vegetables, jazz, or another person—when one confesses love for or a crush on another for the first time, *suki* is the appropriate word. But "liking" alcohol (*sakezuki*), like Yamakawa's use of alcohol for "stress release," often can be a euphemism for serious health problems, including alcoholism.

In a juvenile case, for instance, a fourteen-year-old's shoplifting was explained in part because his father "did not have money because he liked alcohol [*sakezuki*] and had to change jobs frequently,"[203] language that elicits pity for the teenager. In a 2012 case the drunk-driving defendant "liked to drink [*inshu ga suki*] and drank with dinner [*banshaku*] at home every night,"[204] another benign reference to a pattern that seems potentially problematic.

Sometimes courts more deliberately juxtapose "liking" alcohol with the undesirable consequences that follow. In a 2001 case, a deceased man was described as follows: "Taro liked alcohol, and almost every day, he would drink four or five *goụ* of sake, and had been treated for alcohol-related liver damage."[205] In a 2003 divorce case the court described the plaintiff husband: "The plaintiff claims that he does not drink much, and that he usually is not intoxicated, but we affirm the defendant's testimony, which states that the plaintiff liked alcohol, consuming at least one-third of a *shou* bottle every day."[206] And in a 2003 case, the court described the family life of a woman who attempted to murder her sixty-nine-year-old husband: "They usually got along well, but they both liked alcohol and when they would drink they would have intense marital fights."[207]

The court offers no commentary on "liking" alcohol in these cases, but the focus on individual facts seems to suggest that attendant negative consequences are to be expected.

Some opinions suggest a harsher normative stance. In a 2009 opinion, for instance, instead of describing the defendant as a person who likes alcohol, the court described him as someone who "refused to give up his much-liked cigarettes and alcohol even as his daughter and her husband attempted to help him stop."[208] The court pushes the language from "like" (*suki*) to *daisuki* ("much-liked," or perhaps "loved"), and the implication is clearly negative.

Finally, in a real estate law case from 2003, the Tokyo District Court stated that the plaintiff "liked drinking and was an alcoholic" (*sakezuki de aruko-ru izonshou*).[209] That phrase seems an accurate description of some of the people in the previous cases as well, but courts generally avoid the direct correlation. Rarely do courts attribute alcoholism to a defendant, and never is it criticized, perhaps because alcoholism in Japan is seen as a moral failing and not a disease, and courts tactfully choose to avoid that particular extralegal conversation.[210]

* * *

Given what we've learned so far, what are socially appropriate Japanese drinking norms? The law, accompanied by some external evidence, suggests the following: Drink alone or drink with friends, preferably workmates, as drinking is an important part of one's job. Drink shochu and beer in izakaya, whisky and water in snacks, and sake wherever you wish—but not the really cheap stuff. Drinking at home is fine as long as you don't overdo it. Drink for pleasure, drink to solidify relations, drink to reduce stress, drink during free time, drink whenever. But a warning to anyone who plans to follow these rules: How you drink says a lot about who you are, who your friends are, how others might perceive you, and what kinds of acts you're likely to commit. Let us now turn more specifically to those acts.

3

Drunk Crimes

A Ministry of Justice survey asked prisoners in Japan—yes, prisoners—how a sentence for murder should be affected if the defendant "was drinking at the time of the crime and wasn't able to make sound judgments." Thirty percent said that the punishment should be increased greatly, and 16.6 percent said it should be increased somewhat. A little less than 34 percent said that the drinking should have no effect on punishment, and nearly 18 percent thought the punishment should be decreased, either a little (13.1 percent) or more (4.8 percent). A similar survey of people on probation found that nearly 54 percent favored higher penalties for murderers who had been drinking, and about 8 percent favored lower penalties.[1]

Of course, prisoners might not be Japan's most representative subpopulation. Precisely because of their incarceration, they might seek stiff penalties for others, based on feelings that a person should not be allowed to commit a crime *and* have the luxury of a drink. Or maybe those for whom intoxication led to imprisonment feel remorse. Whatever the reason, this population has experienced the justice system, and for whatever reason the collective take of the majority seems to be that alcohol adds a layer of blameworthiness to criminal acts.

Importantly, though, the prisoners had contrasting views. Judges are no different, and in this chapter we explore the expression of those diverse views through the cases. Japanese law regarding the role alcohol plays in criminal culpability differs significantly from American law but is relatively straightforward. Still, because application of the law is difficult, courts generally turn to one of two methods. The first, psychiatric testing, is inexact, but an aura of scientific precision surrounds it. The second, analysis of drunkenness according to subjective factors, is arguably even more tangled, as courts are predictably unpredictable in their treatment of different individuals.

Drunk Japan. Mark D. West, Oxford University Press (2020) © Oxford University Press.
DOI: 10.1093/oso/9780190070847.001.0001

Categorically Drunk

In Japan, as we saw in the "drinker's paradise" case, intoxication can lower or even entirely eliminate a defendant's liability. Here's how it works. With few exceptions, the Japanese Penal Code (art. 38) requires a prosecutor to prove criminal intent for any crime. The Code then provides in the subsequent article (art. 39) that people who suffer from "loss of mind" (*shinshin soushitsu*, alternatively, "unsound mind") are not punishable and that weak-minded people (*shinshin koujaku*) may have their penalty reduced.

Each of these terms—"loss of mind" and "weak-minded"—are purely legal terms of art; the Penal Code sets forth no accompanying biological or psychiatric standards. But a 1931 Supreme Court case that effectively defines the insanity defense elaborates on the terms to create evidence-based definitions. The Court held that "unsound mind" or "loss of mind" occurs when a "mental disease renders a person without the ability to appreciate the difference between right and wrong, or good and evil, or to control actions on the basis of the distinctions." By contrast, "weakness of mind is a lower impairment that does not eliminate responsibility to the same extent."[2]

Courts use psychiatric evidence to determine whether a defendant meets those conditions, but that evidence is not dispositive. A prominent example in the case law, often cited as precedent, is a 1984 Supreme Court case in which the defendant, a member of the Naval Self-Defense forces, proposed marriage to the sister of a high school friend. She rejected him because of her family's political affiliations. The spurned defendant broke into her home and attacked her sister, her sister's three children, and people who were awakened by the noise, leaving five dead and two seriously injured. The psychiatric expert witness found no "loss of mind," but the Court concluded on its own, after evaluating the defendant's situation holistically, that he suffered from a "weakness of mind" and therefore had some, but not full, culpability.[3]

Readers familiar with U.S. law will find Japanese insanity law familiar. Like some U.S. jurisdictions (and the Model Penal Code), insanity in Japan requires a mental disease and has both a cognitive component (ability to appreciate the difference between right and wrong) and a volitional component (ability to control actions). However, the Japanese standard in intoxication cases looks much more like the so-called M'Naghten rule (the insanity standard used in most U.S. states), which lacks a volitional component.[4]

Where Japan differs—dramatically—is its designation of intoxication as a form of insanity. In Japan insanity is a condition that can constitute "loss of mind" or "weakness of mind," and thus intoxication can completely exculpate a defendant. By contrast, in the United States a defendant does not have a constitutional right to present evidence of voluntary intoxication.[5] Most states do not admit intoxication evidence, allow it only as a defense to crimes that require purpose or knowledge, or allow it only for crimes that require specific intent.[6] Only rarely does alcohol consumption arise in the American insanity context; for instance, one outlier of an opinion allowed a defendant to argue that his longterm alcoholism caused neurological damage that excused his conduct[7]—but even that case clearly stated that "voluntary intoxication may not provide the basis for an insanity defense," and as such differs from the Japanese usage.[8]

Because Japan treats intoxication as a form of insanity, pursuant to the Code of Criminal Procedure a prosecutor (art. 223) or a judge (art. 165) can order a psychiatric evaluation of an individual who claims intoxication or otherwise appears to have been intoxicated at the time of the crime. Sample psychiatric evaluations are widely available. Large but ordinary Japanese bookstores (which sell an extraordinary range of books) carry both guides for conducting evaluations and anonymous sample volumes by well-known psychiatrists. Like court opinions, the structure of evaluations is standardized. They usually include a statement of the circumstances of the crime, family history, adult history, recorded dialogue, the results of various psychiatric tests, and a description of the defendant's psychological disposition at the time of the crime.[9]

The theoretical mooring in the Japanese psychiatric community for the determination of whether a person experiences loss of mind or weakness of mind as a result of intoxication is the work of the Swiss psychiatrist Hans Binder (rhymes with "cinder"). Binder, the Japanese literature asserts with hagiographic reverence, was born in Zurich in 1899. He was an only child. His mother was a housewife and his father a doctor. He eventually rose to prominence at Universität Basel, where he authored more than seventy articles. He is virtually unknown in the United States, and an internet search in English will produce few results. But his most prominent article, published in 1935,[10] is said (in Japan) to have received worldwide acclaim.[11] Beginning in the 1970s, Binder's work became the basis for intoxication analysis in Japanese courts.[12]

Binder's 1935 article classified intoxication into two categories: simple and abnormal. Abnormal intoxication is further divided into two categories, complex and pathological, for a total of three. There are no strict blood alcohol requirements or other physiological measures. As the Tokyo District Court explained fifty years later:

> Traditionally, the analysis of intoxication is based on the widely used taxonomy of the Swiss psychiatrist Binder (published in 1935). . . . Simple intoxication is regular intoxication, with a showing of extremely

> common signs of intoxication. Complex intoxication is quantitatively different from simple intoxication, occurring when an individual's excitement level and endurance is quantitatively much stronger and often appears abruptly, with flare-ups of periods of stupor, with a generally irritable mood, frequently leading to crimes of violence and injury. In principle, the actions of such a person can be understood from the surrounding circumstances, but due to a loss of control, the person's usual personality changes. Broad memories are maintained, and widespread memory loss is rare. By comparison, the acts of a person experiencing pathological intoxication cannot be understood from the surrounding circumstances. The person shows a transformation into a fantasy-like state of disabled consciousness, and the development of amnesia is common.[13]

Japanese courts often convert these three categories of intoxication—simple, complex, and pathological—from Binder-based psychiatric evaluations directly into legal categories. The Tokyo District Court states dogma: "Simple intoxication results in full capacity, complex intoxication results in limited capacity, and pathological intoxication results in complete lack of capacity."[14] "Complex intoxication," which is believed to occur easily in people with diseases such as alcoholism or arteriosclerosis, is said to be the most common form of intoxication seen in crimes that involve intoxication,[15] but "pathological intoxication" is more prevalent in the published case law. Not all courts follow such rigid categorization,[16] and sometimes courts must manage competing evaluations (for instance, one evaluator might find complex intoxication; another, simple intoxication),[17] but the parlance is common. Even when courts do not cite Binder, they often still rely heavily on his classification system.

Consider a case from 2013 in which the court worked around Binder's categories even as it cited an evaluation that relied on them. On September 10, 2011, at an apartment in a Tokyo municipal housing building—and therein lies an unmistakable class marker—with two friends, from 6:30 until 11 p.m., the defendant drank nearly seven *gou* of sake, roughly a couple bottles of wine. His friends left him, and he began to shout "Why are you leaving?!" He attempted to destroy his friend's apartment, then left with a tomato box in which his friend had kept shoes by the door. He put his drinking glass in the box, wandered around the complex, and shouted, "Who the hell are you?" at a resident who tried to avoid him. The defendant chased after the resident and hit him with the box. The resident called the Japanese emergency number (110), and the police arrived to find the defendant wearing no pants. When they questioned him, he punched one of them. They took him to jail.

A psychiatric expert conducted an evaluation. Although the defendant's nakedness at the time of the crime suggested pathological intoxication, the psychiatric evaluation's conclusion was merely complex intoxication. But, the court noted, "according to the doctor's psychiatric evaluation, intoxication can vary widely based on the defendant's mood, the emptiness of his stomach, his blood glucose levels, and various psychological factors, and because these factors are different at the time of the test and the time of the crime, the test showed not pathological intoxication, but complex intoxication." The court found the defendant to have been pathologically intoxicated and therefore lacking capacity.[18]

The court's out-of-hand rejection of the expert's conclusion in the evaluation is curious, but the more interesting language here is the discussion of "the test." The court is referring here to a specific methodology for determining Binder categorization: a drinking test (*inshu shiken*). Until this point, Binder analysis might seem merely simplistic, though its simplicity might give it a certain elegance. But the drinking test turns Binder from simplistic to odd, as the test is exactly what it sounds like: An expert induces intoxication in the defendant and observes.

Drinking tests have a few varieties.[19] In a "reproductive drinking test," an evaluator attempts to reproduce and observe the exact state of intoxication that the defendant experienced at the time of the crime. But because of the challenges involved in replicating the amount of alcohol, the type of alcohol, and the time of drinking, two other methods are commonly used. First, in a "provision-based drinking test," the evaluator reproduces the blood alcohol content that was recorded at the time of the crime and evaluates behavior based on that amount. In this case, alcohol can be input intravenously, but the usual method is simply to have the defendant drink until his blood alcohol reaches the appropriate level.[20] Second, in a "free drinking test," the evaluator allows the defendant to drink at his own pace and then observes his behavior.[21] No matter which Binder drinking test is used, simple and complex intoxication are the most common results.[22]

Before we go further, let me be clear: Japan is a far outlier here. Japanese researchers report that besides Japan, only China uses Binder categories. Within Japan the only actor that uses Binder outside of psychiatrists and the courts is the Ministry of Health, Labor, and Welfare.[23] Laypeople do not use these words, and they have never appeared in the official proceedings of the legislature or any of its various committees. Despite the fact that Binder wrote in German, the Japanese criminal law scholar Kondou Kazuya reports that Germany never considered using Binder's categories, as it had revised its Penal Code along different lines (using blood alcohol levels) just two years before Binder's publication appeared.[24]

So why Binder? Binder analysis entered Japanese courts because a generation of Japanese criminal psychiatrists preferred it, and it filled a vacuum in which no detailed legal standards existed.[25] With little more than that, Binder analysis became a standard part of a psychiatric evaluation.[26] Like other forms of psychiatric evaluations, a defendant can refuse the drinking test, but doing so means forfeiting the intoxication-based insanity claim.

Binder analysis (and drinking tests in particular) is a clear expression of individual justice in alcohol-related cases, as courts look beyond legal categories, beyond factor-driven tests, and directly to personal responses to alcohol in their determination of culpability. (And they can then disregard the evaluations if they wish.) To better appreciate these personalized dynamics, it is useful to examine a few evaluations. I provide one evaluation for each of the three Binder categories.

First, a case of "simple intoxication." The defendant was accused of robbery and attempted rape of a bar hostess. In his evaluation the evaluator describes the crime, the defendant's family history, and his physical characteristics. He then conducts a preliminary psychiatric examination unrelated to intoxication, focusing on IQ and Rorschach tests. Then the drinking test begins. The evaluator explains:

> In order to evaluate the defendant, he was administered a drinking test. According to his testimony, his affidavits, and the affidavits of related people, at the time of the crime, from 10:00 p.m. until the time of the crime, a period of approximately two and one-half hours, he drank five shochu "high sours," a medium-size bottle of beer, and three glasses of whisky (Suntory White) on the rocks. Approximately three and one-half hours after the crime, at 4 a.m., his breath alcohol content was measured at 0.40 milligrams per liter, and it is believed that he was in an intoxicated state at the time of the crime.
>
> For the test, the defendant drank whisky (Suntory White) mixed with water, at his own pace, without breakfast. He was also provided with dried squid and rice crackers, and as his state of intoxication was observed, blood samples were drawn at regular intervals and alcohol levels were estimated using gas chromatography.

The evaluator appears to be using a combination of a reproductive drinking test and a free drinking test. The test does not seem particularly arduous, as the defendant is given snacks of the sort that are typically eaten while drinking; squid and rice crackers go with Japanese whisky like cheese goes with wine. (Such snacks, called *otsumami* when paired with alcohol, appear in the case law twenty-four times but signal nothing. Only four of those cases are criminal cases, and *otsumami* help establish a timeline in each but present no apparent pattern.)

The testing begins, and the results are recorded as follows (the note-like quality of the prose reflects the original Japanese reports):

> 10:00 a.m. Beginning of Drinking Test. First blood draw. Blood alcohol 0 mg/dl. Began to drink whisky mixed with water at a ratio of two parts water to one part whisky. Looks slightly nervous. Drinks normally and the subject of conversation turns to drinking establishments. Asks for more after the fourth cup (one cup = 90 cc of whisky).
>
> 10:30. Begins to speak loosely but there is very little change in mood. Talks about singing karaoke at "R." Turns to water as he prepares to sing, but doesn't sing. Pace quickens and begins to drink in large gulps.
>
> 11:00. Has drunk 360 cc of whisky. Third blood test. [The report omits a second blood test.] Blood alcohol level 209.5 mg/dl. Can somehow stand on one leg. Able to walk to the bathroom alone. No major change in outward appearance but eyes begin to droop.
>
> 11:30. 450 cc of whisky. Fourth blood test. Alcohol level 290 mg/dl. Cannot stand on one leg. Sits stunned in silence. Face is white. Hardly touches seventh whisky, has hardly touched snacks. Talks about how he drunk-dials people and how strict his father was. Obviously tongue-tied.
>
> 11:45. Begins vomiting. Takes guard's shoulder and is led to the toilet. Sobs there. Returns to the room with tear-stained face. When asked about the situation recalls things from the past and cries.
>
> 12:00 p.m. Fifth blood test. Alcohol level 364 mg/dl. Eyes are watery, vomits in room, passes out.

The evaluator then records blood alcohol content for the following three hours.

The evaluation next describes the defendant's psychological state at the time of the crime. It repeats the previous facts, explicitly citing Binder, and delivers the bottom line: At the time of the crime, the defendant's intoxication was "simple."[27] Apparently vomiting, crying, and memory loss are insufficient to achieve a Binder result that reduces culpability; based on this evaluation, a court would likely find that the defendant had complete responsibility for his crimes.

A second drinking test, in a case that results in a diagnosis of complex intoxication, uses similar methodology. The defendant allegedly committed arson of his own home. After reciting the particulars of the case, the evaluator explains the drinking test:

> According to the testimony of the defendant and related parties, on the night before the incident, beginning around 6 p.m. and ending around 11 p.m., the defendant consumed nine beers, five brandies, and two *gou* of sake. Replicating the defendant's drinking is difficult, but the brandy that he drank on the night of the crime (Suntory V.S.O.P.) was prepared, and a free drinking test, in which the defendant drinks at his own pace, was conducted. He was also provided with dried squid and rice crackers, and as his state of intoxication was observed, blood samples were drawn at regular intervals and alcohol levels were estimated using gas chromatography, in order to confirm the degree of the defendant's alcohol habit and his abnormal intoxication.

In this case, then, the defendant receives the free drinking test, again with his personal brand of brandy and snacks. The test proceeds:

> 10:00 a.m. Beginning of drinking test. First blood draw. Alcohol level 0 mg/dl. Subject begins drinking brandy mixed with water. Talks about relations with T.M. and O.S. Doesn't remember O.S. being present at the time of the crime. Talks about going to a bar and a drinking place were a certain Philippine woman is.
>
> 10:30. 270 cc of brandy consumed. Second blood test. Blood alcohol level 105.2 mg/dl. Body shakes when standing on both legs. Can stand on one leg. Says that when he drinks three bottles of beer at home, starts barhopping and stays out all night drinking. About twice a month has to take a day off from work. Becomes insolent and talks about problems at work, complaining about his father-in-law and the young workers. Voice shakes (a little excited) and says, "I get angry. What kind of idiot burns down his own house?" Requests and is given a cigarette. Says he wants today to be his last day of drinking, that he is reading a book on Zen, and sadly utters that this incident is a punishment determined by Zen and so on, but shouts angrily that wasn't aware of the incident and that he didn't do it.
>
> 11:00. 450 cc of brandy has been consumed. Third blood test. Blood alcohol level 239.7 mg/dl. At the time blood is drawn, shouts "Why are you drawing blood?" and has a glazed look in his eyes. Smokes a cigarette. Staggers back to seat and shouts, "I did nothing wrong, screw you," "Don't screw around with that 'you committed arson' stuff, screw

> you." Speed of drinking slows, slurs words. When a clock chimes, says "Shut up, screw you, be quiet" while grabbing the back of the collar of the examiner's smock. Eyes are glazed, speech becomes difficult, words become sparse, and pace of drinking slows.
>
> 11:15. Brandy 450cc consumed. Anger and excitement become extreme, evaluator feels danger, and drinking is halted. Defendant smokes a second cigarette. Expression is tired. Mutters snippets about angels, human failures, asks to be saved, says he is innocent, and so on. Puts cigarette in ashtray on table in front of him, but leaves it there without putting it out.
>
> 11:30. Fourth blood test. Blood alcohol level 371.3 mg/dl. During the blood draw, is agitated, and shouts "You idiot, don't screw with me." Eyes glazed. Slams fist on table and shouts "Stop screwing with me!" Handcuffs and chain around the back are put in place. Does not ask to drink. Becomes quiet, mutters to himself indistinctly. Suddenly begins pounding the legs of the chair, shouting, "I did nothing!!" Guards at his sides restrain him, continues to shout at the guards "Let me go!" Smokes third cigarette. Throws it in the trash without putting it out. Leaning in his chair, suddenly bites the back of own left hand. Guards at his side hit him in the head, and when they hold him down, he says "Sorry" repeatedly like a child. Until he is released he pounds the table, and when he is restrained, he repeatedly says "It's my fault, sorry" to the guard. Facial expression is troubled and he appears ashamed.

Blood is then drawn every hour until 3 p.m. Unable to walk on his own, the subject is led away with a guard holding both of his arms.

The evaluator considers the evidence, presumably along with his subjective views about how the defendant "appears ashamed," and pronounces the subject to have been in a state of complex intoxication at the time of the crime.[28] A court in this case, upon examining the report, is likely to find the defendant suffering from a weakness of mind. Accordingly, if the court finds the defendant guilty of arson, it will give him a lower sentence than it would give a sober arsonist.

Now consider a case of pathological intoxication and a more contextualized and detailed psychiatric evaluation. Three characteristics are initially used to categorize the defendant: thirty-two years old, male, married. The crimes are then described: On the streets of Osaka, beginning around 11:50 p.m., the defendant, using a hunting rifle, shot thirty-eight-year old male A in the back and twenty-one-year old B in the chest. A died immediately and B died later from blood loss. The defendant then went to a taxi in a parking lot, where he shot twenty-one-year old female C, the passenger, in the stomach, and twenty-four-year-old male D, a passerby, also in the stomach. C died eight hours later from blood loss. D lived. The defendant then returned to the street, where he shot a thirty-two-year-old police officer in the stomach and legs. The officer lived. Ten minutes later the defendant attacked, but did not shoot, an unidentified woman before he was arrested.

An interesting point lurks here: Gun crimes in Japan are extraordinarily rare. Rarer still are gun crimes that lead to psychiatric evaluations, as a psychiatric evaluation is required to obtain a hunting rifle. The evaluation merely notes that the defendant enjoyed hunting with his grandfather, obtained a permit at age twenty-five, bought a rifle, and began hunting birds—facts that are necessary in the Japanese context to make sense of the gun possession.

The evaluation describes the defendant's history, beginning with his birth to an unwed mother. He had a rocky childhood, ending in petty crimes at ages seventeen and eighteen, for which he spent time in a juvenile facility. He married at twenty-four and had two children. At the time of the crimes, his wife was seeking a divorce.

He began drinking at age sixteen. He usually drank alone, and he drank "beer, never sake or whisky." His common practice was to drink one can of beer with dinner at home and fall asleep. As he reached adulthood, he began to enjoy drinking in bars and snacks and began to drink up to two beers, but the instances in which he drank more than that amount soon increased. He began to become violent when he drank.

The evaluator conducted a physical examination, and then a psychiatric one in which he determined, among other things, the defendant's IQ to be 77, 87, or 81 depending on the test used.

Two drinking tests were conducted. For each test the evaluation contains a chart that shows blood alcohol levels and amount of alcohol consumed over time. In the first test, a provision-based drinking test, the defendant was given 180 milliliters of sake at noon. (Note that the evaluation has previously stated explicitly that the defendant does not drink sake; the purpose of the drink was simply to raise the defendant's blood alcohol level and apparently not to reproduce his drink of choice.) After twelve minutes the defendant felt ill and had a headache. After twenty minutes he began repeatedly to express discomfort. After 324 milliliters of alcohol, the evaluator halted the drinking. After thirty minutes the defendant could not stand, and after an hour and twenty minutes he fell asleep. He remained in a stupor. After four hours the evaluator called to the defendant, who replied, "My head is numb" and "My arms and legs are strange."

In the second test, a free drinking test, the defendant was given beer at one in the afternoon. Within thirty minutes of drinking 933 milliliters, he was silent and unable to stand. After an hour he had consumed 1.266 liters. He put his head on the desk and said, "I can't lift my head." After an hour and fifteen minutes and

1.659 liters (remarkably the evaluator has allowed the drinking to continue), his breathing became labored and it became difficult for him to move, and finally alcohol consumption was stopped. He asked to visit the restroom and had to be assisted by two physicians. He fell asleep after one hour and forty minutes, again in a drunken stupor.

From these two tests the evaluator extrapolates a timeline of the defendant's intoxication levels during the events leading up to and including the crime, at each step noting the amount of alcohol consumed. (The defendant drank four beers and 190 milliliters of whisky in a three-hour period.) The evaluator carefully codes each step with markers that designate the extent to which the defendant had memory. The evaluator finds that the time at which it was unclear whether the defendant had memory was at 11:30 p.m., before the shootings, at the time he retrieved the key to open his gun locker. Each event, each moment, each interaction is described in extensive detail.

Finally, the evaluator gives his psychiatric conclusion (pathological intoxication), his conclusion based on the law (the defendant was unable to discriminate right from wrong), and even his formal legal conclusion (the defendant had no capacity).[29] A court, then, likely would find the defendant not guilty, as he was of unsound mind.

Again, outside of Japan this kind of analysis is unusual. A postarrest drinking test that determines culpability is not the kind of thing that U.S. (or most other) courts would contemplate, not only because of questions of evidence and manipulability but also because the practice simply seems unlikely to yield useful information. If there is merit in the practice, though, it lies in its ability to individuate. Through Binder-based drinking tests, Japan has established a system in which two people with the same external physical characteristics who commit the same crime after drinking precisely the same amount of alcohol can have wildly different levels of culpability.

To see how courts employ the evidence from drinking tests, consider a case from the Fukuoka District Court in which a man was accused of stabbing a woman in her sleep while he was under the influence of alcohol. According to the court, the defendant was a chronic alcoholic, living in and out of the hospital, where he often was kept in padded rooms. On the day of the incident he had six *gou* of sake, four or five highballs, and a large quantity of beer, all with a friend, at a cabaret (*kyabukura,* a drinking establishment like a snack but generally differentiated by charges by the hour, a customer's ability to choose his female companion, and often by permission to date the companions). They then finished the evening at a snack. The defendant, the friend, and the victim fell asleep at the victim's home. In the middle of the night, the friend was awakened by the victim's groaning. When the friend asked what was happening, the defendant said, "It's none of your business. Go back to sleep."

Unbeknownst to the friend, the defendant was stabbing the victim in the abdomen at the time.

When the friend awoke, the defendant said, "I did nothing" and "It's not a big deal." The two took the victim to the hospital in a taxi. The defendant then took another taxi to a liquor store, where he bought whisky. He considered hanging himself but was arrested before he could do so. He was charged with murder.

Two psychiatrists conducted drinking tests on the defendant. As always with published opinions, we don't have the actual evaluation to consult, but the court quotes it at length. In the first test the defendant hallucinated, punched the wall, ate cigarette ashes, and drank his own urine. (Given the steps required to achieve that last act, it is not clear how or why this occurred or was not prevented.) In the second test the psychiatrist allowed the defendant to drink so much that he passed out, so the results were not as clear as in the first test, but it is clear that the defendant hallucinated. The psychiatrists, and subsequently the court, concluded that the defendant was pathologically intoxicated at the time of the crime and thus had no responsibility. The court thus found him not guilty.[30]

From a U.S. lawyer's perspective, this case is amazing. The court, relying primarily on evidence of what happens when the defendant drinks in front of evaluators who have a say in his criminal culpability, has determined that *at the time of the crime,* the defendant was not culpable because of his drinking. His sentence wasn't merely reduced because of his drinking. Nor was it increased, as it would be in some legal systems, or pursuant to the opinion of a plurality of the surveyed prisoners from the beginning of this chapter. He walked. The court does not mention the negligence or recklessness that might have been involved in his decision to drink; he simply is not guilty of stabbing the victim to death.

Courts sometimes question drinking test procedures (and as they do so they affirm the procedurally valid version of the test). In a 2006 case, a psychiatrist determined a defendant was pathologically intoxicated at the time of his crime. Over the course of a drinking test lasting two and a half hours, the defendant was given one liter of beer and 850 milliliters of shochu, for a total of roughly 262.5 grams of alcohol. The psychiatrist measured the defendant's blood alcohol level four and a half hours after he began drinking in order to approximate the blood alcohol at the time of the crime—which occurred four and a half hours after he began drinking. The evaluator found a blood alcohol level of 258 milligrams per deciliter, noted that the defendant was unable to speak and had no control over his bodily functions, and determined he was pathologically intoxicated pursuant to a Binder analysis.

The court's problem with the test here wasn't the result but the calculation on which it was based. The psychiatrist determined the amount of alcohol to be used in the test by looking at the amount of alcohol purchased according to a liquor store receipt. But that receipt and the amount of alcohol it represented was split seven ways, so it was difficult to tell exactly how much the defendant had drunk. That receipt-based calculation assumed that the defendant had consumed two or three glasses (280 to 420 milliliters) of beer and three or four medium mugs (750 to 1,200 milliliters) of shochu on the rocks—but, the court noted, the defendant drank twice that amount of beer in the drinking test. In the police report, the defendant said he had three or four glasses of beer and three or four shochu on the rocks, but in court he claimed that he had had roughly the equivalent of a medium mug of beer and three or four beer mugs of shochu on the rocks. "It is difficult," the court said, "to estimate objectively the amount of alcohol that the defendant consumed from statements made by witnesses, and it is clear that the amount of shochu drunk depends on the size of the glass and the amount of ice. Accordingly, it cannot be said that the amount of alcohol that the defendant consumed in the drinking test was the same as what he actually drank [at the time of the crime]." The court found the examination unreliable, the defendant not pathologically intoxicated at the time of the crime, and, logically and naturally pursuant to Binder analysis, the defendant not suffering from a loss of mind. Based on the defendant's demeanor and blood alcohol level at the time of the crime, however, the court found independently that he was "weak-minded," thus allowing for a lower sentence. The court dismissed the psychiatrist's evaluation based on its own detailed examination of the amount of alcohol consumed and, without further consulting the evaluation or ordering another, simply used the available evidence to reach its conclusions.[31]

Sometimes courts struggle significantly with psychiatric evaluations. Consider, for instance, a murder case from the Osaka District Court that relied heavily on evidence regarding alcohol consumption. In this 2008 case the defendant was accused of stabbing to death a "delivery health woman." (The delivery health industry dispatches, or "delivers," women to visit men, where they legally may engage in any sexual activity besides vaginal intercourse. Illegal activity surely occurs behind closed doors.)

The defendant confessed but claimed that he was pathologically intoxicated at the time of the crime. The court analyzed the claim with great care:

> From the age of 20, the defendant started drinking, and at around age 24 he drank a large bottle of beer or two every night. At 26, he began working in the nighttime entertainment industry [*mizu shoubai*], and his drinking increased to the point that he drank two beers and half a bottle of whisky every day. He drank at work but his drinking was never discovered, so he seems to have held his liquor [*sake ni tsuyoi*] well. When he married and began working at a company, he would drink one or two "One Cup" sake before going to work. Before his divorce,

> he began to feel sick from drinking, so he stopped, but he soon began drinking beer again, and afterward the volume increased, and at izakaya and snack he would drink four or five large bottles of beer. From his late 40s he began to become drunk more easily, and he reduced his consumption to three or four large bottles of beer. He began to have hangovers, which he had not experienced before. . . .
>
> In May of 2003, the defendant's hangovers became more severe, and he began to tell his colleagues at work that he was sick and skip work. To feel better, he drank sake and shochu, and when his life became worse he drank more. During this period, he stopped eating. A few days after this period, he was unable to stand, and he called an ambulance and was admitted to the hospital. At the hospital, he experienced auditory hallucinations in which he heard voices in the sounds of air conditioners and rain.
>
> For the next two months, the defendant did not feel like drinking, but he soon began to go out drinking with his friends, drinking for five days in a row. He recovered a bit by taking liver medication. He did not hallucinate during this period.
>
> The defendant did not drink for about five months, but beginning in early 2004, starting with just one drink, he fell into a weeklong period of drinking during which he became unable to move. His friend J came to his house and took him to his own home. During this period, the defendant stared at the wall and hallucinated that the wall was moving. He did not drink during this period, and began to have breakfast at his friend J's house. Occasionally he would have a drink, but because he continued to eat, he did not fall into lengthy periods of drinking.

This is a considerable amount of drinking history for the court to sort through and use officially as part of its legal analysis. In essence, it is doing the work of psychiatric evaluators, perhaps copying from their reports or perhaps analyzing on its own; it's not clear. In any event, the only issue before the court is still the defendant's state of intoxication at the time of the murder. Although the background can help inform that determination—and the mention of One Cup gives quite a bit of context—it does little to tell us how drunk the defendant was at the time of the crime. The court offers it, of course, so as not to provide routinized justice to the defendant; it purports to tailor its analysis to the specific individual with all the baggage that he brings to court.

And yet, despite the focus on the individual's intoxication history, when the court described the circumstances of the crime, it offered little concrete information regarding intoxication. It began its narrative of the crime three days before its occurrence:

> A few days before the crime, around December 16, 2004, the defendant, after a long absence, visited three snacks, and drank beer.
>
> At around 9 a.m. on the eighteenth, the defendant called his friend J, and in a listless voice said, "Let's take the day off." J understood that the defendant had been drinking again, and said, "You're drinking again? At the end of the year, let's give this a better shot," and went to work. Between 10 a.m. and 11 a.m., the defendant's friend K called him, and K thought that the defendant was drunk.
>
> On the nineteenth [the day of the crime] at 10 a.m., J called the defendant, and it was clear that he was completely drunk, saying meaningless things like "aaaa—uuuuu." J became angry and hung up.

It's not clear why the court began its narrative three days before the crime. I can speculate, but those guesses would make the most sense if the court also spent significant time on the criminal act and the defendant's level of intoxication at the time. It didn't. When the court described the crime, it merely said that the defendant visited his English class to complain to his teacher, ordered the delivery health worker, paid $80 in advance for a sixty-minute course, and eventually killed her as she phoned her employer, screaming into the phone, "Help! I'm going to be killed! Send a driver!"

The court described the scene with crime-drama-script specificity: "On the eastern side of his six-tatami-mat room was a sofa, stained with blood, on which lay the victim's down jacket, and on the western side there was a delivery health advertising flyer [*chirashi*] stained with blood." The court briefly discussed the fact that the defendant might have been experiencing alcohol withdrawal symptoms and seemed to have been intoxicated for some period of time after his return visits to the snacks. But it said no more in its own voice about the crime or the defendant's intoxication.

The core of the intoxication analysis is the court's examination of two psychiatric evaluations. One, by doctors "S and T," stated that there were four empty bottles of shochu on the defendant's table, which the court suggested must surely be the doctors' mistake because elsewhere in the evaluation it was claimed that on the day of the murder the defendant drank only one or two bottles. (The court had noted only one bottle in the "facts" section of the opinion.) The court stated that this discrepancy did not make the entire opinion unreliable—but it is interesting that the court thought the discrepancy worthy of mention, as it would seem to have little bearing on the conclusion.

The "S and T" evaluation found that the defendant was not pathologically intoxicated but in fact was suffering from "simple" intoxication. But the court found other faults with the test. The court said that during a drinking test, the defendant was told to drink as quickly as possible, as the effects of the alcohol would be difficult to observe if he drank slowly. "Regardless of whether this was a free drinking test (or some similar drinking test) or a provision-based drinking test, this method of conducting a drinking test in an evaluation leaves suspicions." The court found that the S and T evaluation was difficult to use properly.

An additional evaluation, which the court labels the "U" evaluation, asserted that cases of complex intoxication are difficult to re-create in a drinking test, and accordingly it examined only the facts of the crime and the defendant's likely mental state at the time (using, the court noted prominently, "facts that the S and T evaluation did not consider"). The U evaluation concluded that the defendant was in a state of complex intoxication. The court found the U evaluation credible and adjudicated the defendant to have been "weak-minded" at the time of the crime, resulting in a six-year sentence, much shorter than the fifteen years that prosecutors had sought.[32]

The court's opinion is thorough. It parses through years of the defendant's background, criticizes the S and T psychiatric evaluation (perhaps rightly so), and painstakingly reaches its own conclusion that the defendant was merely weak-minded, a conclusion derived from Binder taxonomy that seemed inevitable from the beginning.

Perhaps it comes as no surprise that vocal critics of the Binder method, such as the writer of the U evaluation, have emerged, most of them arguing that better, more widely accepted methods of psychiatric evaluation exist.[33] Another easy criticism here, and there are many, is that context matters; the place at which you drink, the time when you drink, and the people with whom you drink can have markedly different effects on how your intoxication is expressed. Binder tests make no attempt to mimic any of those contextual factors, and few drinking environments seem more sterile than drinking alone in front of an examiner, pen in hand, guard at the ready.

The 2009 implementation of a lay judge system in Japan that requires ordinary citizens to sit on panels together with professional judges to decide certain classes of criminal cases highlights additional concerns. Before May 2009 judges tried all cases in Japan and could use professional discretion to decide how and when to apply the results of a Binder analysis.

Japan's lay judge system has two particular features that could call into question evidentiary concepts like the Binder method. First, the involvement of lay judges *only* in serious criminal trials, including murder and dangerous driving causing death or injury, means that lay judges are likely to see intoxication issues as a significant percentage of their docket. Second, unlike U.S. jurors, the assigned role of lay judges in Japan includes the investigation and questioning of the facts of a case. The Binder method, and its potential direct link to a legal outcome, could complicate that role.

These concerns were raised specifically in 2011 meetings led by the Ministry of Justice to evaluate the success of the lay judge system. Speaking to an investigative panel, Kuroda Osamu, a prominent psychiatrist with the Tokyo Metropolitan Matsuzawa Hospital who frequently conducts psychiatric evaluations, described the difficulties involved in conducting an examination for a lay judge panel:

> As most of you know, an evaluation usually is quite long, with tens of pages. But in a lay judge trial, the lay judges have only a few days during a public trial to read the documents, so the document must be heavily abbreviated. In these cases, the main portion of the evaluation is usually the only portion that is used, without the background factors such as the diagnosis or how the psychiatric injury influenced the crime.
>
> To accomplish this, first, the evaluation form was greatly simplified. . . . Additionally, for lay judge trials, the use of oral evaluations, such as the in-court use of PowerPoint presentations, has become common. . . .
>
> [In one particular case on which I worked,] the defendant claimed that he had ingested alcohol at the time of the crime, so it was necessary to create a chart that detailed the relation between alcohol and drunkenness. To do so, I had to explain the influence of alcohol on a person, including a brief introduction to the chemical background, such as how alcohol changes the body and how blood alcohol levels change over time after drinking alcohol. . . .
>
> Traditionally in cases of intoxication during a crime, the three-category Binder method has been used for many years, but I realize that lately that method is seen to have little scientific basis, so instead of giving that explanation, I explain the Anglo-American system that focuses on blackout.[34]

Three aspects of Kuroda's statements are worthy of note. First, the lay judge system has altered the nature of the evaluation from a long discourse to a summary model, either because lay judges cannot digest "tens of pages" in a few days or because the evaluation of intoxication evidence is always a new exercise to them (unlike judges, who review many cases). Second, Kuroda says that he no longer uses the Binder method due to its lack of a scientific basis. If other psychiatrists follow Kuroda's lead, use of the method will decline. Third, apparently the judges in the case do not complain about the use of methods other than Binder. All three factors point toward a system in which lay judges in particular make judgments about capacity and criminal responsibility without reference to rigid categories, even with professional judges serving on the same panel. It is the exercise of precisely this kind of everyday, commonsense judgment that many who supported the lay judge system desired, and it is likely to lead to justice that is even more individualized.[35]

Subjectively Drunk

As we saw in the pantless drunk case in the previous section, courts can stray from Binder analysis to apply their own subjective concepts of drunkenness, with little discussion about why they are doing so. But sometimes patterns underlie those subjective judgments. Law and medicine scholar Tanaka Keiji's study of intoxication in Japanese criminal law finds that when courts decide alcohol-related weakness-of-mind cases, they usually cite in their reasoning at least one factor of the following eleven: the defendant had a motive, was aware of himself and his actions, had considerable judgment, had substantial memory of the incident, was coherent, had the ability to move and speak normally, had stable behavior before the incident, had behavior with an understandable purpose, did not have impaired consciousness, is not a chronic alcoholic, and becomes violent only when he consumes large amounts of alcohol.[36] Here I want to consider how courts apply three of the more commonly used of those eleven elements to determine whether a person is drunk: judgment, motive, and understandable purpose given the circumstances.

Judgment

In a Chiba District Court case, the defendant was accused of sexually assaulting and murdering a five-year-old whom he had lured with the promise of chocolate. Three psychiatric experts testified that the defendant suffered from pathological intoxication, which should lead to a not guilty verdict. However, the court noted that although that might be the judgment from the perspective of psychiatry, there were other factors to consider. In this particular case, the defendant had the presence of mind to take his victim to an isolated place and appeared normal after the incident. The court bypassed Binder analysis, substituted its own judgment, and sentenced the defendant to death. The defendant's ability to use judgment to move the victim overcame psychiatric evidence of intoxication.[37]

The Fukuoka High Court used similar logic in an arson case (not to be confused with the arsonist's evaluation in the previous section). In 2009, on Valentine's Day, the defendant, an "alcoholic" who was "unable to stop drinking, unsure of his health, self-loathing, and, uncertain of his future, fought with his (then) wife, and when his wife left he decided to set fire to his own house." The fire burned the house and an adjacent storage space to the ground. The district court found that the defendant was under the influence of alcohol and sleeping pills, in a state of "damaged consciousness." His memory was spotty, but he had motive and acted rationally, so he was merely "weak-minded" and not of unsound mind, and his sentence was reduced.

Or at least that is how the high court summarized the district court's (unpublished) opinion. The high court then delved deeply into the facts, starting long before the time of the crime, to create a richer narrative. In November 2006 the defendant established an izakaya. Already we have some indication of social status; the defendant has enough money to open a small establishment. He began to drink with customers. His alcoholism eventually caused liver damage. He required hospitalization. The narrative then jumps to include other tangential details: In May 2007 he fought with his wife and attempted to commit suicide by slitting his wrists, and although the court does not explicitly blame the wife for this event, her role is at least strongly implied. He recovered and spent the next year or two struggling (the court goes into significant detail of the struggles) with both alcohol and the financial viability of the izakaya, which was open only intermittently.

On the day of the arson the defendant was attempting to declutter his izakaya in order to reopen. As he did so, from nine or ten in the morning until one or two in the afternoon, he drank three or four *gou* of sake. He napped. His wife, who had been out, returned home, and he drank more as he ate his dinner at 6:30. Around 7:30 his wife left again, and he drank still more. Around 8 or 8:30, as he continued to drink, he began to imagine that his wife had left the house to get away from him. When she returned, he became angry with her and yelled, "You're late! Get yourself in line!" At 8:50 she left again. The defendant regretted the verbal harshness he had expressed to his wife (*iisugi*, literally, "saying too much"), but around nine, when he realized that his wife had once again left the house, he thought she might not come back, considered suicide, and took thirty sleeping pills with his drink. At around ten he dragged a futon to the entrance of the home, poured kerosene on it, and lit it on fire. He then ran to his next-door neighbor's home, banged on the door, and shouted "Fire, fire!" His neighbor called the fire department. When firefighters arrived, he told them kerosene had spilled when he tried to fill his heater (kerosene heaters are commonly used in Japan in February) and that the fire began when he turned the heater on. He began to become violent and yelled, "Do you have any idea how much I've had to drink?!" Police took him into custody. His blood alcohol level when measured in custody was 0.23 and was estimated to be 0.39 at the time of the crime.

The court focused on these meticulously laid out facts, including the noteworthy role of the wife—and not, interestingly, the defendant's objective blood alcohol level—as it attempted to construct a logical story of considered judgment. Those details make the defendant's thought process look as if it could not be anything other than purposeful. The defendant had the wherewithal to inform his neighbor of the fire, had sufficient wits about him to give false statements to the police, and had enough memory of the event to make his claims of a lack of memory or judgment questionable at best, as evidenced by his subsequent statement to the police:

> I decided to set a fire. First, I took the futon [a *kotatsu* futon, a heavy blanket that traps the heat from a heated table on the floor] from the living room and dragged it to the dining room. The futon was made of nylon and decorated with red flowers. I went straight from the living room to the dining room. Then I poured some oil that I already had in the house onto the futon. I can't actually recall if what I poured was kerosene for the heater or oil from a tank that I kept in the storage shed, but I'm sure it was one of those. I tried to set fire to the futon with a cheap lighter, but the lighter didn't work very well, so I added some newspaper advertisement fliers, lit the paper, and put that on the futon. Then the futon with the paper on it began to burn. As it began to burn, I left the house, either through the entrance or out the side door.

The court has attempted to impose a bit of precision by focusing on the purposive nature of the defendant's behavior, noting only a small gap in his memory. Despite that determination, however, the court found that the defendant was under the influence of alcohol and sleeping pills and based on that decided "that his decision-making power was impaired," though the power was clearly not entirely absent. The court finally punctuated its opinion with an official approval of a Binder-taxonomy evaluation that found the defendant was in a state of "complex"—not pathological—intoxication, but Binder seems hardly to have mattered.[38]

Motive

A 2010 Tokyo District Court case begins with the following language: "On July 22, 2009, at around 2:30 in the afternoon, in xxx number of xxx co-op, Meguro, Tokyo, with intent to kill, the defendant stabbed his father's 44-year-old girlfriend [*kousai aite*] in the right thigh, right chest, and right abdomen with a 14.3-centimeter kitchen knife several times, and accordingly, at 2:20 in the afternoon in the Red Cross Treatment Center in Hiroo, Shibuya, she died as a result of blood loss from a laceration of her right femoral artery." And then: "In the fourth open court session, the defendant stated that he thought the victim would die when he stabbed her." He "confirmed that instead of trying to save the victim, he set fire and ran away . . . and accordingly there is sufficient evidence of intent to kill."

Compared with the opinion in the arson case, those details are sparse, and they seem almost too sparse if the court is truly trying to convince anyone of intent to kill. The court did not describe what the defendant drank or how much; it merely noted that intoxication due to alcohol consumption was the primary issue in the case. The court discussed psychiatric evaluations, one of which included that the defendant was either in a state of simple or complex intoxication, the other of which simply recounted symptoms (easily excitable, hallucinations), but that took all of a paragraph.

The court focused instead on motive. The victim had called the defendant to ask him to help make his father's lunch. When he said he would not help her, the victim said, "If you're not going to help, you should go home. Don't you understand Japanese?" Normally those aren't fighting words, but in this particular case the court wants us to believe that they are, as they offer a clue about the particular defendant's psyche. The defendant, the court says, "had been raised in the United States as a child, and his memories of how hard he had worked on his Japanese in the past remained strong." To the court, those comments (whether it matters that they are uttered by a woman is unclear) and the victim's subsequent anger explained motive. "It cannot be said," the court stated, "that at the time of the crime he had full capacity for understanding his motive."

The court seems to be struggling here. The defendant had a motive—a backlash of anger over his upbringing and language ability—but he was drunk and mentally ill, so what work do the motive-related facts do, other than to tell us who the defendant is? The court then delved further into his "personality": "The defendant's mother testified that the defendant was kind as a child, and surely it can be said that in his childhood, the defendant was kind. But the defendant's middle school records show that he dabbled in marijuana (a far more serious offense in Japan than in the United States), punched his friends, and so on, so it cannot be said that the defendant had absolutely no relation to crime. However, there is insufficient evidence to determine to what extent this type of personality influenced the crime." Again the court appears to waffle.

Because of the U.S. connection, the unique motive, and the court's apparent indecision, I was especially curious about this case. The press widely reported that the defendant had an unusual given name, Shaka, which was easily searchable.[39] He was twenty years old at the time and unemployed. His father is Japanese; his mother testified in English. I have no desire to pry further, so suffice it to say that he has been released from prison, is using his non-Japanese-sounding nickname, and appears to be doing well, or at least well enough to be active on Facebook.

The court gave none of these specific facts as it took the middle road in its verdict: Motive plus mental illness and alcohol equals weak-minded but not unsound mind. After asserting that it must be considered that the defendant was raised separately from both parents and that he was sent to Japanese middle school with no understanding of Japanese—all of which apparently is relevant to individual motive—the court sentenced him to seven years, not the twelve requested by prosecutors.[40]

It is especially worth noting here that a lay judge panel decided the case. As such, perhaps the facts needed less exposition than in other opinions, in which judges might feel compelled to spin a complex narrative. Perhaps more significant, the panel was also the first ever to view a video of a defendant's police interview, which in this case occurred soon after the murder. One lay judge publicly stated after the trial that the video was determinative in establishing that the defendant was weak-minded from alcohol at the time.[41] In any event, what all decision-makers in the room seem to have found convincing, from whatever evidence, either as a manner of increasing the penalty from zero or decreasing the penalty from the prosecutor's request, was the "motive" of pent-up anger. Even under the influence of alcohol, the actions made sense.

Purpose

Similar to motive as a loose factor for determining intoxication-related culpability is the third factor, "an understandable purpose under the circumstances." Let's explore that factor in another case in which the defendant claimed that he was of unsound mind. It is from the 1960s and bears some historical artifacts, and yet there is consistency over time. Upon graduating from high school, the Gifu District Court tells us, the defendant went to work at a steel auto parts company as an apprentice but quit after a month. He moved in with his parents and helped in his father's delivery business. That information should help us code him.

In December he went drinking with eleven of his coworkers at an end-of-the-year party, where they drank 1.5 *shou* of sake. He began dancing with a geisha—a fact that evokes the 1960s but that also makes clear, among other things, that the delivery business is prosperous enough to hire a geisha for a year-end party. One of his coworkers, a thirty-four-year-old man described by the court as one who "takes to alcohol badly" (*sakeguse no warui*), told him, "Stop being so loud. Shut up." The defendant responded sarcastically, "You should teach me better." His senior colleague replied, "You young folks have to grow up." The group continued to drink, an argument ensued, the defendant pulled out a knife, and he stabbed his coworker to death.

A psychiatric examination, based in part on a drinking test in which the defendant drank six *gou* of sake and seemed to lose memory quickly, found that the defendant was pathologically intoxicated. The court disagreed and ignored the psychiatric evidence. The defendant was surely intoxicated, it accepted; unlike his victim, however, he did not take to alcohol badly. The victim yelled at him, he became uneasy and excited, argued back, and simply exploded. He never lost his ability to tell right from wrong; his judgment simply was diminished. The court was able to spin a narrative of understandable purpose under the circumstances, and accordingly found the defendant weak-minded.[42]

When the actions of the defendant stray from "an understandable purpose under the circumstances," courts often find the defendant to be of unsound mind and therefore not culpable. In a Tokyo case, the defendant beat, raped, and strangled a sixty-seven-year-old woman. He claimed that he was pathologically intoxicated. The psychiatric evaluations agreed, but at the same time suggested the possibility of manipulation that we saw earlier:

> [Dr.] Tanaka's evaluation and statement concludes, based on the defendant's violence during his drinking test, which in turn were acts based on his inability to understand his surroundings and an injury to consciousness, that his symptoms are particular to pathological intoxication. The same evaluation and statement also state that during the drinking test, before the defendant became violent, he told evaluator Tanaka three times, "This level of drunkenness won't make me abnormally intoxicated, and I'll be guilty, so I'd like you to keep giving me more alcohol until I show signs of abnormal intoxication." He also said, "Whether I'm guilty or not guilty, what will happen to my time in prison if there is an appeal," and so on, showing that he was very interested in his criminal responsibility and guilt or innocence.

The court disregarded those statements and found the defendant pathologically intoxicated. That finding reflected the psychiatric evaluation, but it also arose from the court's inability to discern an understandable purpose, as it found that "a normal, healthy young person like the defendant would normally never have a sexual interest in a 67-year-old woman or make her an object of sexual desire." The defendant was clearly drunk according to observers, and he recounted, "I don't know which house I went into, but I know I had sex with whatever woman was there."[43] That evidence was sufficient for the court to find the defendant of unsound mind. The Tokyo High Court affirmed, stating that the defendant's judgment was so impaired by alcohol that he had no idea what he was doing at the time.[44]

Set aside the issue of whether sexual desire (and not power or violence) was actually at issue in the case; the judges said it was, as Japanese courts often do. The broader point is that the defendant's actions made no sense to the court, and the court gave us very little in the way of background facts about the individual defendant to help us make sense of them either. Two psychiatric evaluations aided the court in making that decision, but even after considering those evaluations the court noted, "[T]here are many factors both before and after the crime that are unclear, and the defendant's intoxication is not a textbook case." Still, the fact that the defendant was intoxicated and his actions could not easily be stated in a comprehensive narrative guided the courts' decision.

It is in these cases of possible pathological intoxication that the evidence in an opinion can get especially murky. In a Fukuoka case of random violence, the defendant drank whisky, sake, and beer and then stabbed two strangers to death. He claimed that he was pathologically intoxicated. There was significant evidence to support his claim: Two days before the incident he went to the hospital, telling doctors that he needed to drink and that he was hearing things. He said that he could hear voices that sounded like "a running Tarzan," and he believed that flies and turtles were in his futon. (Neither flies nor turtles have particular cultural salience.) He was diagnosed at the time with mild alcohol withdrawal symptoms. Two psychiatric evaluations found that the defendant's pathological intoxication was not "textbook," but diagnosed it nonetheless. The court, noting that it could find no motive, agreed, and found the defendant not guilty.[45]

Prosecutors appealed. The high court noted that the defendant's claimed hallucinations varied from day to day; he once said he thought he was fighting a giant jellyfish at the time of the crime, but the next day he said it was a human woman. His memory was hazy, but he was able to recall the basic issues of the crime, including the fact that he was brandishing a knife. He was an alcoholic, and yes, he saw flies and turtles that weren't there. But his degree of intoxication on the night of the crime could not be confirmed, and his capacity was merely diminished, not absent. His basic behavior of "lying in wait for the victims to pass by for his attack and orderly planting himself for that attack were actions that were not completely incomprehensible for a normal person." Because his actions could be understood in some way, his mind was weak, not unsound, and the court accordingly sentenced him to seven years.[46]

Again, the court seems to be attempting to achieve a certain level of personalized justice, even delving into discrepancies regarding the subject of the defendant's hallucinations. But the court just doesn't seem to understand this person or his actions. We learn nothing about him that would make him appealing or relatable. The court can't identify with him, doesn't seem to feel the need for readers to, and leaves him in the middle ground of diminished capacity.

Contrast that case with a 2015 case of simple intoxication to see how a court can reduce complex behavior to a simple story. The defendant was born in 1978 and excelled in baseball as he entered high school. In his senior year he fought with his teammates and quit the team. He quit school and failed to hold a job. At nineteen he joined an organized crime syndicate, tattooed his back and arms, and entered a life of petty but violent crime. (In Japan these three events often come as an unfortunate set.)

With that, unlike the jellyfish fighter, we have a good sense of who this person is and a sense that the court understands him (or wants to) and his place in society. The crimes of which he is accused don't occur until December 3, 2014, when the defendant is thirty-six, and yet the court has given us many years of personal history. He's poor, he lacks a high school diploma, and his membership in an organized crime syndicate at least suggests that he might be either an ethnic or social minority.[47]

On the day of the crime he was angry about his job, upset that he had to work so much overtime, and yelled at his boss in front of his coworkers. He drove his "dated model Toyota Crown" (a common luxury sedan in Japan) to meet a coworker at a parking lot. And here is some detail:

> On his way home, at 4:28 p.m., he stopped at a convenience store to buy a beer ("Asahi Super Dry," 500 milliliters) and a beer-like alcohol product ("Clear Asahi," one can, 350 milliliters). He drank them while watching a Blu-ray [disc] he had rented from the video rental store "Geo Matsushita" the roughly 100-minute violent feature *Mad Max 2* (the story of a protagonist who seeks revenge upon those who do wrong and that contains chase scenes and scenes of cutting).

The defendant became "excited by the violent scenes, and when the film finished," at 7:12 p.m., he went back to the DVD rental store to get the sequel (presumably *Mad Max Beyond Thunderdome*, one of the few details the court did not explicitly provide). He then went drinking at a karaoke snack called Q, where he drank half a bottle of Asahi Super Dry, talked to a hostess about his work troubles, and drank glasses of his kept bottle of Oita barley shochu Nikaidou, on the rocks, approximately 79 millimeters per glass. (The court is being quite precise, presumably based on precise police reports; no one orders a 79-millimeter glass.) He then performed karaoke, singing "Kenka Joutou" by the artist Kishidan,[48] and dancing with customers he didn't know. He paid $60 of his $85 bill ("It's fine, it's fine, you can bring the rest next time," he was told, which seems reasonable for a snack owner to say to a member of an organized crime syndicate) and went to his car.

The actions that followed are unsurprising given the setup. At 11:45 he began a minor rampage. He crossed the street against the light and kicked a car that almost hit him, damaging it. He drove his car to a nearby ramen shop, where he paid his bill as well as that of three non-Japanese customers he didn't know, laughing as he did so. He then punched a man in the face, causing injuries that required two weeks to heal. He went home and watched ten minutes of the "*Mad Max 2* sequel DVD." Finally, he went back outside with a small knife and cut two men, giving them wounds that required two and three weeks, respectively, to heal.

The crimes here, random attacks on strangers, are not so different from the previous case, though of course the result—death—differs. But note how much more detail this court gives than in the previous case. The court is overloading with facts, presumably to tell a narrative that leads to a conclusion, and here it is: The defendant, the court says, was motivated by the excitement of watching violent movie scenes. The court then took a paragraph to explain that according to a psychiatric evaluation using the Binder method, the defendant suffered merely from simple intoxication, and as such he had full responsibility for his actions. No other evidence is offered from the psychiatric evaluation. No evidence is offered for the court's own pseudo-psychiatric evaluation of the defendant's *Mad Max*–induced mental state. The court sentenced the defendant to three years in prison.[49]

This is armchair psychology at best, but for a cause: It yet again humanized the defendant. By telling a set of specific facts, the court offered a theory of the defendant's mental state that wasn't contemplated by the law, or apparently even by the psychiatrist, but it was understandable in the case of this particular defendant on this particular night. He had a purpose.

Courts, then, apply the insanity-grounded, Binder-based, factor-driven standards that are specified by both Penal Code and Supreme Court precedent in what could perhaps generously be called a holistic approach. These judgments require and allow judges—and lay judges—to exercise considerable discretion.

Of course there is nothing grossly offensive to notions of justice about such an approach. In fact it seems unfair, at a minimum, to rely solely on the faux precision of evidence such as free drinking tests and blood alcohol levels in many of the cases discussed in this chapter. Japanese judges often seem to be asking "What would I do if I were in that situation?," a question that necessarily implicates an amalgam of factors that seem impossible for a legislature to articulate in a statute. When they do so, they need to spell out much more about "the situation" as well as about the defendant's particular background, to determine and explain how "I" would react in the defendant's shoes. The outcomes that result might fit the particular defendant but create ripples that can make the system appear malleable and uneven. If judges are using other factors behind the scenes of the opinion to counter that observation, they aren't telling us.

Japanese judges grapple with two tensions as they make such determinations regarding intoxication. First, they face a tension between the commonplace and the unique: between typical patterns of intoxication and unique individual reactions to alcohol. Some aspects of intoxication can of course be as generally applicable as police checklists suggest, and accordingly courts sometimes approach cases of intoxication as if its symptoms are universal. And yet when courts attempt to place individuals into those patterned forms of intoxication, they consistently point to specific characteristics and actions to highlight the degree to which a particular person fits, or doesn't fit, the expected pattern.

Second, judges face a tension between objective and subjective methods of evaluating intoxication. Regardless of the accuracy of Binder tests, they at least use established psychiatric criteria, just as Kuroda's so-called blackout analysis does, that help determine intoxication. Sometimes courts take Binder seriously, and sometimes they don't. Sometimes they utilize a judicially established factor-based analysis, and sometimes they don't. The differences cannot be explained by an underlying predictable pattern; rather, the glue that holds the opinions together seems to be the court's desire to tailor justice in each case, for each person, based on particular facts. Or at least those facts as presented by the court—including *Mad Max*, limited Japanese-language ability, and a history of baseball—often suggest.

4

Drunk Driving

In the criminal cases discussed in the previous chapter, defendants attempted to show that they were too drunk to be culpable. In drunk driving cases the opposite is true: Defendants obviously attempt to show that they were not drunk *enough* to be culpable (with one rarely seen exception to be explored: If the defendant is so drunk that he doesn't know he's driving after drinking, his culpability lessens).[1] The two types of cases share a common theme: Despite clear standards, whether based on Binder analyses or breathalyzer results, courts avoid mechanical justice and focus on people and their circumstances. Again courts navigate between the commonplace and the unique, and between the objective and the subjective. I first explore the ecosystem, legal and otherwise, for drunk driving, and then turn to the application and extension of the law. We will see drunk drivers again—I examine their sentencing in chapter 6 and drunk-driving-based employment terminations in chapter 7—but let's start with the basics.

The Drunk Driving Ecosystem

Japan has experienced two well-known drunk driving cases; here is the first. On November 28, 1999, fifty-six-year-old Taniwaki Keiichi, a professional truck driver, rear-ended the Inoue family car with his truck on a Tokyo expressway. The car caught fire. The father, Yasutaka, was pulled from the car, his back on fire. He required several operations to recover. The pregnant mother, Ikumi, crawled out of the car just in time to see the back seat area explode, killing their three-year-old daughter, Kaneko, and their one-year-old daughter, Chikako. Three others were injured in the accident.

At 12:30 p.m. on the day of the accident, Taniwaki had stopped for lunch at a rest area, where he drank a can of *chuuhai* (sho*chu* *high*ball). He also drank 280 milliliters of whisky, roughly six (U.S.) to nine (U.K.) shots.[2] He dozed for an hour and then resumed driving. The accident occurred at 3:30 p.m. At 4:15 he

Drunk Japan. Mark D. West, Oxford University Press (2020) © Oxford University Press.
DOI: 10.1093/oso/9780190070847.001.0001

took a breathalyzer test, which showed a 0.63 breath alcohol content, roughly equal to a 0.13 blood alcohol content (more on these measures soon).

Prosecutors charged Taniwaki with death by negligence in the performance of work or gross recklessness (Penal Code art. 211), which carries a maximum penalty of five years' imprisonment, and driving under the influence, which at the time carried a two-year penalty (Road Traffic Law arts. 117-2 and 65). Taniwaki made a terrible defendant for sentencing purposes. The Tokyo District Court noted that he made no attempts to negotiate a settlement with the family, did not submit a written apology to the court until the second public hearing in his trial, and did not appear apologetic. He had a record of poor driving. And immediately after the accident he said to the mother, "Why were you stopped? If you stop so quickly you're gonna get hit," and subsequently yelled, "I wasn't drinking and driving" and "I wasn't drinking; it's just cold medicine!"

When the court sentenced Taniwaki, it first noted this lack of remorse and apology. It then countered itself with mitigating factors: He had a long history of driving without incident; he had been fired and would not receive retirement pay; he had already been subject to "considerable social sanctions"; his company would help pay damages; and his wife and children would help him make a return to society. He was sentenced to four years in prison, a sentence many thought too short when balanced against—if this is possible—the tragic death of the children.[3]

Prosecutors, who had sought five years' imprisonment, appealed the sentence. The Tokyo High Court noted the seriousness of the crime and the influence that it had on society but, citing Taniwaki's newfound remorse and loss of employment, affirmed the four-year sentence.[4]

The Inoues brought a separate civil suit for damages against Taniwaki and his employer. Writing in 2003, the Tokyo District Court focused on the horrific nature of the children's deaths, whose cries could be heard as they burned. In so doing the court was sending a message—to the defendant as well as to those who read of the well-publicized judgment—as the precise nature of the deaths was only marginally relevant to Taniwaki's civil damages. The court further admonished, "Even as the plaintiffs told their children to follow social rules such as 'wear your seat belt,' an adult couldn't follow fundamental rules and took the children's lives." The court awarded a record $2.5 million judgment, including $340,000 for the life of each girl, to be paid in installments annually on November 28, the anniversary of the accident. The date was purposely chosen.[5]

November 28 became significant for another reason: On November 28, 2001, the second anniversary of the incident, the Japanese Diet (parliament) unanimously passed a new law criminalizing "dangerous driving causing death or injury," which we will examine in the next section, that allows for significantly higher penalties in a case like Taniwaki's. The new law came about in part as a result of a social movement sparked by the Inoues, which, the Tokyo District Court explained in the civil case, resulted in a petition signed by 374,000 people calling for increased penalties. A few months later penalties for drunk driving were increased and legal blood alcohol limits were lowered.

The post-Inoue legal regime for driving under the influence is strict. Article 65(1) of the Road Traffic Law broadly prohibits drunk driving: "[A] person may not drive a vehicle under the influence of alcohol." Two additional provisions in article 117 of the same law clarify "under the influence of alcohol" by dividing drunk driving into two types. First, article 117-2 states that a driver who is "in a drunken state (a state in which there is a fear [*osore*, 'risk' or 'danger'] that the driver cannot drive normally due to the influence of alcohol)" is subject to up to five years' imprisonment and a fine of $10,000. I will refer to that provision (*sake yoi unten*) as driving while intoxicated, or DWI. Second, article 117-2-2 provides penalties of up to three years' imprisonment and a fine of up to $5,000 for an intoxication level that is specified by ordinance. That ordinance, revised in 2002, sets the limit for intoxication as 0.15 milligrams per liter of breath or 0.30 milligrams per liter of blood. That measure translates in U.S. parlance to a 0.03,[6] but Japanese courts normally speak of breath alcohol levels. I will refer to that provision (*shukiobi unten*) as driving under the influence, or DUI.

The scheme results in two primary paths to criminal punishment for drunk driving, and the details are important. DUI, which carries the possibility of three years' imprisonment, is based on an equivalent blood alcohol level of 0.03, a level that is lower than any U.S. state (California, for instance, is 0.08),[7] and can result for many people after one beer.[8] DWI, which carries the possibility of five years' imprisonment, is based on a subjective determination by police that the person is unsafe to drive due to alcohol (and here California has a similar provision that gives prosecutors an avenue for conviction without a blood alcohol level).[9]

Cases of DUI, with its low, objective standard, might seem easier to prove. But Japanese courts, as one might infer from the use of Binder analyses, often take into account the fact that different bodies process alcohol differently. Accordingly, even in DUI cases, courts sometimes rely on subjective factors in addition to blood alcohol levels. The Miyazaki District Court, for instance, using medical tests and relying on evidence regarding the strength of the odor of alcohol on the driver's breath, found a driver not guilty of driving under the influence even when he exceeded a 0.25.[10] In a Kagoshima case, the driver blew a 0.35 but was found not guilty because he showed no other signs of drunkenness.[11] Conversely, the Tokyo High Court has held that cases of driving under the influence depend not only on a "scientific evaluation" but also on the amount of alcohol consumed, the circumstances of the drinking, and the amount of time after the consumption. Applying that standard, the court found a man whose breath alcohol measured 0.40 (in excess of the then-standard 0.25) guilty based not on the breathalyzer evidence but on evidence that he had consumed, on an empty stomach, four beers and five or six glasses of whisky and was in an excited state at the third bar he visited in one night.[12] Other courts have followed the Tokyo High Court's lead, noting that the chemical standard is not necessarily dispositive.[13]

Again there is no discernible pattern in the cases as to when a court will rely on objective tests like breathalyzer results and when it will use its own subjective judgment. Courts simply exercise their authority to do so, presumably based on their sense of how best to administer justice in each particular case.

Prosecutors are far more likely to charge breath-based lower-penalty DUI than police-observation-based DWI. Each year approximately forty thousand people are arrested for drinking and driving. Of those, fewer than one thousand are charged with the more subjective, higher-penalty DWI; most are charged with DUI.[14] All of these numbers are relatively low; by comparison, police make 1.4 million arrests for driving under the influence in the United States each year.[15]

Like the number of arrests, the number of alcohol-related automobile accidents and fatalities is relatively low in Japan. Japanese police determined that there were 3,355 automobile accidents in 2018 in which alcohol was involved, a figure that accounts for 0.8 percent of all automobile accidents in Japan.[16] There are roughly two hundred fatalities per year in those accidents.[17] In the United States in 2017, the number of alcohol-impaired driving fatalities was 10,874, more than fifty times greater than in Japan.[18]

What can account for such a large difference? Except for the fact that Japan drives on the left side of the road, as in the United Kingdom, U.S. and Japanese driving environments are not facially dissimilar. Driving in Japan is neither chaotic nor strictly orderly by comparison. My personal sense is that, compared to the United States, more drivers in Japan run red lights and allow others to merge, but each is a matter of degree. Another similar facet of driving in the two countries: Stereotypes of polite Japan notwithstanding, road rage occurs there as in the United States; the Japanese National Police Agency reported 13,025 incidents in 2018, nearly double the previous year's number, but the Japanese word for road rage (*aori unten*) can also simply mean "tailgating," which makes comparisons difficult (though for what it's worth, U.S. estimates from the 1990s suggest roughly 10,000 cases per year).[19]

Still, the U.S. and Japanese driving environments differ in important and measurable ways: The United States has roughly three times the drivers and the vehicles as Japan,[20] and Americans drive between roughly two to five times as many miles annually as Japanese, depending on how one counts.[21] But the drunk driving measures differ by far greater multipliers: The United States has fifty-four times the fatalities and thirty-five times the arrests. Perhaps people in the United States simply drink and drive more than people in Japan, or get caught more often, but several other factors have explanatory power: Speed limits are generally lower in Japan; Japan has fewer highways; large SUVs are relatively less common; and public transportation is abundant and efficient, at least in urban areas. (No prefecture has a lower per-capita drunk driving violation rate than Tokyo, with its sprawling public transportation network.)[22]

But even in the most urban areas, trains stop running around midnight, long before bars close. What should a drunk person do? One forty-four-year-old, reportedly drunk office worker named Nagao Shigeki found out the hard way in 2018 that one should not attempt to hold on to the doors of the last train and disrupt service for twenty minutes. (He was arrested.)[23] A popular tactic is to wait until the trains start running again around 5 a.m. Taxis are another answer. Even in small towns, due to zoning restrictions taxis often queue up in front of rows of buildings full of snacks and other drinking establishments. Japan offers an additional service to those who have driven to the bars and become too drunk to drive home: driving agents (*unten daikou*). To use a driving agent, one calls a service and requests one taxi with two drivers (at a premium price). One driver drives the taxi and the other drives the passenger's car; after the passenger and the car are dropped off, the two drivers leave in the taxi.[24]

The failure to use a driving agent service often contributes to a narrative of culpability. Consider a 2009 case in which a high school teacher appealed to the court after the Osaka Board of Education fired him for drunk driving (more on this kind of case in chapter 7): "At around three in the morning, the plaintiff called a driving agent service, but was told he would have to wait 40 to 50 minutes. Because the friend [with whom he was drinking] needed to go home early because of work, he let him get in his car, drove the car, took him home, and the driving-under-the-influence incident that is the subject of this case occurred."[25] In a Sendai DUI case three people were killed and fifteen injured: "Knowing that 'A' had been drinking continuously for six hours, but thinking that a driving agent service was troublesome and that he was quite sleepy, and wanting to go home soon and sleep, he thought that he wanted him to drive him home."[26] (The lower court in the case was more blunt and had a slightly different take on the facts: "He didn't even think of using a driving agent service.")[27] And in a similar case from Saitama in 2008: "The defendant, after continuing to provide 'A' with beer and shochu, instead of arranging for a driving agent service or a taxi, or asking a family member to pick him up, even knowing that A was quite intoxicated from his behavior at the drinking party, did nothing to prevent A from driving drunk."[28] And from Sendai in 2006: "Even though he had fallen asleep while drunk driving in the past, and he thought he should hire a driving agent service to take him home, he did not have enough money, so he thought he would just drive as far as he could."[29]

In each case the court makes clear that the mistake of drunk driving could easily have been avoided simply by using an assumed element of Japanese drinking life.[30] Courts are able to ask what the defendant should have done—perhaps based on what most people would do or perhaps what judges themselves would do—after the fact. It is likely that the particular events would indeed have been avoided if the defendant had done as the court said, but the more salient point is consensus on what constitutes responsible behavior.

The high-publicity nature of drunk-driving cases and the flexibility of courts even regarding objective blood alcohol levels lead police and prosecutors to take special care. Police follow especially detailed procedures that attempt to catalog a wide range of human behavior into tight descriptions. Pursuant to the Code of Criminal Procedure (art. 321(3)), police can use as evidence a Drunk Driving Identification Card. The card is a checklist and fill-in-the-blank list of factors that, in addition to blood alcohol level, include entries about a suspect's voice, manner of walking, body stance, smell, eye condition, hair condition, hand condition, clothes condition, facial condition, drinking place, drinking companions, and facial color (an especially important and often cited characteristic; studies show a facial flush in approximately 40 percent of East Asians when they drink).[31] The card also includes the question "Why did you drink?," a common answer to which in this context is "I finished work."[32] One manual states that suspects are likely to answer "I don't remember" to questions about timing, place, companions, and motives, but that police must persevere to get specific answers.[33] Another prosecutor-penned guide encourages police to obtain very specific statements from drivers—not merely "I was drunk" but, for instance, "[I] was so drunk that my head was spacey and my legs were shaky. Even though I knew it was dangerous to drive, and even though I thought I might be punished for drink driving, I still thought I wouldn't be caught, so I quickly made the decision to drive."[34] The same manual presses police to gather evidence about the circumstances of the drinking: "For instance, if the drinking took place at a drinking establishment like a snack, the police should go to that place, interview the manager about the defendant's drinking, obtain a copy of the receipt, and take photos of the bottle and glass that the defendant used."[35]

At least two factors drive the police need for detail in drinking-and-driving cases. First, police manuals state that the need arises because defendants often claim in court that police fabricated the timing of the alcohol consumption.[36] Second, prosecutors are required to prove intent—knowledge—in both DWI and DUI cases. In the case of driving while intoxicated, prosecutors need not show that defendants recognized that they were driving in an abnormal manner due to the influence of alcohol; rather they must show that drivers knew that they were driving after having consumed alcohol.[37] In the case of driving under the influence, the same must be proven, though the prosecutor is not required to prove that the defendant knew that his blood alcohol content exceeded the statutory level.[38]

Police, then, attempt to elicit from suspects statements that they knew they were drinking and driving. Sometimes these statements come not at the arrest stage, at which one manual suggests eliciting statements such as "I drank, but I thought I had sobered up" or "I drove but I didn't think I had had enough to be driving under the influence."[39]

Another leading police manual focuses on the postarrest stage and gives detailed examples of affidavits for suspects to sign. The examples are practically fill-in-the-blank precedent documents; the officer needs only to revise the names, dates, and drinking places and add in a few details, all in a specified style, about circumstances, words spoken, road conditions, and the like. All affidavits begin with an expression of understanding that the affidavit is not required, then spell out the events in minute detail. Most affidavits end with an expression of remorse. It is from these rich and ostensibly precise details that courts attempt to construct narratives of their own.

Applying the Law

In August 2006, seven years after the Inoue crash, the second major drunk driving incident that received national Japanese attention occurred. Ogami Akio, his wife, Kaori, and their three children, ages four, two, and one, were riding in their Toyota Land Cruiser on a bridge near Fukuoka in southern Japan. Behind them was twenty-two-year-old Imabayashi Futoshi, a low-level municipal official, in his Toyota Crown Majesta.

Imabayashi had come home after work at six that evening. He lived with his parents. He had a beer with his father, followed by three 180-milliliter glasses of shochu on the rocks. "Because," the court said, the next day was a Saturday and he did not have to work, he went drinking with two of his friends. That "because" is interesting. I know what the court means here: Imabayashi felt more free to drink on a night before a day off than before a working day. (Many people in Japan seem to share the sentiment, as the period when most drunk driving accidents occur is between 9 p.m. Saturday and 7 a.m. Sunday.)[40] But it's not clear whether the court is implying "he normally wouldn't drink this much; cut him a break" or "he would drink all day if he didn't have to work the next day; don't be generous to him" or something else entirely.

The court has pointed out a few other things with more clarity. We know, for instance, that Imabayashi is young; the court gives his age and notes that he lives with his parents. We also know that he has money somehow, or at least his family does, as he has the means to drive a car that at the time was Toyota's premium flagship sedan.

Imabayashi and his friends went to an izakaya, where, from 7:45 to 9:20, he drank five or six glasses of shochu. When he left, as he tried to put his shoes back on (he presumably had removed them to sit on the tatami mats that are a staple of traditional izakaya), he lost his balance. He told a restaurant worker flatly, "I'm drunk."

He and his friends then went to a snack. After leaving the snack, Imabayashi went to his car and with his friends drove to a nearby park, hoping to, as the court says, *nanpa*, loosely meaning "pick up women." (The phrase is gendered; "pick up men" is *gyakyunan*, or "reverse *nanpa*.")

The court is not exactly fostering sympathy with this information. It was repeated in the press, usually in a tone that suggested objectivity, but the underlying sentiment is nevertheless something like "he caused a tragedy because he went out drunk cruising for women." It was often repeated in 2-channel textboard internet threads, a popular site for anonymous commenting and posting, especially at the time of the incident—and there the tone was anything but objective. ("Die!" was a frequent response.)[41]

After a few unsuccessful minutes at the park, they returned to the snack, staying there from 9:35 to 10:35. Upon arrival Imabayashi told a hostess, "Today I'm drunk." She later testified that she agreed with that self-assessment. He gulped down a brandy mixed with water, but his pace slowed on his second glass. When he returned from the restroom and tried to sit on a stool, he lost his balance and spilled the hostess's drink on her skirt. Standing tipsy by the bar, he bent down, resting his elbow on his thigh, stretched, and sighed loudly. The hostess later testified, "Now that I think about it, when he left the bar and began to drive his car, I felt like he might fall asleep along the way."

Imabayashi and one of his friends then decided to again try to pick up women. At 10:40 Imabayashi sat in his Majesta's driver's seat, with one friend in the passenger seat and another in the back seat. They failed again in their search. They dropped off the passenger-seat friend, and the back-seat friend took his place in the passenger seat.

Imabayashi drove on an elevated bridge at a speed of between 80 and 100 kilometers per hour (about 50 and 60 miles per hour). His passenger friend asked, "Do you always drive this fast?," to which he responded "No, I don't." Ten seconds later, after eight seconds of apparent inattentiveness, his Majesta plowed into the Ogami family's Land Cruiser at 100 kilometers per hour, sending it over the railing of the bridge and into Hakata Bay. The parents survived; all three children drowned.

Again notice the details that the court has provided, and how they align with some things we already know. Imabayashi decided to "go drinking" (*nomi ni iku*)—an outing for the purpose of imbibing. He had a first party and a second party (broken up by a search for women). The court notes these two parties matter-of-factly, as Japanese has words for the first party, *ichijikai*, as well as the second, *nijikai* (a third party, an after-after party, would have been a *sanjikai*—yes, there is a word), words grounded in an assumption that one does not usually end one's drinking at the place where one begins. The language is common: The most consecutively numbered parties listed in the case law comes from a 2018 case that involved five, by firefighters at a farewell party for a nurse from a local emergency room; their locations, in order, (1) hot pot restaurant, (2) karaoke box (the small rooms or trailers for singing karaoke), (3) izakaya, (4) bar, and (5) another karaoke box. It was at the fifth party that a firefighter sexually assaulted the nurse, resulting in the loss of his job.[42] (A combination of three or more parties is often termed a *hashigozake*, or pub crawl, literally "ladder liquor," a clear harbinger in the case law of bad behavior.)[43]

Back to Imabayashi and his story's alignment with expectations. Notice that he drank location-appropriate drinks: shochu at an izakaya; brandy and water at a snack. He went drinking with his friends but spent a lot of time with a hostess. The hostess knew he was drunk (in retrospect?) but seems to have said nothing; perhaps pointing out his inebriation would have insulted him somehow, or perhaps her words just wouldn't have mattered. His passenger voiced no qualms about getting into the car—though he worried as the drive continued. The court has normalized Imabayashi even as it seems to show disdain.

Imabayashi was charged with the crime of dangerous driving causing death or injury (Penal Code art. 208-2[44]): "A person who drives a vehicle with four or more wheels in a state in which the driver cannot drive normally due to the influence of alcohol or drugs, and thereby causes injury, shall be punished by imprisonment with work for not more than fifteen years when the person thereby causes injury. The punishment shall be imprisonment with work for a definite term of not less than one year when the person thereby causes death." The statute had been passed in response to the Inoues' case and the fiery death of their children, a case with obvious parallels to Imabayashi's.[45]

Here we must analyze the law a bit more carefully to see an oddity in the statute. The critical language is similar to the statute that prohibits drunk driving: The driver cannot drive normally due to the influence of alcohol. But the dangerous driving causing death or injury statute removes the subjective "*fear* that the driver cannot drive normally," as the time for fear has passed, and it adds two other factors. First, it requires a result: death or injury. Second, with the word "thereby," in "thereby causes injury," the statute introduces a hurdle for prosecutors by requiring a causal link between the act and the result. In other words—and this is crucial—prosecutors must prove not only that Imabayashi was under the influence of alcohol but that it was that influence that caused the deaths. Imabayashi could argue that although he was indeed quite drunk, it was negligence in some form—perhaps he is just a bad driver even when he's sober—that caused the deaths. If he could prove that, he still could be found guilty of other crimes—gross negligence causing death, hit-and-run, driving under the influence—but not dangerous driving causing death or injury. That causal requirement is nearly unique to Japan; although there are a few exceptions, the trend in most U.S. jurisdictions is not to require prosecutors to prove that death was caused by intoxication, or even that intoxication affected operation of the vehicle.[46]

The court first considered Imabayashi's intoxication. After recounting the steps leading up to the crash, it focused on the events that occurred immediately after. Imabayashi noticed that he was in the lane of oncoming traffic, pulled back into his own lane, and attempted to accelerate, but the engine was damaged and he had a flat tire, so he pulled off to the side of the road. When his friend asked, "What happened?" (*dogen nattan desuka*), he responded, "Even I don't know" (*ore ni mo wakaran*). He then turned on his hazard lights and exited the car with his friend.

Again the court has recounted a conversation in the local dialect in which it was said to have taken place. Dialect in this case indicates geography but not necessarily class or education. A written U.S. equivalent is difficult, but if this conversation were converted into American English, the oral counterpart might be a Texas, Boston, or Maine accent.

Dialect can trigger stereotypes and assumptions. A Japanese reader knows immediately but perhaps only semiconsciously not only that the speaker is from Fukuoka or a nearby prefecture but that the speaker is almost certainly male—very few women speak like this, and if they did in a court opinion the language would suggest a certain kind of woman in Japan. The combination of geography and gender here conjures up a particular form of masculinity: that of the "Kyushu man" (*Kyuushuu danji*). The Kyushu man is said to be strong, stubborn, strict, gruff, and a heavy drinker.[47] The term rarely appears in the case law, but the meaning is clear in a 2016 defamation case in which a plaintiff claimed he was insulted when someone questioned whether he was a true "Kyushu man" with a crude reference to his sexuality.[48]

Let's put Imabayashi on hold a bit to consider the effect of dialect in a different drunk driving story, from the driver's point of view. A former electronics company manager named Kawamoto Kouji was arrested for drunk driving, served a three-month prison term (it was his third offense), and wrote a book about his experiences. Most of the book is just a fish-out-of-water story about an executive in prison, but the story of his arrest is interesting for our purposes. Kawamoto reports all the usual themes of drunk driving: He left a company party, someone asked if he was okay to drive, he said yes, and he knew he was in trouble when he saw police cars. When the police officer approached the car, he "knocked two or three times on the window" and said, "I know you are very busy, and I apologize. But could you please present your license?" When Kawamoto rolled down his window (and usually in the case law keeping the window up means the driver is about to flee),[49] the officer realized that he had been drinking and said, "Excuse me, but it seems as if you've been drinking. Sorry to trouble you, but could you please get out of the car?" Kawamoto reports that the words were "polite but strict."[50]

Here the politeness catches the ear (a few pages later the more brusque tone of the prosecutor has a different effect)—not because there are no polite cops (there are plenty) but because the language is different from the rest of Kawamoto's narrative. This effect is arguably easier to achieve in Japanese, with its many regional dialects, various levels of formality, and clear differences between written and spoken, male and female, and young and old language. When the court quotes parties directly, perhaps it is merely striving for accuracy, but one effect, intended or otherwise, is to imbue the speakers with characteristics that differentiate them from others. So when Imabayashi and his friend speak with a Hakata accent typical of people from or near Fukuoka, we don't necessarily know much more about them than the fact that they are from Fukuoka, male, and probably not strangers, but we know more about them than if the court had not quoted them directly.

Back to the core of Imabayashi's story. According to the court, the first thing he did after getting out of the smoking car "to hide the fact that he had been driving drunk" was to call a friend and ask him to bring water "to try and cover up the fact that he had been drinking, even if only a little bit." That friend brought two-liter bottles of water to the scene. Imabayashi then called another friend, saying (again in local dialect), "I caused some kind of accident. But the other guy's not here" (*Jiko o okoshitattyan. Jiko shita aite ga oran*).

After discussing this incriminating evidence, the court examined the police report. According to the report, when the police arrived at 11:20, they surveyed the scene. Meanwhile Imabayashi guzzled water until police ordered him to stop. Even after drinking the water, Imabayashi had a breath alcohol content somewhere between a 0.25 and a 0.30, clearly over the 0.15 limit for driving under the influence. The police officer's examination card noted that Imabayashi was speaking normally (and not one of the other check-the-box options: shouting, fighting, crying, being silent, muttering, being violent, incoherent, or verbose), that he could walk a straight line, that the alcohol smell on his breath was "strong," that his facial color was blue (not red or normal), and that his eyes were bloodshot (not normal or teary). The conclusion the officer wrote on the card was that Imabayashi was driving under the influence.

After examining all of this evidence, the court concluded that the defendant was drunk. This was unsurprising, and the court's opinion seemed headed toward that inevitable conclusion from the first paragraphs. But his drunkenness, the court then explained, was immaterial, and here is the plot twist in which the statute constrains the court. Imabayashi was able to drive through the curves of the highway, stopping at crosswalks on a narrow street, and was able to pull the car back into his own lane after the accident. At 80 to 100 kilometers per hour, the speed of the car could not definitively be said to be abnormal. So although he was drunk, his drunkenness did not *cause* the accident: He was not unable to drive normally *due to* the influence of alcohol. Instead, according to the court, Imabayashi was driving inattentively, literally, "looking aside while driving" (*wakimi unten*). The court did not address whether the "looking aside" could have been caused by drunkenness. There was a dichotomy: Either he was drunk or he was looking aside. The court chose looking aside.

The court found other crimes, including gross negligence, fleeing the scene, and driving under the influence. As it sentenced Imabayashi, it criticized him heavily for being selfish, for driving simply to meet women, for drinking and driving on the highway. It mourned the death of the children: "The three children were given the utmost love of their parents, being raised not only like treasures, full of joyful and happy days, but also attempting to achieve their lifelong hopes and dreams." But in sentencing him, it also considered mitigating factors: his apology letter to the children's parents, his youth, the fact that his insurance would help compensate the victims, his family's support, social sanctions he had already suffered as a result of media exposure, and the loss of his job. The court sentenced Imabayashi to seven years and six months—a disproportionately low sentence given the twenty-five years that prosecutors had requested.[51]

The court has provided an abundance, perhaps an overabundance, of narrative. In doing so it revealed which imprecise factors can establish drunkenness and the extent to which they matter. Imabayashi was drunk when he left the snack, falling all over himself; his blood alcohol was over the limit; and the police had concluded at the scene that he was intoxicated. And yet, the court concluded, he was not guilty of the crime because he was simply driving inattentively, for reasons unrelated to his drunken state. He was still going to prison, but he was not going because he killed someone when he was drunk—that fact was immaterial to the dangerous driving causing death charge.

Public outrage followed, and prosecutors appealed the sentence. On appeal, the Fukuoka High Court took a completely different interpretive tack. It first noted the district court's conclusion that the cause of the accident was Imabayashi's "looking aside while driving," but said that the length of "looking aside" would have been 318 meters, or about twelve seconds. Because he was drunk, his reaction time was limited. He had said that the scenery of Hakata Bay had caught his eye, but all he could remember was that he had seen "a machine that was shaped something like a giraffe." (It was a crane; the "giraffe" line makes him sound not only drunk but silly, and I have to wonder if that incongruous lean is intentional, especially when the district court didn't include it.) The high court concluded that "looking aside" was *not* the cause of the accident—again the court sees a dichotomy between looking aside and being drunk, perhaps because that is how the lower court presented the issues. It then focused on the defendant's alcohol consumption, going through each step just as the district court had, and, having ruled out "looking aside," found his drunken state, as evidenced by the same facts on which the district court relied, to be the cause of the accident. Again the court took into account the defendant's apology, loss of employment, social sanctions, lack of record, and family support—but it sentenced him to twenty years, much closer to the prosecutors' request. (And as chapter 6 will show, twenty years is a much more typical sentence than seven and a half when prosecutors request twenty-five.)[52]

Imabayashi appealed to the Supreme Court. Supreme Court opinions in Japan are usually unanimous (opinions by all other courts are required to be), but in this case justices issued both concurring and dissenting opinions, showing again the heterogeneity of opinion on alcohol-related issues. A majority of the Court affirmed the high court's decision. The defendant, the Court said, had drunk all the drinks listed by the lower court, and the Supreme Court punctuated the amount by noting the total volume consumed in a single sentence and highlighting the fact that he had drunk "at his home and at two eating/drinking establishments." The defendant had admitted he was drunk, had lost his balance, and was found by police at the scene to be intoxicated. The Court concluded that if he was inattentive, and if he was unable to notice the car in front of him, given that he was intoxicated, it was appropriate to assume that alcohol was the cause. The majority then affirmed the twenty-year sentence that the Fukuoka High Court had issued.

In a concurring opinion, Justice Ootani Takehiko stated that the fact that the defendant didn't notice the car in front of him for at least eight seconds, with nothing to distract his attention, was clear evidence that the defendant was not "looking aside"; rather his abilities were weakened by alcohol. Again the dichotomy: Either he's drunk or he's looking aside, and Ootani concluded that he was drunk, and presumably looking ahead. Ootani closely examined the facts of the defendant's intoxication, as closely as the lower courts and more closely than the majority opinion. He concluded that if the defendant had been sober, he would have examined the condition of his car.

Justice Tahara Mutsuo dissented. Dissents are rare, and former lawyers are more likely to write them than career judges.[53] Tahara, a former bankruptcy lawyer,[54] argued in his dissent that the defendant did not have difficulty driving normally. The defendant had tried to conceal his crime by drinking water, so he seemed to be thinking logically. He drove well, or appeared to, until the accident. The defendant's blood alcohol level of 0.06 (converted to blood from breath), he noted, was just above Japan's pre-2001 (pre-Inoue incident) standard of 0.05, and for that matter was near the threshold for other countries, including, the justice pointed out, the United States (0.08), the United Kingdom (0.08), France (0.08), and Germany (0.05). He was not "considerably intoxicated," as the majority "unclearly" stated, but merely "slightly intoxicated." All the negative factors reported on the police examination card—the smell of alcohol, the color of his face, and the bloodshot eyes—referred to external characteristics and not motor functions. Accordingly, to Justice Tahara, even the objective factors in this case showed that the accident occurred due to negligence and not the influence of alcohol.[55]

The judges in the cases at each of the three levels of the judiciary disagreed not only about the outcome but also about what factors are sufficient, necessary, or helpful to determining intoxication. The three district court judges found that Imabayashi was intoxicated according to the totality of the evidence, piling on fact after fact, but that his ability to drive normally meant that the accident could have been caused by looking aside. The three high court judges dismissed the "looking aside" claim based on the evidence, but found drunkenness based on the same basic facts as the district court. Of the five justices on the panel of the Supreme Court's third bench, three (two career judges and one career attorney) relied on a simpler version of the facts, focusing on the volume of alcohol, the admission of intoxication, and the police report. One justice (a career judge) thought that a more careful review of the facts was in order and added a supposition about what the defendant would have done *had he been sober*, an extraordinarily imprecise measure. And one justice (a career attorney) set all these things aside and found the defendant, based largely on the breathalyzer and mentioning none of the details of the defendant's evening or condition other than the positive aspects of the examination card, only "slightly" intoxicated, without clarifying what "slightly" means.

The outlier here, of course, is Justice Tahara, who focused on the science and a very precise element analysis, ignoring many objective indicia of intoxication. The other judges focused on messy evidence: how Imabayashi acted primarily in situations outside of the accident, how much he drank, where he drank, and his physical condition, each of which is much more easily observed by laypersons. Except for Justice Tahara, the judges knew intoxication when they saw it; they disagreed only on the issue of causation. When asked about the case three years later in an interview printed in his memoir, Justice Tahara continued to argue that the defendant in the case did not have difficulty driving normally:

> A person must be conscious and aware. I want to say, "Do you know what it's like to look but not really see?" As a representative case, for instance, sometimes if you begin to succumb to sleepiness, your eyes will close, but you're still "driving." If you recognize that you're falling asleep, we can still recognize that you're acting consciously. . . . Of course, you're not allowed to fall asleep. But as you're falling asleep, sometimes your head starts to fall forward. If you're aware of that, we can say that you're conscious.[56]

I won't attempt to parse that; suffice it to say that the justice seems to have held his views strongly.

Each of the judges, then, has in mind a particular image of drunkenness. This is not unusual; there is a commonplace definition of intoxication. But the court seems to have in mind a particular image of drunkenness in which blood alcohol content is only one element. The variation in images makes application to individuals necessarily imprecise.

As in the Inoue case, the public response to the Imabayashi case was considerable.[57] Imabayashi was a municipal employee in Fukuoka City's Animal Control Center, and a higher level of care is expected of public officials, even at Imabayashi's level. The mayor's office received nine hundred complaints, leading the mayor to hand Imabayashi a disciplinary dismissal, cancel events related to Fukuoka's Olympic host city bid, give himself a 20 percent pay cut, and issue pay cuts and reprimands to departments and officials connected with the Animal Control Center.[58] This is the mayor, a publicly elected official, far from Imabayashi in the hierarchy, whose leisure activities he could not possibly control, taking responsibility for Imabayashi's actions.

From an American perspective, this might seem odd, as the mayor's office was not directly to blame. But these actions are not about blame and duty in any legal sense; they are about culturally appropriate reactions to tragedies that receive national attention. The mayor did not have a duty to stop Imabayashi, but he had a responsibility not to enjoy his full salary after the deaths. The city had no way of stopping Imabayashi, but it would have been odd to host celebratory events after the children's very public deaths.

The social movement that erupted again resulted in legal change. The legislature increased the penalties for driving under the influence (to three years or $5,000) and driving while intoxicated (to five years or $10,000). The only other time that penalties for drinking and driving had been increased since 1960 was the legislative response to the Inoue case. The legislature also added provisions for the same or slightly lower penalties to complicit third persons: to those who supply alcohol to a person or encourage a person to drink when there is a possibility that the person will drive under the influence (Road Traffic Law art. 65(3)); to those who loan a vehicle to a person who is under the influence (art. 65(2)); and to those who ask a person they know to be driving under the influence to drive them (art. 65(4)).

The cycle is clear: One high-profile case in 2002 led to a new law, which was used effectively in another high-profile case in 2007, which led to further increased penalties. High-profile cases spark social action, and social action sparks legal change. Reported drunk driving incidents decreased after each case, though it is unclear whether the decrease was due to changes in the law or to media attention.[59]

Extending the Law

Even before the post-Imabayashi revisions, courts had become tougher on some aspects of drunk driving, extending the reach of the law in civil cases even further to find persons *other than the driver* derivatively liable for the driver's actions. To see how courts employ facts in such cases, consider first a criminal case from the Sendai District Court. The defendant drank ten glasses of shochu between 9 p.m. and 3:30 a.m., mostly at a snack, following a single beer at an izakaya. He ignored a red light and hit eighteen people who were on a walk rally for charity, killing three. Most of the victims were fifteen years old. The defendant reeked of alcohol, could not stand straight, could not speak well, and had a breath alcohol content of 0.30, twice the legal limit. The court sentenced him to twenty years' imprisonment.[60]

Because of the anonymity of the parties in Japanese case reporters, it is often difficult to match multiple lawsuits that concern the same set of events. But a civil case based on the same number of people killed and injured at the same spot on the same night sheds new light on what is decidedly the same case. In the criminal case the court merely said that the defendant was taking "a friend" home. The civil case brought against the passenger-friend by four victims provided more detail about the individuals. In that case the court noted that both the driver and the passenger were *bousouzoku*, members of an adolescent motorcycle subculture—basically, gang members—that sometimes serves as a breeding ground for yakuza recruits. The passenger was senior (*senpai*); the driver was junior (*kouhai*). The senior passenger had asked the junior passenger to drive him around to drinking establishments and take him home at the end of the night. They drank together. The senior passenger knew the driver was drunk and did nothing to stop him. The court gave very few other facts; it simply applied basic principles of derivative tort liability and awarded the four plaintiffs \$1.1 million.[61]

Why did the court in the civil case mention gang status when the criminal opinion did not? Perhaps the prosecution didn't offer it in the criminal case but the civil plaintiffs did. Perhaps it was useful to show the senior-junior relationship in the civil case to establish passenger liability and unnecessary in the criminal case because the passenger's liability was not at issue there (and the prosecution might not have thought the argument to be exculpatory). I suspect that the latter is the case, but even if that hunch is wrong, it remains curious that one court, and not the other, chose to trot out that fact given that it causes readers to look differently at the parties involved.

Another combination of civil and criminal cases in the passenger liability context similarly presents the facts differently in the two cases. In a Tokyo civil suit two passengers and a driver drank "single-serving sake" (probably One Cup, but the court did not specify) from convenience stores and whisky and water until they were drunk at the "Philippine pub" Club Manila Garden, where the driver sang, danced, and played the tambourine while a hostess sang. The two passengers were found liable when the driver hit a nineteen-year-old moped rider.[62] In the criminal case against the driver, the court gave far fewer facts, omitting the Philippine pub frivolity altogether.[63] The driver's culpability was clear; it was the culpability of the passengers that needed to be more clearly established by examining their individual bad acts. Giving readers more information about them, turning them into humans, however flawed that night, makes the civil judgment more understandable.

Other cases—here are three, briefly—further highlight the need to find significantly blameworthy acts for a passenger to be civilly liable for harm caused by a drunk driver. In a 2006 Yamagata case in which a driver ran a red light, fled from police, and hit a college student in the crosswalk, eventually receiving seven years in prison, the parents of the student sued the passengers, who knew the driver was drunk. The court awarded \$300,000 to each parent while highlighting the facts that the driver hit and ran, that the passengers each had five or six 500-milliliter beers, and that they ate Chinese food and ramen and continued to drink after the incident.[64] In a 2010 Osaka case in which a passenger and a driver had drunk eight beers each at a snack, the passenger clearly knew the driver was drunk, and the driver hit and killed a sixteen-year-old boy after running a red light, the court found liability for the passenger. The court showcased the fact that after the boy had been hit, the driver said, "We'll go to the cops," and the passenger responded, "Well, let's calm down a bit. Let's sleep on it."[65] And in a slightly different context, in a 2006 case involving comparative negligence in the city of Tsu, a boss went drinking with his employee at two izakaya, where they had beer, sake, and shochu. The employee planned to sleep in the office, but the boss, knowing they were both drunk, asked the employee to drive him and another colleague home. The car crashed, they all died, and the wife and child of the boss sued the parents of the driver. The court reduced the damage award by half because of the comparative negligence of the passenger.[66]

Courts, then, seem to look carefully at the facts of both the drinking and the driving when determining liability. In each case, whether as a matter of legal analysis, as a matter of framing, or both, courts find liability for passengers when drivers clearly are drunk, when passengers do nothing to stop them, and when passengers also were drunk and unsympathetic, whether because they callously eat and drink after a hit-and-run, because they encourage drivers to flee, or because they're the boss or otherwise senior to the driver and therefore have more power.

Courts also impose criminal liability on *non*passenger third parties. Contrast the concept of *kanpai* toasts from chapter 2 with that seen in a 2011 Saitama District Court case: "Until that time, C had always observed proper etiquette toward his superiors. Defendant A, who disagreed with him, fought with him about a money issue, and when C *yobisute* [called by his last name without the honorific –san] defendant A, the defendant A began to hit C's head and so on. After the fight, the defendants reconciled, and defendants A and C, with the liquor ordered by [another person], did *kanpai*."[67] *Kanpai* in this situation is a way of making up after a fight, not a formal ritual and not a way of beginning a party. It isn't even quite "cheers," but rather a way of expressing the concept of coming together over a drink.

Consider the interaction in a bit more detail. To the judges it is a benign expression of the everyday. But from an outsider's perspective, the *kanpai* is only the tip of the iceberg that helps establish hierarchy in a more complete way than in the junior-senior case of gang-member passenger liability we reviewed. The statements come from the testimony of a worker at the restaurant at which the *enkai*, as the court refers to it—a drinking party often for work-related purposes, often used interchangeably with *nomikai*, literally, "drinking party"—was held. According to the employee, "C," with sunken eyes, "ate the remaining cold ramen off of other people's plates and drank their soup. He staggered as he went to the restroom, he didn't use proper language with his superiors, and he was slurring his words." The court uses two words here—*senpai* for superiors, and *tameguchi* for improper language—the meanings of which are not adequately conveyed by literal one-word translations. A *senpai*, a superior in age and rank, can exist only if a *kouhai*, a junior, exists. In this case, C was thirty-two years old and A was forty-three; they both worked for a moving company. C had worked there for seven years, A for twenty.

The second word, *tameguchi*, is not included in most dictionaries; in fact the court says *iwayuru tameguchi*, or "so-called *tameguchi*," as courts often do when introducing an uncommon or slang term. It is not clear in this example precisely what C did, but presumably he used language that should be used among friends, ignoring hierarchy, perhaps leaving off polite sentence endings like *–desu* or *–masu*, suffixes that would create the minimum midlevel politeness necessary to address work superiors.

Were it not for the other evidence of bad behavior, it is possible to code this as a simple mistake. Some rules of drinking etiquette are clear; people in Japan in some instances pour not for themselves but for others (*oshaku*), for instance. But after the drinking has begun, rules are relaxed, and, as we saw in chapter 2, people "let go," sometimes to the extent that hierarchy dissipates. Donald Richie, the author and film historian (among other things), who seems to have experienced and journaled every aspect of Tokyo social life during his fifty years living there, colorfully describes the abandon that followed at a typical party he hosted:

> [Construction executive Tani Hiroaki] became noisy in this company-president kind of way, opened his pants and pulled up his shirt to show off his scar, a stomach operation for ulcers—he had worried *that* much making his millions. Also, since this is the way men in his world act when together, he began joking about the host—complaining about me all of these years, said I never once bought him anything but a suit and he still had it, he took *that* good care of it.[68]

As Richie and the cases suggest, once everyone in the group has begun to drink, the rules change. In some settings, C—to return directly to the case—could have spoken his mind and used his overly familiar language with no consequences. In this case, however, C was out of order, perhaps because, according to the employee's testimony, he had had a beer and seven glasses of shochu mixed with oolong tea, an amount that the employee said was more than C's usual. Defendant A thwacked him on the head in a "What's wrong with you, huh?" sort of way, and the two eventually reconciled with the *kanpai*.

Why might these details matter to the court? Because in this case, defendant A and another superior, defendant B (forty-five years old, with fifteen years' experience working at the company), did not stop the etiquette-ignoring C from drunk driving and were being prosecuted as accessories to C's dangerous driving causing death, the crime that emerged from the Inoue accident. C killed six in the resulting crash, and establishing that A and B were superiors was important in showing their ability to have stepped in. In the sentencing portion of the opinion, which came after this recitation of facts, the court chided A and B specifically because "both defendants were in a senior [*senpai*] position in the workplace"—a relationship we already know from the facts. Each received a two-year prison sentence, eventually affirmed by the Supreme Court.[69]

In the absence of either some kind of bad behavior or a power relationship, however, courts seem reluctant to impose criminal liability on third parties. For instance, the Sapporo High Court in 2007 decided a case in which the passenger who was the subject of the suit did not know the driver was going to drink, and the driver looked as if he could drive. The court found that the cause of the accident was not the driver's intoxication but his inattentiveness—he was "looking aside," as in the Imabayashi case—as he adjusted the car stereo, while driving, the court explained, on a snowy morning in northern Japan. The passenger had also been drinking, but the court seems to have sympathized with him, as he asked the driver to turn around to see if the person who had been hit was injured. (The driver fled instead, and in the process not only completed a hit-and-run but also violated a duty to rescue imposed by the Road Traffic Law, art. 72.) The passenger, with no bad behavior and no obvious power relationship to the driver, had no liability.[70]

Japanese courts do not require others to take responsible actions in vain. In a 2016 Kyoto case the wife of a drunk driver sued to have her driver's license reinstated after the Kyoto Public Safety Commission suspended it for a two-year period. Her transgression: She had asked her husband to drive her, knowing that he was drunk. According to the court, on June 2, 2013, at 2 a.m., the plaintiff-wife had called down from the second floor of their home to her husband on the first floor, where he was watching a DVD, and asked him to take her out to eat barbecue (*yakiniku*, literally "grilled meats"). (Perhaps the court wants us to know that the wife was unable to check the husband's ability to drive as they were on two different floors of the house.) He complied, and on the way he bought two beers and drank one. At the restaurant he drank two medium mugs of beer (it goes with barbeque in Japan). They returned home at 5 a.m., and at 8 a.m. he drank two more mugs. At 11 a.m. she asked him to take her to eat ramen, and he agreed. Along the way he stopped at a convenience store and bought another beer. The police pulled them over around noon and arrested him for drunk driving.

The court provided much more detail than one might expect for a case of a driver's license suspension, including the husband's history of alcohol abuse and liver disease and the wife's allergy-related impairments to her sense of smell that limited her ability to notice her husband's drinking. But in the end, the court's decision came down to the wife's actions on the day of the arrest. According to the testimony from the husband's drunk driving case, the wife said (in humanizing Kansai dialect), "Are you going to drink and drive? Stop it" and "Why are you drinking? You know you shouldn't drink. Let me drive for you instead. Stop here." To which her husband replied in less endearing dialect, "I'm okay" and "Shut up, stupid" (*urusainja, boke*). The court further noted that because the husband was male and the wife was female, the wife did not have the physical power to stop him. It found, then, that the wife had not aided her husband in driving drunk, and as such she should not have been punished.[71]

I must admit, I didn't know which way this case was going; it wasn't until the court referenced the differences between men and women that the outcome became clear. Unlike the correlation between One Cup sake and tragedy, I was also initially unsure what the court was implying—other than hinting at class—by reciting the couple's dining habits (barbecue at 2 a.m.; ramen in the late morning). I'm still not entirely sure. But doesn't the inclusion of "Shut up, stupid" in the narrative at least suggest what the judge might be thinking?

5

Drunk Others

Liability for passengers in drunk-driving cases raises a broad question: What are the general responsibilities of sober people for drunk people? In this chapter I look at three categories of cases: criminal suits that seek to punish people who fail to perform duties to the intoxicated; civil cases filed by family members of university students, just above or just below legal drinking age, who die as a result of accidental alcohol poisoning; and civil suits brought by potential beneficiaries against insurance companies after their insured relatives die as a result of alcohol. In all three types of cases the framing of the facts is as important as the legal results the courts reach. And here again courts shape the facts in ways that inevitably lead to the rarity of tragedy, but along the way they offer glimpses of the everyday that allow defendants to be understood, differentiated, and categorized.

In each case the parties act against a social backdrop of general responsibility for self and others. Studies have shown that people in Japan, more than in the United States, tend to assign responsibility to groups, as opposed to individuals.[1] As Lee Hamilton and Joseph Sanders found, people in Japan "seem to see the responsible actor as embedded in a web of close and hierarchical ties with others, including victims."[2] More broadly, another psychological study finds that Asians "are inclined to attribute behavior to context and Americans tend to attribute the same behavior to the actor."[3] When something goes wrong in Japan, then, studies suggest, the individual is less likely to be found at fault than in the United States. But at least in the settings in this chapter, courts in Japan tend to place responsibility with the individual, not the group.

Responsible by Relationship

In the United States a person usually is not required to rescue another from harm unless the law imposes a legal duty, either by statute or by a few judicially created categories. Those categories are predefined: People have a duty to rescue others

Drunk Japan. Mark D. West, Oxford University Press (2020) © Oxford University Press.
DOI: 10.1093/oso/9780190070847.001.0001

when they have certain status relationships with them, when they contract to care for them, or when they have tried to help victims and in so doing secluded them from others who could help.[4] We can imagine scenarios in which those conditions might apply to a drunk victim, but U.S. law is not so specific.

Japan creates a more precise duty to rescue the intoxicated. The Japanese Penal Code (art. 218) punishes people who are "responsible for the protection of" certain categories of others, including the sick, when they require, and do not receive, protection. The Supreme Court has specifically defined "sick" in the statute to include "intoxicated."[5] Still, there are only a handful of cases in which courts employed the provision for intoxication, perhaps because it is difficult for prosecutors to prove that a person is *responsible* for a drunk person pursuant to the statute (and perhaps because, as we have seen, police routinely "protect" drunk people by putting them in jail before they require protection by others). Here are three cases; each occurred years ago, and the facts are extreme. In a 1961 case three friends drank heavily together. With arms around each other's shoulders, two of them helped carry the third as he drunkenly stumbled. The drunk became angry with the other two, telling them, "Leave me alone!" and "Don't treat me like a kid!" The drunk's friends felt "resentment" (*fungai*) and let him fall from their arms. The place where he fell was a railroad crossing; it was late at night, and the two knew that the trains were still running. The drunk man died in the manner one might expect. The court found the friends guilty.[6]

In a case from 1968 the male defendant found his female companion drunk at a train station in the middle of a cold January night. (The case reporter ambiguously calls the companion *joukou kankei*, or lover, but the defendant's briefs, unsuccessfully relying on a 1926 Supreme Court precedent, argued that a married man owed no duty to his mistress [*joufu*], thus clarifying the relationship.) He tried to take her home, but she sat in the road and didn't move. In an alleged attempt to sober her up, he removed all of her clothes. She still would not walk, so he left her in a rice paddy. He said he did so to sober her up; prosecutors said the couple had an "abnormal" sadomasochistic relationship. She "froze to death." Guilty.[7]

Finally, from 1985: A man found his alcoholic common-law wife drunk when he came home from work. To sober her up, he put her in the bath and left her there for four hours in their wooden house in January. She died of hypothermia. Guilty—but given a suspended sentence, in part because, according to the court, "it cannot be said that the victim bears no responsibility" and in part because the defendant was needed at home to continue to raise their young daughter.[8]

In each of these cases more is happening than mere failure to rescue. First, the victims weren't strangers; they arguably fit the status relationships of the U.S. duty-to-rescue law cited earlier, whether as co-adventurers, lovers, or spouses. Second, the defendants affirmatively hastened death, through negligence or more, or at least seemed to harbor ill will. In each respect the alcohol-related duty-to-rescue cases are not unique, as a similar thread of relationship plus something extra runs through drug-related cases. In a well-publicized case that began in 2009, for instance, the actor-singer Oshio Manabu was convicted of leaving his bar-hostess sex partner to die after she overdosed on Ecstasy (MDMA). The Tokyo High Court, noting that the defendant could have prevented her death, finding that his affidavit was "extremely unnatural" (he self-described his behavior as something from the films *The Exorcist* and *The Grudge*), and focusing on the sex-and-drugs relationship with the hostess, affirmed a lay judge panel's sentence of two and a half years in prison.[9]

A specific legal duty to protect the intoxicated can arise in another context in Japan: in employment, through the charge of professional negligence resulting in death (Penal Code art. 211). Those duty-to-the-drunk cases are relatively more common because the employment relationship, and hence the duty, can be determined more easily than situations that lack neatly defined legal categories. Take a relatively recent case that made headlines. In the early morning hours of February 12, 2012, an eighteen-year-old bartender named Akiko, two years too young to drink legally, was found dead at the "girls bar" in Osaka at which she worked. A girls bar is similar to a snack or cabaret with hostesses in that the primary commodity is attention from (usually young) women. But unlike such establishments, women in a girls bar keep the male patrons company with conversation not in a cozy setting but from behind the bar, as bartenders. There is no *mama* at a girls bar, where the women are usually in their twenties and the setting is said to be more casual.[10]

At the particular girls bar in the Osaka case, named Sora (named in the press but not in the case reporter),[11] management used a "drink back" system, through which the female bartenders were compensated each time their customers bought a drink. (Compensation at these establishments, as in many other forms of nightwork, is often of questionable legality.) Customers frequently bought drinks for the bartenders, which they apparently chugged (*ikki*) with them.

Akiko drank four or five brandies in a row, each at 37 percent alcohol, for a total of at least 640 milliliters—roughly equivalent to downing three bottles of wine or thirteen beers at once. She passed out on the floor. The manager said she was just drunk and sleeping it off and did nothing; she died from sudden alcohol poisoning. The court issued the following commentary as it sentenced the manager:

> The "drink back" compensation system used by the defendant harbored a danger that his employees drink excessively. Nevertheless, the defendant did not sufficiently acknowledge the health conditions of his underage female employee, causing her to die without seeking

> emergency care. The defendant's weak awareness and sense of responsibility as a manager is also to blame. Moreover, the sadness and grief that accompanies the loss of life of an eighteen-year-old is large. However, the cause of the victim's inebriated state is also due to the customer who asked her to take a shot [*ikki*] of brandy, as well as herself, so it is not appropriate for the defendant to bear full responsibility for the victim's death.
>
> Furthermore, the defendant has reached an agreement through which he will pay the victim's family $150,000 in installments, and he has already paid $35,000. The sentiments of the family to punish the defendant, which initially were quite harsh, have also changed. The defendant has also said that if he had not hired underage workers to begin with, this problem never would have arisen, and although it cannot be said that he fully grasps his own issues, after a considerable period of being incarcerated before posting bail, he has begun steps to seek new work out of the nightlife industry.[12]

The court sentenced the defendant to one and a half years' imprisonment, suspended for three years, but it placed responsibility on all three parties: the victim, the defendant, and the person who asked her to drink. The defendant bore legal responsibility in part because of the victim's age and in part because of his negligence. As in the duty-to-rescue cases, it is those additional factors that shift some of the liability from the drunk to the other; without it, liability would seem to stay with the intoxicated, even though the intoxicated in this case was only eighteen, still legally a minor.

And yet the penalty is low. I will discuss sentencing in more detail in the next chapter, but here I note that Japanese sentences (like civil damages) are low across the board,[13] on average less than half as long as in the United States.[14]

As in so many other areas of the law that we have seen, it's unclear how much of the court's language is universal and how much is determined by individual circumstances. Six months after Akiko's death, twenty-one-year-old host Tanaka Yuya died from alcohol poisoning while on the job at the Osaka host club Black Pearl. He was three years older than Akiko, no longer a minor, but like her, he drank as part of his job. His parents sued, and in February 2019 they won a civil case against the defendant company in Osaka District Court, which awarded damages of $730,000. The court made clear that Tanaka was pressured to drink; he chugged bottle-keep shochu and tequila after his senior hosts said, "Why are you just sipping?" (*nani chibichibi nondennen*), "Drink up!" (*nomeyo*), "Drink more! (*motto nome*), and, after Tanaka vomited, "Don't throw up the liquor that you receive from our customers!" (*kyaku kara moratta sake hakunayo*), each of which is more a demand than a request and has just a bit of an edge due to the slight Osaka accent. Unlike Akiko's case, this was a civil case, and as such the court had plenty of opportunity to examine comparative negligence on Tanaka's part, but it did not do so. Perhaps the pressure was just too strong in this case, and the court accordingly felt no need to chastise the victim.[15]

Tanaka's family pressed further still, in a widely publicized campaign.[16] They urged prosecutors to indict the pressuring senior hosts, but unlike in Akiko's case, prosecutors declined to file charges. Tanaka's family filed for workers' compensation with the government, arguing that drinking was part of their son's job. The government denied their claim, and again they sued to overturn the decision. The Osaka District Court once again sided with the family, finding, for the first time ever, that drinking in the night industry is work-related, removing the blame from individual employees.[17]

The decision is remarkable and has ramifications for the entire service industry. Alcohol rarely even appears in workers' compensation opinions—when it does, it is when the government argues that the worker was an alcoholic, evidence to which the court usually pays little attention[18]—but here the court has used it against the government. But what does it say about individual responsibility? Perhaps the pressure senior hosts placed on Tanaka put him over the tipping point at which the fault for drinking is no longer his own. And yet, unlike in Akiko's case, prosecutors declined to bring criminal charges, presumably because they believed the circumstances differed in such meaningful ways that they would not win their case.

University Tragedies

A troubling thread in the case law involves university students who drink themselves to unintended death, occasionally in pressure-filled situations that bear some resemblance to Tanaka's case. In the United States we would characterize many of these incidents as hazing; in Japan they are known as *ikkinomi* (chugging) or *aruhara* (alcohol harassment) incidents. According to a nonprofit agency that monitors such incidents, thirty-four university students died from sudden alcohol poisoning in Japan from 2005 to 2014.[19] I will go back further than usual in history here to look at four court cases, from 1980, 1985, 2006, and 2011.

I have chosen cases that occur over a period of more than thirty years to show that despite student turnover and changes in higher education, the narrative is unfortunately uniform; I have not simply captured a static moment in university time. Moreover, despite a few details that might seem particularly Japanese, the stories are not terribly dissimilar from facts that one can imagine in the American and perhaps some other university experience. All four of the deceased students are male. In only one case do the plaintiffs prevail in their suit; the facts of that case are extreme and the damages awarded low.

A caveat applies. In Japan all criminal defendants receive full trials, even if they confess. But civil cases like these reach the courts and make their way into opinions only when settlements cannot be reached. Often parties settle rather than go to court. For instance, after a highly publicized incident at the prestigious University of Tokyo, the parents of a deceased twenty-one-year-old filed suit against twenty-one members of their son's tennis club, seeking a total of nearly $1.7 million in damages (about $80,000 each; at the time of writing, the case is pending). According to press reports, ten members of the club had already settled with the parents for $2,400 each, far less than the parents demanded but not a bad settlement from the parents' perspective given that, as the following cases suggest, the face an uphill battle in court.[20]

To take the earliest court case first, the Tokyo District Court's 1980 decision involves a student at what is now the Tokyo University of Marine Science and Technology. The student, Fumio, attended his university's welcome *konpa*. *Konpa* (from "company") in this context are organized student drinking parties. Usually a student organizer or party planner is in charge of the evening, which begins with a toast and might end with a cheer. In between, students play games and get to know each other—according to the timetable of the organizer. All-you-can-drink izakaya trips and drinking games are common.

The court doesn't tell us whether Fumio actually played drinking games, but if he did, it's not unlikely that one of them was the Yamanote line game (*Yamanotesen geemu*). The Yamanote train line circles Tokyo with twenty-nine stops, all but two of which connect to other railway or subway stops. It plays a more central role in Tokyo life than any public transportation system in any American city. In the game, players sit in a circle, clapping in rhythm, and each player must name a station on beat and in turn. A player who can't name a station (that has not been previously named) in rhythm has to drink. The game can be played with any other list of places or items, but the Yamanote line is standard.

The number of cases in which the Yamanote line game arises is small—there are only three mentions—but each mention occurs in a sexual assault case.[21] Even more curiously, in each of the cases the court finds the defendant not guilty, as the alleged victim's testimony is not sufficiently reliable. Of course the Yamanote line game is not the only action depicted in the opinion, but I suspect that it appears in the facts as a plot device for showing camaraderie ("How could he have assaulted you after you were playing a game together?"), drunkenness of the complainant ("You drank so much as you played the game that you couldn't possibly remember"), or both.

In any event, in Fumio's case the *konpa* was specifically designed as a welcome party for new students, a well-traveled rite of passage at many universities—a rite with which many of the judges are familiar because they experienced it firsthand. Fumio drank beer there. Then he returned to his dorm with upperclass students and began a "room tour" (*heyamawari*) in which he was pressured to drink at each room. According to testimony, the room tour was part of a more extensive ritual: "Each year the so-called student welcome *konpa* was held, and it lasted as long as a week, during which period new students in dormitories were forced by senior students to drink for several days, and that occasionally the nature of the force was outrageous, and new students would suffer alcohol poisoning, vomit, and pass out." Fumio experienced a similar fate; he eventually died of asphyxiation. His parents sued, arguing that the university had a duty to prohibit introductory ceremonies or to ensure that students at the *konpa* did not drink too much.

The university, the court said, had a duty of care for students that went beyond classroom instruction and included health and safety, but that activities like drinking in dormitories were the province of student self-governance. Moreover, students had been warned at orientation about alcohol (at the urging of the dean of students, who thought that there was too much drinking the previous year); the president of the university had urged self-control in drinking; and signs warning of the dangers of alcohol had been posted in the dorm's lobby. The university had fulfilled its duty of care.[22]

The finding of a lack of liability is not surprising, as the university played no direct causal role in Fumio's death and took some measures to prevent the conduct that preceded it. But we should not take that result as a given. The law could establish a duty for a university to protect its students in the same way that it establishes a duty in the employment context; it does not. Norms might require university officials to atone in the same way that the Fukuoka mayor did following the junior official's drunk-driving accident; that did not occur in this case. But the court's opinion is straightforward and shows a rather standard view of vicarious liability.

There is an omission here, though, that I find glaring. Unlike in previous cases, the court gives us virtually no information about the victim (or anyone else) other than that he was a male and a new student. His class and social status are apparently irrelevant, as we are not provided those facts. He is simply a student, with no additional details given to cause us to either feel sympathy or cast aspersions.

A 1985 case that occurred at Miyazaki Agricultural Junior College tells us much more about what is—or more precisely, what is not—required of a university. The victim died of alcohol poisoning after at a volleyball victory party held in one of the dorms. Like college students everywhere, the victim split the cost of the evening's supplies—two giant bottles of beer (about a gallon total) and six one-*shou* bottles of shochu (altogether, about three gallons)—with several other second-year students, each throwing in $5. The victim drank approximately five paper cups of beer and three paper cups of shochu.

Again we've learned little about the student, but we've learned something about college drinking, even from a small data set. University drinking cases tend to involve specific events or groups—a welcome party, a volleyball victory party, a tennis club. Although random bursts of drinking among friends who are unrelated by a particular activity certainly take place, they don't usually reach the case law in Japan. Headlines in Japan after student deaths rarely say merely "Student Dies after Drinking"; instead the headline names the group or event that provided the context for the drinking, thereby providing an easy shorthand for the case in conversations in the media and elsewhere.

It's important to note the particular prevalence of sports clubs—especially tennis—in such cases.[23] Japanese sports clubs, two Australian researchers found, are the safe space in which Japanese students can learn how to drink at future, more adult drinking parties. The clubs teach rituals, provide an environment for conversation, and encourage group solidarity. Part of the learning involves "getting really drunk" through "heroic drinking."[24] I'm not confident that that dynamic differs significantly from the U.S. (or Australian) case, but in that friendly heroism lies a social distinction between the university cases and the pressured drinking that we saw in Tanaka's host club case.

In this volleyball party case, the court, like the court in the 1980 welcome party case, made clear that universities had a duty to their students. Then it focused on the reality of the (Japanese) university setting:

> In the management department of the school, students enter at the age of at least eighteen, after graduating from high school. Many students reach the age of majority [twenty] in their second year, and by the time they graduate all students have reached that age. More than half of the student body, then, is eighteen or nineteen years old. Underage drinking is prohibited by law, but students who graduate high school at eighteen have lots of interaction with more senior students, and university social life often results in a mixing of students who are of the age of majority and those who are not. Many underage students have drinking experience, and, beginning with their parents, have been in environments in which drinking is relatively tolerated. Many students have experience drinking even before they matriculate.

The court here has taken note of reality: University students in Japan, as elsewhere, drink. (And alcohol availability is not an issue; for instance, the University of Tokyo's on-campus co-op sells university-branded wine, sake, and shochu.) Using that premise as a stepping stone, the court then places the burden of intoxication squarely on the student and not the group, finding that "students should be trusted to govern themselves, make decisions, and act responsibly."

The court is using the language of student responsibility to foreshadow its legal determination that the university is not liable for students' behavior. In doing so, the court goes further than the 1980 case, stating that drinking and intoxication are decisions made by the individual—even by underage individuals. The court then put limits on what is required of the university, saying, "It is sufficient for a university to publicly inform students of the ban and take measures to increase their awareness of it. It is unnecessary that they make rounds of dormitory hallways or conduct inspections of rooms in order to prevent violation or to prevent occurrences of incidents such as this that occur as a result of drinking."[25]

The court is placing its faith in the self-responsibility of minors, going beyond a legal holding that the university is not legally liable to a more philosophical point about when one is responsible for one's own actions. If the action is drinking, the court seems to say, one becomes responsible when one goes to university, if not before, even if one is not of age (unlike Akiko in the girls bar). And note again that the court tells us little in the way of background facts about the individuals involved.

The third case, from 2006, comes on appeal to the Fukuoka High Court and involves a medical school's rowing club. The court doesn't name the school, but media coverage clarifies that it was the Kumamoto University School of Medicine.[26] Like the 1980 case, it involves a *konpa* to welcome new students. The event—the first party (*ichijikai*)—had fifty attendees, including ten new students. After the first party came the inevitable second, or after-party (*nijikai*), held on the third floor of an izakaya, which was a five-minute walk from the first party. The second party was a "relaxed" event in which new students could interact with upperclass students and alumni. They drank beer and shochu and had speed-drinking contests (*hayanomi kyousou*). "Because the new students had little drinking experience," the court explains, "many drank more than their limits, drinking lots of alcohol and becoming drunk."

The experience of the twenty-year-old victim—the court names him Ichiro, but the press identified him as Yoshida Takurou—at the second party began with self-introductions and beer and proceeded as follows:

> Ichiro leaned against the table and speed-drank with Oozuka, downing two to three centimeters of shochu shots [*ikki*] in 160 to 180cc glasses. After Ichiro finished drinking the shochu, he did a "guts pose" [a fist raised victoriously as a sign of "heroic drinking"] and appeared to be in good spirits. He then drank another glass of shochu. The appellee Oozuka was a second-year student, and stood in the position of one

> who takes care of new students. He had been told by Nekoda, a more senior student, to be careful not to drink at the second party, so he drank very little there, and when he speed-drank with Ichiro, he drank only the water that others had poured for him.
>
> Ichiro talked with the appellee Chazono [an unusual name from Kagoshima prefecture, alternatively pronounced Chaen], in the same place where he had been speed-drinking with Oozuka, and had a drinking contest with him. He drank a glass of shochu on ice (it is unclear how much ice was in the glass), while Chazono drank shochu mixed with water (the ratio of water was high). Ichiro won that contest, and said to Chazono, "*Senpai* [Senior], it's late. How about one more drink," and Chazono said "I'm done" and moved to another place in the room.
>
> Ichiro appeared to be a bit drunk, but he was completely conscious, and he had a speed-drinking contest with appellee Aitani. He drank a glass of shochu (the appellee Aitani's shochu was straight).
>
> During the drinking contests, people applauded and cheered, and the three appellee alumni Ushiyama, Kajima, and Kanemoto went to Ichiro's spot to join in. They began chugging beer and shochu with the new students. When a person lost a contest, people around him pushed him to drink more. Some drank another beer, but those who lost stopped drinking, and at the most, they had three or four cups of alcohol.

The court again has given little information about the individual victim but has provided a dense account of college drinking, or at least of college drinking that lands in court cases. The *konpa* begins formally with self-introductions. The fun apparently lies in the same sort of activity in which American university students so unwisely engage: drinking contests. And these students drink *a lot*: The beer and shochu (note no expensive or high-alcohol-content drinks) flow like water. Some people actually drink water. In fact they *compete* with water, which carries its own dangers. The person who did so in the narrative, Oozuka, was the person who was told not to drink much because he was an alcohol monitor of sorts for the new students.

Which brings us to a final question: Why is no one helping the new students? They are competitively chugging, and those who are in charge do not step in; rather they encourage them. And recall who these participants are: *medical students*, including alumni, on their way to becoming doctors. Survey data suggest that although doctors smoke far less than the general public, they drink about the same,[27] and medical students are notorious for drinking parties.[28] But still, shouldn't a little medical knowledge help? The court, at least in this portion of the opinion, is neither praising nor criticizing; it simply is apparent by omission that no one steps in.

The result toward which the court's narrative has steered eventually occurs: Ichiro passes out. One student says, "He's not answering; this is alcohol poisoning," and another responds, "He's probably just sleeping. He's okay." They carry him away to a student's apartment to sleep. He vomits, he passes out again, he snores, and then the snoring stops. Eventually he dies alone in the apartment.

Ichiro's parents sued both the attendees and the head of the rowing club, a professor. The case thus differs from the previous two, as the defendant is not the university. Yet the court is faced with a similar decision of how to apportion responsibility for drinking among (a) the intoxicated deceased and (b) those around him who might have changed the outcome.

In an unpublished opinion, the district court rejected the parents' claim, finding that alcohol was not necessarily the cause of Ichiro's death (because the precise cause of death was unclear). The high court, however, easily found that alcohol, whether through poisoning or asphyxiation, was the cause of the death. It then said that because the defendants had no plans to get the defendant drunk, they had no immediate duty to rescue or care for him. However, the defendants recognized Ichiro's intoxicated state, watched his condition worsen, and had a duty to take him to seek medical attention. The court found most of the defendants, including the supervising faculty member, liable, for total damages of almost $1 million.

Except:

> At the time of the event, Ichiro had just turned 20, and cannot be called a true first-year student. He was worthy of being called an adult, and with that classification come expectations. With respect to drinking, Ichiro was expected to be responsible for his actions and exercise self-control. However, it is clear that his methods of drinking, such as his aggressive speed drinking and drinking more than he could handle, were grossly negligent. Still . . . the defendants violated their duty to protect, and it is appropriate to apportion the responsibility according to principles of comparative negligence as 90 percent to Ichiro.[29]

The court has reduced the damages to be paid by the defendants from a little less than $1 million to a little less than $100,000, based on its judgment that Ichiro was far more blameworthy (90 percent) than the others in the room. In doing so, despite the final ruling of liability for the defendants, the court came to a conclusion that lies close to those of the other two courts: Young people in the university setting, even those just past the age of majority, even in a roomful of medical students, even amid questionable power dynamics, are responsible for their own behavior. The group bears some responsibility, much like the relationship-driven duty-to-rescue cases from the beginning of this chapter, but without any additional bad behavior they were liable for only 10 percent.

Consider finally a 2011 case involving a nineteen-year-old, Haruo, and his experience with the tennis club from the Electrical Engineering Department of an unnamed university. The tennis club met each Wednesday and Saturday, and a drinking party (*nomikai*) was held at a member's house after every gathering. The court telegraphs its position early in its recitation of the facts: "Participation in tennis and drinking was voluntary. The deceased Haruo regularly attended the drinking parties."

Haruo began the drinking party, held at a member's apartment, by drinking a large can of beer with the other first-year students. At around two in the morning, one of the more senior students told the five first-years, including Haruo, that they had not yet had enough to drink. He had a plan to fix this: He took an inexpensive (about $13) and large (2.7 liters, equal in volume to seven or eight cans of beer, but with at least four times the alcohol content) bottle of Daigorou-brand shochu, placed it in front of them, and told them to drink straight out of the bottle, as much as they could, and then pass it on to the next person. It was called, according to the court, not chugging (*ikki*) as in most cases,[30] but "Daigorou racing" (*reesu*). Unlike chugging, in which drinking amounts are fixed so that participants can compete, in racing each participant drank as little or as much from the bottle as he wanted on his turn, a fact that should benefit the defendants. The first-year students drank and were applauded and cheered. The upperclass students joined them.

After the first round, one person dropped out. A second person then went to the bathroom, vomited, and went home. In the second round, three others dropped out. One of the first-years had had enough, and he hid the bottle behind a washing machine. The court doesn't elaborate on this fact, but packed somewhere in that action there probably is a story about how a first-year student in this situation who felt he could not simply leave or stop drinking chose the socially discreet strategy of hiding the bottle.

The tactic worked, and the drinking stopped. But one of the upperclass students found the bottle, and the game began again. At around three in the morning, Haruo and another member finished the bottle. At around four, Haruo passed out. At around noon, people noticed that Haruo wasn't breathing. He had died of alcohol poisoning.

Again the facts show all the maddeningly poor choices that accompany youth binge drinking: the lack of inhibition, the encouragement, the games, the cheering, the inability to leave the scene without losing cool points. The court again paints a picture that could easily be imagined in the United States. The only difference is the type of liquor, shochu, weaker than vodka but far stronger than beer.

The parents sued the upperclass students. Prior court decisions had made clear that they were the only possible defendants. If universities were not liable for drunken deaths in their own dorms, they surely were not liable for deaths in a private home after an informal tennis club meeting.

The court first questioned the voluntary nature of the drinking game. It recognized that a bit of psychological pressure resulting from the age "gap" between the first-year students and the upperclass students might have played a role, but the participants appeared to enjoy themselves and were free to drop out. Finding next that Haruo did not appear to be so intoxicated that he was on his way to losing consciousness, the court found no duty for the defendants. The court concluded that under the circumstances, the death was unforeseeable. The defendants were not liable.[31]

Each of these cases is representative of those involving college drinking in school-related activities. All show the things that people of that age occasionally do when alcohol is placed in front of a group. In each case the plaintiffs essentially lose; only in Ichiro's case did the court find the defendants blameworthy, and they were only 10 percent at fault despite being medical students who voiced the concern that the deceased might have been suffering from alcohol poisoning. As one plaintiff's lawyer in such cases summarized the situation to the press: "People and society still think it was the victim's fault for drinking in the first place."[32]

Finally, in each case, the court offers little in the way of personal detail that characterizes opinions in other types of drinking cases. The students are merely students. Although the court provides a few details that might give away certain significant aspects of their lives ("medical school rowing club"), as compared to some other types of cases, the court does relatively little foreshadowing by repeating their personal histories, conspicuously omitting their individual journeys with alcohol. Perhaps that is because in these cases, the students are victims and not defendants. But the court also gives us little information about the defendant university or professors, and information about the students might have been useful. Courts seem to be withholding information about parties—a reminder that they can do so when they choose.

Insured Drunks

Courts enforce self-responsibility on the intoxicated in a third patterned area of facts and law: cases in which people seek damages from insurance companies for acts that occurred while policyholders were intoxicated. The insurance cases are of two types: auto insurance and life insurance. We will examine a few of each; as in the previous settings, each is representative of many. In almost every case courts deny plaintiffs' claims and find them or their heirs responsible for their drunken behavior.

The first auto insurance case comes from the Osaka District Court, writing in 2007. The driver was a used car salesman. The day of the accident was his day off, but he drove in to work anyway, and at 6 p.m. returned home, where he ate dinner with his family. He did not drink with his meal, the court tells us. (Without these words, readers might logically have assumed that he did, given *banshaku* customs.) He left home at 8 p.m. and stopped at a "kitchen bar" (a bar that serves café-style food and usually also includes seating apart from the bar) about ten to fifteen minutes away, in front of the Amagasaki train station. He parked at a parking meter, and he ate at the bar and drank draft beer with a group of four or five friends. The court points out that this was the day on which the Hanshin Tigers baseball team won the Central League pennant, and customers were celebrating. The reason for the inclusion of that bit of information isn't immediately obvious, but perhaps it is intended to suggest that many customers, and by extension our driver, were celebrating with more alcohol than usual. At the end of the night the driver left in his car. He crashed, and both he and the driver of the car he hit died.

The drinking driver's heirs sued the insurance company for payout under the policy. The insurance company pointed to a clause in the policy that stated that there would be no payout if the driver/policyholder was—and here the court quotes verbatim from section 2, paragraph 1, provision (6)(1)(2) of the policy—"under the influence of alcohol, under circumstances in which there was a fear [*osore*, 'risk' or 'danger'] that he would be unable to drive normally."

This is a strikingly vague provision from the U.S. perspective. The ambiguous terms—"under the influence," "fear," "circumstances"—all would likely be resolved against the insurer in the United States pursuant to a principle of contractual interpretation known as *contra proferentem*, which states that ambiguous words will be interpreted against the drafter of the contract. U.S. insurers typically use more objective language in policy exclusions, like "illegal activity," which is easier to verify with a police report.

Japan has no such interpretive principle. The court had little evidence of the driver's intoxication. There were no reliable blood alcohol test results. The manager of the kitchen bar said that he had no idea how much the driver had had to drink. The driver was dead, and apparently there were no other significant witnesses. (We apparently have no testimony from his drinking companions; perhaps here the Hanshin Tigers reference is relevant.) The court focused largely on the accident itself, finding a violent impact on a safe road and that there was no sound of braking—both of which were not necessarily the result of alcohol. But the court wrote:

> It is reasonable to find that the accident was caused by the deceased's inability to exercise control or care as a result of judgment that was impaired by the influence of something. Considering that he drank and considering the time that elapsed after he drank, the cause of this impaired judgment must be the influence of alcohol. The exact amount he drank and his level of intoxication are unclear, but looking at the circumstances of the incident, it is clear that he was under the influence of alcohol.

The court summarily dismissed other evidence as speculative:

> The plaintiffs claim that when the deceased commuted by car, he never drank outside the home, and had never been arrested for driving under the influence or driving while intoxicated, and accordingly they argue that he could not have been drinking before the incident. But he usually drank at the above-mentioned kitchen bar and drove home thereafter. Therefore, the fact that he never was arrested for driving under the influence is not a reason to deny the facts of this drunk driving case.

I assume that the court included that language to ensure that the plaintiffs knew that it had considered their argument, but the language is a bit sharp in a case involving death. It is not an unreasonable point, but it comes without a court's usual sympathy for the dead, without, anywhere in the opinion, an expression about the tragedy of the accident, how it could have been avoided, how unfortunate it was that the plaintiffs would have to deal with the expenses without insurance, or how the judges understood the sentiment but were unable to act on their behalf under the law. In any event, the court rejected the claim.[33]

A second case was decided two years later. In 2006, a year after the incident that led to the first case, many insurance companies, in the wake of deregulation, revised the drunk-driving provisions in their policies. Instead of the subjective standard that we saw in the contract in the first case, insurers switched to new language that denied auto accident claims *not* if the driver was "under the influence of alcohol and there was a fear that he would be unable to drive normally" but if the driver was "driving under the influence pursuant to article 65(1) of the Road Traffic Law, or in a corresponding state." As we saw in chapter 4, article 65(1) is the broad prohibition of drunk driving: "A person may not drive a vehicle under the influence of alcohol." This provision would seem to make the judge's job easier (and its explicit connection to the law more closely resembles the U.S. model).

The case before the court involved such a clause in an auto insurance policy. The plaintiff-driver rear-ended a car stopped at a traffic light. The question was the influence of alcohol on the driver in the accident. The only scientific evidence was the result of a blood alcohol test, which measured a mere 0.10, below Japan's low limit of 0.15, a result that easily could have resulted from one beer.

And yet the court began with a set of facts designed to avoid the objective breathalyzer evidence and to support its own subjective judgment of intoxication. The driver, the court said, did not habitually drink at night, but during periods when he had lots of drinking parties (*enkai*) he drank considerable amounts. He had liver damage from alcohol use. When his father died a year earlier, he did not eat for two or three days, drinking nothing but shochu, and was diagnosed with an inflamed liver as the result of alcohol. This personal history is of course not explicitly connected to the question of whether the driver violated section 65(1) on the night in question; the court is simply setting the stage to let its readership know that the driver drinks heavily—a stage the court chose not to set in the university student cases.

The first detail the court gives us regarding the night of the incident is that the driver left home at 8:30 p.m. on a Saturday to buy a bento box meal for dinner for his daughter at a nearby store. On his way home, his friend and business associate Kitagawa, the manager of a company that ran an izakaya, called him on his phone and asked him to come to the izakaya. He agreed to do so.

The reason for the court's inclusion of these facts could simply be to explain why the driver is driving: He went out to buy dinner and was diverted by a phone call to an izakaya. But the court had no need to include the detail about the daughter and the box meal; it's never mentioned again, and it's a Chekhovian gun that never fires. Or did it? The court could be hinting at the driver's responsibility for his daughter (who is to receive a box dinner at 8:30 p.m. on a Saturday night, raising questions about her age, the whereabouts of other caregivers, and the lack of dining options) and his inability to fulfill it, as the court does specifically say that after being invited to drink, he went to the izakaya "without returning home."

The court then lands what seems like a more direct blow to the driver. It had no real need to describe his associate Kitagawa, but it did so anyway. It noted that Kitagawa had been arrested and was under detention for violating a law that prohibits the storage of one's automobile in a facility more than two kilometers from one's home, usually achieved through illegal registration. A person might do that simply because parking is cheaper elsewhere or because they forget to change their address after a move. But the court here uses the term "garage skipping" (*shakotobashi*), which at a minimum suggests (along with the arrest) that

Kitagawa did so to skirt emissions regulations regarding cars with diesel engines. Perhaps the court is suggesting that he was doing something more sinister, as organized crime syndicates are often involved in the illegal movement and purchase of vehicles (among other reasons for the practice, syndicate members can't get auto loans without a legal source of income), especially the foreign vehicles that don't meet emissions standards.[34] So again the court is saying something about status: The combination of Kitagawa's management of an izakaya company and his arrest for garage skipping shows that he might not be an ordinary business associate.

The court then turned the arrest into an arguably relevant point: It uses the fact that the driver had gone to visit Kitagawa in jail to establish that the two were close. It also notes that police refused to allow the driver to see Kitagawa because they were *too* close. That statement of closeness, combined with what we already know about Kitagawa, suggests that both men might be gangsters. I suspect that that is the reason for the mention of Kitagawa's arrest, as the closeness of the men should have been clear from the fact that they were drinking buddies, and the arrest is otherwise entirely unrelated to the elements of the case.

At 9:30 the driver arrived at the izakaya, began with a beer *kanpai* with Kitagawa, and talked about Kitagawa's detention and the national news of the day. They lay down on benches in the izakaya as they talked through the night, dozing on and off. Just past six the next morning, the driver left. A few minutes later an accident occurred; he hit another driver.

The court then jumped through two hoops—one legal, one factual. The legal hoop is a bit complicated, but it's worth exploring to see how the court handles it. The issue is based on the insurance contract's incorporation of article 65(1) as its drunk-driving standard. In a criminal drunk-driving case, as we saw in chapter 2, article 65(1)—"a person may not drive a vehicle under the influence of alcohol"—is connected to two other articles in the same law and an ordinance. When combined, those rules define the words "under the influence of alcohol" in article 65(1) to mean a breath alcohol level of over 0.15. The driver tested at only 0.10, and as such, he argued, he was *not* driving under the influence according to the language of the policy.

The court rejected that argument. Article 65(1), the court said, stood on its own in this context, without the other provisions that define intoxication by a breath alcohol level. Even if in a criminal case a 0.15 was necessary to show a violation because of the two additional provisions, the language of the policy specified *only* article 65(1): "under the influence of alcohol." That language says nothing of blood alcohol content and does not reference the two other legal provisions. Therefore the definition under the insurance contract should have nothing to do with blood alcohol content.

What, then, should the definition be, if article 65(1) is to stand on its own? How should "under the influence of alcohol" be interpreted? The court says the definition should be as follows: "According to the sense of society, a person is under the influence, specifically, whether that person has a higher level of alcohol in his body than usual, as can be recognized by facial color, breath, and other external features." That language comes not from a statute but from (among other sources) a standard legal commentary book on the Road Traffic Law[35] —but the court did not cite a source.

To be clear, that's not an unreasonable ruling. But it has the effect of taking a potentially objective measure out of the policy and giving the court discretion to make a subjective judgment. I suspect the outcome would have been different in the United States because of the interpretive principle of finding against the drafting insurer in cases of ambiguity, but that is simply a different choice and not necessarily a correct one.

The court then needed to make the factual judgment. Again, recall that the driver's blood alcohol level was consistent with his story that he had had only one beer, or even less. But the court found other evidence. The driver fell asleep at the izakaya and stayed all night; surely he had had more to drink. He had a receipt from the evening that showed an order of one beer, two bottles of cola, and peanuts, but the court expressed strong suspicions that the receipt was fraudulently created by Kitagawa (who, after all, had been arrested for another crime and whose relationship with the driver was apparently unusually strong). For the defendant to have drunk nothing while dozing and talking all night at an izakaya was "strange." When he hit the car at the traffic light from behind at 40 kilometers per hour, with no signs that he tried to brake, he could have done so only if he was under the influence of alcohol. The insurer need not pay.[36]

The court has thus taught us what constitutes a normal drinking pattern: If a person sleeps and talks at an izakaya all night long, he must have had more than one beer. I don't necessarily disagree, but the record in this particular case does not contain a lot of evidence to support that fact. Perhaps more important, as in the first case, the court almost seems to show contempt for the driver (and his friend) and searches for cracks in the evidence to show that he was driving drunk—despite evidence to the contrary, which it did not address, choosing instead to make its own subjective decisions. The facts tell us not only what happened but how the court will rule.

Next, consider cases involving life insurance and accidental death insurance. Unlike the first set of cases, we know in these cases that someone, usually a family member of the plaintiff, has died. Courts might be more sympathetic to the deceased and be less likely to find intoxication.

Insurance policies in these kinds of cases usually have a clause that covers claims only if the incident that caused the death was "sudden and unexpected" (*kyuugeki, guuzen*) or sometimes "sudden, unexpected, and external" (*gairai*). In Japan courts must determine whether a death occurred from drinking, in which case death might be expected, or from some other, more surprising force.

In the first case, from 2001, the court described the deceased as follows:

> Taro, born February 20, 1944, established a construction company on June 22, 1988. His wife, Hanako, handled the accounting. At the time of the incident, he managed the business, which had two employees.
>
> Taro felt unease about his health, and in October 1997, with his wife, Hanako, he joined Reihoukai [a 1950s offshoot of an offshoot of Buddhism], which is headquartered in Kobe.
>
> Taro liked alcohol, and almost every day he drank four or five *gou* of sake. He received treatment for liver damage, and on June 16, 1977, he was diagnosed at Matsuyama City Hospital with an inflamed liver due to alcohol and admitted for treatment.

The court has painted quite a picture of Taro in that short passage, which I have expanded from only three Japanese sentences to six to prevent English run-ons. Curiously, it mentions his membership in Reihoukai, a so-called "new religion." That connection is not wholly irrelevant, as a religious service was Taro's apparent destination on the night of his death, but the reference also serves to portray him as a person who lives out of the mainstream. His socio-economic status is also crystal clear from his work and that of his spouse. The next description is more relevant: Taro "likes" alcohol, he drinks almost every day, and he drinks to such an extent that he requires hospitalization. Still, those facts do not establish his condition on the night of the incident; they simply let us know what to expect.

On the night of his death, Taro drank at home. He appeared to witnesses to be drunk. He walked in the street and fought with drivers. At ten past midnight, he was run over, first by a taxi, and then by a second car. He died. Neither driver was criminally prosecuted.

The court suggested that Taro might have been suicidal, but it need not have gone that far to decide the case. The drinking that night, whatever the volume, combined with his regular drinking habits and a few other hints in the opinion of odd behavior, were sufficient for the court to rule that the death was not "sudden and unexpected." The heirs received no life insurance payout.[37]

Arguably that case did not even turn on a question of intoxication; it simply was sufficient for the court to note it in passing. A second life insurance case, from 2003, focuses more specifically on intoxication. In that case the deceased drank shochu with a friend at a snack called Pepe from 10 p.m. until 11:15. The pair then went to Club Peter Pan (names like these are commonplace), where they drank four or five glasses of shochu mixed with water. The deceased was extremely drunk, with a breath alcohol level of 0.76. The family argued that he "held his alcohol well, and had never been in such an inebriated state." He went to a "completely dark, completely deserted city street, with no street lights." A car ran over him at 2:40 in the morning, and he died.

Again the court must determine whether the death was sudden and unexpected (and, because of the policy in this case, whether there was gross negligence [*juudai na kashitsu*] on the part of the policyholder). But there is a potentially complicating factor in this case: The driver who ran over the deceased also was drunk (he drank sake on ice and beer, the court states) and received a suspended prison sentence for running over the policyholder. The court, however, paid little attention to that legal situation, despite telling us the detail about what the driver drank. The victim was quite drunk, was lying in the middle of the road, and was the cause of the accident—never mind the drunk driver. Again the family received nothing.[38]

And again, as in the auto insurance cases, the court expressed no sympathy. The opinion was short, direct, and used the word *deisui*, a word that, as we saw in the police protective custody statistics in chapter 2, translates roughly to "dead drunk." The court used that word fifteen times—not that the description was undeserved, but without a hint of the empathy that is seen in some other opinions.

A 2010 case focuses directly on intoxication, has no complicating third parties, and determines whether the death was not only sudden and unexpected but also "extraneous" or "external" (*gairai*). The deceased, Akira, was forty-eight years old. Again the court begins Akira's history before the night in question, noting that he had a history of depression and hyperuricemia (high uric acid) and had completed bankruptcy proceedings—perhaps the court's response to an argument raised by the insurer, or perhaps the court's way of addressing concerns about suicide, the risk for which increases in Japan for people with high levels of debt.[39]

As for the night of the death, the court tells us that Akira returned home from dinner, which included alcohol, at 10 p.m. on December 24. He drank *ume chuuhai*, plum wine highballs, in his living room. The court eventually tells us that his blood alcohol level showed that he was mildly intoxicated but doesn't tell us how much he drank. In this case in particular I'd like to know more: What's missing is not only how much he drank but also a more complete timeline of Akira's actions on December 24, Christmas Eve. If Valentine's Day is not the most romantic night of the year in Japan, Christmas Eve is. It is traditionally a time for a dating—often a nice dinner followed by a stroll through Christmas lights, all in preparation for the traditional Christmas cake and Kentucky Fried Chicken, thanks to an amazingly successful 1974 marketing strategy.[40] But the court doesn't tell us anything that happened before 10 p.m.

that day other than the fact that Akira went to dinner. I would not question the omission in a U.S. case, but given the significance and the level of detail provided in other areas of the law, I wonder if we're missing anything. The only other character in the facts is Akira's daughter, Akiko, who, given Akira's age, could be in her teens or twenties. We know with specificity that Akira has been depressed and has too much uric acid in his blood, but we don't know what he did the night of his death at dinner, despite the fact that the contents of that dinner are about to reappear.

In any event, Akira fell asleep in the living room after returning home. At 1:35 in the morning, Akiko went to awaken him and get him to go to bed. He woke up, tried to drink the last remaining bit of his drink, said "Uuuh," and fell over. He died at the hospital as a result of asphyxiation by his own vomit.

The court found that the events had nine stages:

> (1) Drinking, (2) a nap, (3) awakening by Akiko (a family member), (4) drinking the last bit of plum wine highball, (5) saying "uuuh," (6) lodging of vomit in the windpipe, (7) closing of the respiratory tract, (8), asphyxiation, and (9) death. Factors (1) through (4) are part of a conceivable normal pattern [a part of daily life], and are not unnatural; factors (5) through (7) are a result of the influence of alcohol the night before, the effects of which might be exaggerated by anti-depressants; and factors (8) and (9) are a natural cause and effect. Accordingly, when Akira woke up from his nap, his ingestion, or planned ingestion, of alcohol from outside his body [operating from outside his body] became a trigger . . . and unexpected vomiting and closing of the respiratory tract led to asphyxiation. It is reasonable to say that Akira's death occurred in a "sudden, unexpected, and external manner."

Now we seem to have a sympathetic court. Akira drank alcohol and died, intoxicated (depending on how some controversial blood alcohol levels are interpreted, a factor that the court mentioned but did not discuss), in his own vomit, and the court found those events to be sudden, unexpected, and external. The last factor seems to be the most difficult; after all, Akira put the alcohol in his body the same way that the other victims have. But yet the court allowed an internal cause of death—vomit emerging from inside his stomach—to become external. The court awarded $100,000 to Akira's wife and $50,000 to each of his two children—and told us little more about Akira, his life, or his specific drinking habits.[41]

The insurer appealed. The Osaka High Court seemed unimpressed with the trial court's opinion, correcting several minor errors in that opinion, including the ordering of each of the opinion's mentions of *ume chuuhai* (plum highball) to be corrected to *umeshuu no rokku*, plum wine on the rocks. Depending on the brand and whether Akira mixed his own drinks or bought drinks in cans, the latter is likely to have more alcohol content, in which case the difference might matter. But the court did not mention the difference; it just corrected the name of the drink.

The court then went directly to the interpretive puzzle at the heart of the matter, systematically examining the three factors: sudden, unexpected, and external. It began with the external, noting that the term *could* apply to alcohol, but in this case the death was caused by something internal that came from Akira's own stomach. Accordingly "the cause of Akira's death was not 'an external accident,' and it is not necessary to examine whether the other factors, 'sudden' and 'unexpected,' were met. The cause of Akira's death was asphyxiation, and the appellee's claim for insurance damages is unfounded." The Osaka High Court reversed the lower court, yet again finding against the policyholder on relatively subjective grounds.[42]

Akira's heirs appealed to the Supreme Court, and they won. The Court found, with no recitation of facts, that asphyxiation necessarily occurs in the airway, not the esophagus, and therefore "of course" (*touzen*; alternatively, "naturally") any blockage must be external, even if it comes from the stomach. That "of course" turns a concept litigated by parties that could not settle and debated at lower courts into a conclusion that is intended to be obvious. The Supreme Court sent the case back down to the high court, with instructions to reconsider the case in light of its holding.[43] The policyholders appear to have won, but only after two appeals—and they are the outliers in this type of case.

In both auto and life insurance cases, then, it is difficult for plaintiffs in Japan to recover for actions that occurred when the policyholder was drunk. Although each case is grounded in legal rules, a broader interpretation, and one that would be consistent with cases in other contexts, is that in general, intoxicated persons are expected to take care of themselves.

* * *

In three kinds of cases of intoxication, courts find, to state a broad conclusion, that drunks are responsible for themselves. In the relational and employment duty context, duties are enforced only in extreme situations and penalties are generally low, though there is some evidence that the situation might be changing in the service industry. In cases involving university students, whether the defendants are universities or individuals, courts rarely hold others responsible even for the actions of underage drinkers. In cases involving insurance, courts often resolve conflicting evidence in favor of the insurer even if that finding seems to require significant narrative construction to prepare readers for the conclusion.

What becomes of the social science claims of responsibility in Japan from the beginning of this chapter, in which the context is more important than the acts of the individual? At least in civil cases of intoxication, those concerns seem relatively unimportant. Individuals are responsible for their own behavior. People around them—universities, students, professors—are not responsible, and death results from internal not external causes. Individual actors are responsible for their own actions even in cases in which others in the group could easily be held accountable.

As for Japanese drinking life, a few more data points have emerged. University students in Japan, as in the United States, engage in stupid and extraordinarily risky drinking behavior. Sometimes death results. The determination of whether people are drunk depends on many subjective factors—how much they drank, how they looked, how they acted—and sometimes blood alcohol levels are irrelevant. And if people are going to spend the night at an izakaya, they are presumed to have had more than one beer—especially if their friend owns the place, and especially if that friend has unrelated legal problems that hint at larger issues. Even if the results of the cases are predictable in some sense—note again the tension between the necessarily generalized patterns of intoxication and the unique individuals who must act them out—the court is at least required to set up the conditions in the narrative to make it so.

It is possible, of course, that I am overly conflating issues across diverse contexts. The cases in this chapter obviously rely on a myriad of diverse laws, theories, and arguments, and those differences might play a greater role in explaining different outcomes, and perhaps narrative stances, than I predict. Nevertheless when courts go out of their way in one case to quote the precise language used to pressure a person to drink and say nothing in others, or when courts give significant background about parties in some cases and not in others, something else is going on: They are engaging in a kind of analysis that transcends the underlying legal underpinnings of the cases to provide significant information both about individuals and about what it means to be drunk in Japan.

6

Punishing the Drunk

We have now seen a sufficient number of patterned drunk-driving cases that their facts can be summarized, and I will do so here to focus on sentencing, the last stage of a criminal proceeding. Police pulled over a drunk Hashimoto at 3:30 a.m.; he fled and hit a truck, was arrested, and was charged with dangerous driving causing injury.

The Hiroshima District Court convicted Hashimoto and sentenced him to one year and six months' imprisonment. (The sentencing range was between one and fifteen years.) He appealed, lost, and the high court then turned to sentencing. It began by reciting the facts, as courts uniformly do in this section of the opinion. It then stated the harm and blameworthiness of Hashimoto's conduct: He was driving under the influence when he hit the truck, causing injuries to the driver that required 170 days of physical therapy to recover. The victim was a professional driver, and as such he would remember for "a long time" the difficulties that had come as a result of his driving. An hour and a half after the incident, Hashimoto had a breath alcohol level of 0.30. And "as described above, out of fear that his driving under the influence would be discovered, he drove dangerously to escape a police car, and his motivation and circumstances were malicious [or 'blameworthy,' *akushitsu*]. Moreover, he has two other incidents of driving under the influence, and his complete disregard of traffic rules suggests that he is a habitual drunk driver. Accordingly, his criminal responsibility is quite serious."

The court thus began by explaining what was wrong with the defendant and his actions. But like almost every other criminal court opinion in this area of law, the inquiry did not stop there. "Oh wait, hang on," one can almost hear the court say, as it turned to a different set of factors that suggest Hashimoto might not be such a bad person after all:

> The defendant has negotiated a settlement of $19,215.03 for the victim's personal injuries as a result of this incident of dangerous driving causing injury, and after the lower court's decision was issued, he has made

Drunk Japan. Mark D. West, Oxford University Press (2020) © Oxford University Press.
DOI: 10.1093/oso/9780190070847.001.0001

> progress toward negotiating a settlement regarding compensation for damages to property. The defendant has shown remorse, and has sent sympathy gifts to the victim and the company that owned the vehicle. The defendant and his mother have apologized to the victim. The defendant suffered a right tibial fracture and a wound to his left thigh, which required a total of three months' hospital treatment. Because of these injuries, he is not able to move about as he was before. The car that he was driving at the time of the incident is totaled, and because of his crime his drivers' license has been revoked. He has no prior criminal history other than that mentioned above.

The mention of Hashimoto's mother is curious (why is she apologizing for her adult son?), but let's set that issue aside for a bit. Hashimoto has seriously injured a person as a result of his drunk driving—not just any drunk driving, but fleeing from the police because he was afraid that he would be caught for a third time. The court is fully aware of the other two incidents, and yet it praises his lack of *other* criminal history. The court seems to be bending over backwards in this section to present facts in a light favorable to Hashimoto. It continues, focusing more now on factors that are completely extraneous to Hashimoto's conduct or the criminal act (and here comes his mom again):

> The defendant has a wife and young children to support. His mother appeared at a court hearing and testified that she would never allow the defendant to drink and drive again. The defendant's mother and his wife submitted letters to the court stating that they would supervise him. A representative of the construction company that employs him stated in a court hearing that because of the defendant's skills, experience, and ability to guide, he has been given substantial responsibility at worksites. The representative has submitted a statement promising to employ and guide him. Considering all these factors carefully, it cannot be said that the defendant's sentence was too heavy and inappropriate.[1]

After reviewing factors that could both mitigate and aggravate Hashimoto's sentence, the court found that the lower court had sentenced him appropriately. In reviewing those factors, the court focused on Hashimoto (and his mother) as a person with specific circumstances (though perhaps not truly as an individual, given the role of his family), and in that regard the opinion is typical.

How typical? Consider a 2016 drunk-driving case. The defendant had drunk for four hours while he and his friends made their way to a graduation party. He was fiddling with his phone, ignored a traffic light, and hit a victim with his car, killing him. He didn't stop; instead he went to his friend's apartment (with a broken windshield), called his friends, fell asleep, woke up the next morning to search the web for windshield replacement and police accident reports, and eventually was caught by police. The court first berated him:

> The defendant left his house and drove his car knowing he would drink, and after drinking a lot of alcohol over the next few hours, in a condition in which his ability to drive normally was impaired by alcohol, he thought simply that he wouldn't cause an accident, and with no cause for urgency or need whatsoever drove his car to meet his friends, and as he used his mobile phone he missed a red light, causing this accident. The defendant has driven under the influence more than ten times. This time, he carelessly thought that he would not cause an accident. He disregarded the rules of the road, and drove in an extremely dangerous condition. Moreover, the defendant was afraid to have his drunk-driving accident exposed, so he offered no help to the victim and did not inform the police, instead choosing to go to his friend's house. This act is cruel and malicious. The victim was crossing with the green light in the crossing zone when he was hit by the defendant's car, killing him, through no fault of his own, and with grave consequences. His survivors feel not only sadness about the sudden loss of their family member, but also anger over the fact that the cause was not just drunk driving, but a hit and run. They hope for severe punishment for the defendant, whose responsibility is heavy, and he cannot escape harsh condemnation.

Then the court—oh wait, hang on—backed off, examining some of the same mitigating factors as in the previous case: "The defendant deeply regrets the fact that he drove drunk so casually, causing an accident that killed the defendant, ending his life. He has written many letters of apology [*shazaibun*], has voluntary insurance with unlimited compensation, and has made appropriate payments to the survivors of the victim. Even taking into account the fact that the defendant has no prior record, the sentence [of five years] is appropriate."[2]

Note that after the individualized scolding, the court turned to factors that are not dissimilar in the two cases. The two courts seem to be trying to achieve some sort of equity across cases while continuing to acknowledge, even if only through words and not results, the human element in the courtroom. The court followed a uniform, systematic, routine method, and yet it did so while treating the defendants as distinct individuals.

In this chapter we first examine the broad landscape of criminal sentencing in Japan. We then explore the specific ways in which drunk drivers might not be such bad people after all—and if any of it actually matters.

General Sentencing Principles

The Japanese Penal Code provides a specific range of punishment for each crime, but the range is broad. Many penalties were increased in 2004: The penalty range for homicide (excluding life imprisonment and the death penalty), which was once three to fifteen years, rose to five to twenty. The penalty for inflicting injury causing death, once two to fifteen years, rose to three to twenty. The penalty for dangerous driving causing death, once one month to ten years, rose to one month to fifteen years. In each category, penalties were raised in part in response to public opinion polls that suggest fear over an increasing crime rate and general unease, feelings that some scholars have suggested are not warranted by statistics.[3]

Still, as we have seen, sentences remain low. Noting that fact, Dan Foote has described Japanese criminal justice as a system of "benevolent paternalism." The system is benevolent in its focus on "specific prevention," which prevents "recidivism through the reformation and rehabilitation of the offender," and it is paternalistic in that it "is also characterized by the great trust placed in and the broad grants of discretion made to authorities."[4] The Penal Code provides that a punishment may be reduced by half in light of extenuating circumstances (arts. 66, 68). If a defendant has not been imprisoned in the past five years, sentences of up to three years may be suspended (art. 25(i)).

How are judges to apply these broad provisions in a system that affords such discretion? The Supreme Court has given some guidance, noting in a prominent 1966 case that criminal courts must consider "a defendant's character and history, as well as the method, purpose, and motive" for the crime.[5] "And yet," one judge writes about that case, "in practice, sentences are determined according to their market price [*ryoukei souba*]."[6] The Japanese judiciary, with help from prosecutors, has created a so-called market price system that works somewhat like sentencing guidelines. (The defense bar plays almost no part in the process. Although there is little reason to believe that defendants do not receive good counsel, it is also true that there is no significant, organized defense bar in Japan).[7] In the Japanese context, however, unlike the U.S. context, the guidelines are not legislated, leaving Japanese judges with greater discretion than their American counterparts.[8] The purpose of the system is to "apply the same sentence to incidents of the same type, same character, and same degree."[9] According to one judge, the market price system is necessary because "if sentences were too light, too heavy, or varied widely, sentencing would be grossly unfair to defendants and would cause society to lose faith in the justice system."[10]

Prosecutors initiate pricing in individual cases. They file sentencing requests with judges based both on regular internal practices and expectations of the degree to which judges will accept such requests. Courts consider the request, and in most cases reduce the requested punishment, sentencing defendants to roughly 70 to 80 percent of the requested punishment.[11] (Opinions in criminal cases often state both the sentence and the prosecutors' request.) Stated another way: Prosecutors add about 20 percent to the sentences they seek to account for the fact that judges reduce prosecutorial sentencing requests by about 20 percent.[12] The result is the market price.

Precedent also plays a role in determining the market price. As cases have become more easily searchable, a database of sentencing decisions has been built. If a sentencing court gets the decision "wrong," it can be corrected on appeal, and high courts can detail how the lower court missed the mark. And in at least one case, prosecutors discovered that they calculated a heavier sentence than necessary after the fact and took the unusual step of appealing to have it lowered.[13]

The nature of both the prosecution and the judiciary helps maintain market prices. Most prosecutors and judges serve for life, and as such both are similarly restrained within their own systems. Judges and prosecutors are both frequently transferred within their respective systems, usually once every three years. Rarely do either have political ambitions that might drive prosecutors in the U.S. case, for instance, toward harsher penalties.[14] The constant turnover, similar training, and overall cohesiveness and stability of the professions help ensure relative convergence on market prices.

If all of this sounds a bit too neat, consider the cases of defendants who are sentenced according to the lay judge system, through which citizens decide cases jointly on panels with judges. For the benefit of those lay judges, the Supreme Court and local authorities have introduced sentencing databases that include detailed factors such as "defendant's remorse" and "victim's fault." Databases generally are not accessible by the general public—or, for that matter, by attorneys, presumably on the theory that they will attempt to game the system.[15]

Perhaps because of databases, or perhaps because of the presence of professional judges on lay judge panels, the sentences handed down by lay judge panels look roughly similar to judges' professional court opinions. Overall penalties for each crime are similar.[16] The ratio of length of sentence requested by prosecutors to length of sentence actually issued is also similar for both kinds of panels.[17] The standard deviation is larger than in judge-based trials—lay judges, for instance, tend to give harsher penalties to sex offenders[18]—but the sentences are similar, and, like professional judges, occasionally lay judges exceed the penalties requested by prosecutors.

A 2014 Supreme Court case, the first in which a lay judge panel's sentence was reduced on appeal, clarifies that uniformity among lay judges and professional judges is in fact a goal of the system. In that case, abusive parents caused the death of their twenty-month-old daughter when they slapped her head, causing an acute subdural hematoma. Prosecutors requested a term of ten years' imprisonment. The lay judge panel imposed a sentence of fifteen years. The defendants appealed, the high court affirmed, and the Supreme Court overturned the decision. The Court stated:

> The Japanese Penal Code sets forth a wide range of statutory punishments for a crime based on the premise that the elements of each crime can include many different kinds of criminal acts. Accordingly, a court should determine and pronounce sentences that it considers appropriate for the criminal act in question based on the principle that people should be held responsible for their specific actions. Still, the accumulated body of court opinions shows trends in sentencing for each crime. These accumulated precedents are not legal norms, but they have significance as a guide for sentencing. For a sentence to be valid as a judgment of the court, sentencing factors must be valued objectively and appropriately, the outcome of the calculation must be fair, and accordingly it is important that prior sentencing be taken into account to guarantee the appropriateness of the sentencing process. The reasoning is as valid in lay judge trials as it is in trials conducted by professional judges.

The Court found that the lay judge panel deliberately "chose a sentence far heavier than that demanded by the prosecutor, close to the statutory maximum," and that such a sentence would be valid only if the opinion "provides a specific and convincing explanation" for the deviation from precedent. It then sentenced the defendants to eight years in prison, exactly 80 percent of what prosecutors requested.[19]

The Court has thus given us an official account of how sentences are calculated (along with an implicit instruction to stick to the market price system). Additional guidance is available from court practice. An often cited but never formally legislated proposed revision to the Penal Code from 1974 reads as follows: "(1) Punishment shall be commensurate with the culpability of the offender. (2) Punishment shall be imposed for the purpose of repressing offenses and reforming and rehabilitating offenders, in light of the age, character, career, and environment of the offender; the motive, method, result and impact on society of the offense; and the attitude of the offender after the offense."[20]

Most of the factors have little to do with the actual crime; they focus primarily on the defendant's background and, with specific authorization from the Supreme Court, postcrime factors.[21] The use of these factors can be seen in several surveys. One study of 271 defendants in Tokyo District Court finds that judges tend to focus most on motive, criminal record, age, settlement, family relationship, friends, working habits, education, employment, and time of previous convictions.[22] Another survey finds other postcrime factors that play a role: "relation of defendant to friends and organized crime firms," economic situation, family situation, financial reparations to the victim, remorse, and impact on society.[23] And a third study finds that while prior criminal history, age, and other background factors have the highest correlation to sentence length, apology, remorse, settlement, and support of family remain important factors.[24]

Among these factors remorse is a hallmark of the Japanese criminal justice system. Of course an underlying assumption is that judges are able to determine true remorse, based on "remorseful appearance in court."[25] But according even to an Osaka District Court judge, remorse is not always easy to ascertain:

> It is very important in criminal trials to respect the role of remorse. However, it is very difficult to use remorse as a sentencing factor because of the inability to see into the heart of a person. Every judge has seen a defendant express words of remorse in court but then change immediately after the sentence is announced, or has announced a suspended sentence based on a defendant's remorseful words only to see that suspension revoked when the defendant commits the same crime again, or has given a heavy sentence when a defendant is not good at expressing remorse. Doesn't every judge have the experience of seeing the same defendant express remorse two or three times, or of seeing a defendant swear that he will break his ties with organized crime even as organized crime members attend the sentencing hearing and offer moving words on behalf of the defendant? Proving and recognizing the actual existence of remorse is extraordinarily difficult.[26]

We can draw two points from the judge's statement. First, let's not overlook the first two sentences. The judge actually seems to care about remorse; it is not a mere placeholder or part of an elaborate sentencing grid. Other evidence supports the view; in a study of traffic accident apologies, for instance, a prominent Japanese lawyer noted that an increase in damages might increase apologies, especially those forced by insurance companies, but that judges were likely to dismiss those apologies as a sort of punitive compensator measure and not evidence of true remorse.[27]

Second, the judge is correct that judges cannot actually recognize remorse. It's notoriously easy to fake,[28] and judges make mistakes. They base their determinations in part on courtroom demeanor, a factor that courts specifically note in opinions[29] and prosecutors cite as valuable in making their final sentencing requests.[30] Remorse can also be demonstrated by a defendant's ability to reach a negotiated settlement with the victims, a factor dependent in part on the relative class and income of the parties. As David Johnson notes,

"Suspects who have enough money and connections to hire a defense lawyer before the charge decision is made can produce evidence of remorse and forgiveness."[31] One study of thirty automobile accidents resulting in death in the 2002 Tokyo High Court found settlement to be one of the most important factors affecting a change in the sentence on appeal.[32]

Despite the difficulties of making clear determinations about the existence or importance of postcrime factors in the Japanese system, those factors appear in virtually all criminal opinions in which a defendant is sentenced. The rhetorical pattern is consistent: the defendant committed very bad acts, and he is quite blameworthy, but he also has his good side, and "considering all the factors" the sentence is x. Given that construction, in which the judge is never required to specify how much any given factor matters, and for many factors does not need to discuss how the determination of the degree of existence of that factor was reached, one possible conclusion is that these discussions don't matter: The court has determined the market price and is simply inputting text into the opinion to explain it, in part to satisfy the mandate in the Code of Criminal Procedure (art. 335) that arguments on reduction of sentence have been addressed and in part to ensure that the litigants, appeals court judges, and ultimately society will be able to divine punishment similarly.[33]

Lay judge panel practice usually conforms. In a 2010 case of dangerous driving causing death, for instance, after a lengthy discussion of the factors that damned the defendant, lay judges (and the professionals with whom they served) unanimously signed on to the following opinion:

> Considering the above, the defendant's criminal responsibility is quite severe. On the other hand, the defendant has sent a letter of apology to the family [the victim's oldest son], and with the utmost sincerity, he has shown remorse for his acts. He also has stated that he will never drink again, will receive treatment for his alcoholism, and will never drive again. The defendant's second son has also promised that he will guide the defendant toward a return to society, and that he will work with the defendant to treat his alcoholism. The defendant's insurance is paying appropriate compensation, and the award for damages to the house and car has been paid. The defendant's company has terminated him as punishment. It is also recognized that the defendant lived an ordinary life as a hard worker and as a member of society. Accordingly, considering all the factors that are favorable to the defendant, an adjudication of a sentence of seven years' imprisonment is appropriate.[34]

Whether or to what extent the factors that lay judges mention are doing any work in determining the seven years is unclear. It is clear, however, that there is an agreed-upon rhetoric, a ritual for decision-makers, that includes the expression of a predetermined set of factors.

Alcohol-Related Sentencing

Consider more carefully the sentencing factors from Hashimoto's case, the Hiroshima drunk driver from the beginning of this chapter. A few factors from the incident and before the incident mattered: He had no criminal record, he was injured, he had no car and no license, and he had a family to support. But most of the factors that the court weighted occurred after the crime: settlement, remorse, gifts, apologies, and statements from the mother, the wife, and the employer that each will help.

The court has given defense counsel quite a long list of tasks that their clients can perform to improve their position at sentencing. These factors are standard in Japanese drunk-driving sentences; the sentencing portion of a drunk-driving opinion is in some ways as formulaic as other criminal cases. The first paragraph describes the actions. The second paragraph describes the heinousness of the act and the pain felt by others, usually the family of the victim. The third paragraph lists the factors, as in Hashimoto's case, that favor the defendant.

By far the most common defendant-favoring factors in drunk-driving cases are payments to the victims or their families, expressions of remorse, explicit apologies (if the crime has identifiable victims), and the lack of prior offenses. Following closely in frequency are family factors (the attendance of family in court, the testimony of family that they will help the defendant, or occasionally even the mere existence of family), social sanctions (such as loss of job), and pledges of abstinence. Importantly, it is never clear from the record exactly which factors were presented to the court and with what degree of emphasis; the opinions simply create a narrative.

Even in cases with unusual facts we often see a return to form at the sentencing stage. Consider the *Mad Max* case from chapter 3, in which the defendant damaged a car and injured several people after watching a DVD (and drinking). In the sentencing portion of the opinion, after noting the heinousness of the acts, the court stated:

> We cannot say that the wounds were minor, but they were not so severe. We confirm that the defendant has paid $1,200 for damages to the first car. Moreover, the defendant has not disputed the facts of each crime, and has shown remorse and apologized to each victim, and in the first, second, and fourth cases he has already reached a settlement with each victim that involves significant compensation. He has begun

> to pay each . . . and his mother appeared in court to say that she would guide him in the future.[35]

It is unclear, of course, how much influence a mother can actually have over this particular defendant, a thirty-six-year-old member of an organized crime syndicate. The language is simply standard and will not sound unusual if the judgment is appealed.

So standard is the sentencing process that many mitigating factors in the general driving context are not unique to alcohol-related driving cases. In a 2017 case in which a driver hit and killed a nine-year-old, the court listed in his favor the fact that he had compensated the victim's family, had no prior record, had shown remorse, and that his wife had promised to care for him. He received a three-year prison sentence. His driving was impaired not by alcohol but by playing Pokemon Go on his smartphone.[36] In fact if we substitute "smartphone"[37] or, for that matter, "drugs"[38] or "running a red light"[39] or "mistakenly stepping on the accelerator thinking it is the brake"[40] as the cause instead of "alcohol" in cases prosecuted under the catch-all law that criminalizes driving that causes death or injury,[41] the length of the sentence in those cases varies, but the sentencing factors do not.

It might seem, at least in the drunk-driving context, that sentencing is an area in which judges might be seeking justice more generally rather than applying the humanized analysis we have seen in other aspects of cases. But three factors suggest that courts do, in fact, maintain their focus on the individual at sentencing despite their rather uniform approach.[42]

First, many drunk-driving cases rely, at least rhetorically, on unique sentencing factors that are not part of the standard list. In a 2002 case, for instance, the court took into account the fact that the defendant was engaged to be married.[43] A 2008 case found in the defendant's favor the fact that his child had been killed in the accident caused by his own drunk driving.[44] A 2006 case emphasized the tears that flowed with the defendant's apology.[45] A 2011 case noted that the defendant served as a volunteer after an earthquake and distributed tissue packets on the street (a common advertising method) that included anti-drunk-driving warnings.[46] I assume, again, that courts state these facts for a reason.

Second, the common factors encourage individual defendants to at least attempt a show of remorse, which can result in reparations to the victim in a relationship-building process that necessarily focuses on individuals. The system encourages the right individuals, or at least the people who are best able to control drunken conduct, to compensate victims, even without using the resources of the civil courts. The factors also encourage particular people in the defendant's life, especially family members and work colleagues, to play a restorative role, at least at the time of sentencing.[47]

Those expectations might sound Pollyannaish, but a substantial body of literature on restorative justice in Japan suggests that the practice is more than window dressing.[48] Consider an example from chapter 4: the drunk truck driver Taniwaki, whose actions led to the fiery death of the Inoues' children. The Tokyo District Court stated that Taniwaki lacked remorse. Still, as the children's mother, Inoue Ikumi, explained in her book about the incident and the anti-drunk-driving campaign that followed, she continued to interact with Taniwaki and his family after the incident. The driver's wife wrote Inoue an apology letter four months after the incident, and Inoue sent her a photo album of the children—with apparent sincerity—to pass to her husband, who was in jail. Each month thereafter, on the day of the children's death, the wife sent Inoue snacks and fruit. As her husband was about to be released from jail, Inoue wrote the wife and requested that they visit her. (She also requested that she never allow her husband to drink again.)

Shortly after the truck driver's release, he visited the Inoues' home, together with his wife and an unspecified relative. This visit had no legal or financial purpose, as the driver had served his jail time and the civil suit had ended. He apologized again, saying (according to Inoue), "I will never drink again. For that reason, I'm not going to associate any more with the friends with whom I used to drink. Just as I promised in court, I won't ever get behind the wheel again." Inoue expressed her doubts to him: "Most perpetrators in this world forget their remorse three days after they serve their sentence and return to normal life. The reason I agreed to meet you, even though I couldn't prepare myself for it, was because I was afraid that if you went back [home to] Kochi there was a good chance I'd never see you again." The driver responded, "If our positions were reversed, I'd probably feel the same. But I'm not running away. I will keep my promise and carry this burden forever. Please believe me." At the end of the visit Inoue asked him to return, and he promised to do so. He apparently never did. Inoue suggests that he might have started drinking again. Still, years after the incident his wife continued to send fruit and snacks each month, and the visit, which is not unusual in Japan, meant something to the Inoues, and perhaps mattered to the driver as well.[49]

An emphasis in alcohol-related cases on particular alcohol-related factors also shows how judges tailor generalized sentencing patterns to particularized individual behavior. Abstinence, for instance, receives no mention in the leading treatises on sentencing, and family support is mentioned only fleetingly, with a warning that if family members pledge their support for the defendant, a judge must also consider why the defendant, if surrounded by family, committed the crime in the first place.[50] And yet each factor is frequently mentioned in the cases.

These factors merit more exploration; they tell us much about both personalized justice and Japanese drinking life. Let's focus first on oaths by defendants, then on pledges of support by others.

Oaths

Amy Borovoy explains the nexus between family and the pledge of abstinence in Japan outside of the courtroom:

> Danshukai, one of the largest organizations for families recovering from alcoholism (it has forty-seven thousand members, in contrast with AA's five thousand in Japan), is a self-help group where families of alcoholics attend the same meetings as the alcoholics themselves.... While Danshukai shares the AA notion of social support with sobriety as means of recovery, it departs from the Al-Anon notion ... that family members cannot heal their families' illness, that alcoholism is the abuser's problem and not the family members', and that family members should attend meetings to learn to manage and to look after themselves rather than "fix" the abuser. Instead Danshukai adheres more closely to conventional Japanese gender role constructions. At the end of each meeting, after men recite a "Sincerity Pledge" of sobriety, women recite a "Family Pledge."[51]

The case law clearly reflects some of the dynamics Borovoy mentions. Let's look first at the impact of pledges and oaths outside of the sentencing context. If an oath arises in the facts of such a case and not the sentencing portion, its appearance usually indicates that it will be broken before the opinion concludes. In a 2011 case, a pharmaceutical company fired the plaintiff employee. According to the company, the plaintiff had a "very bad alcohol habit" (*sakeguse ga hijouni waruku*), and he often came to work drunk. One of the plaintiff's key failures seems to have occurred at the Shanghai airport, where, in 2008, he missed his flight because he had drunk so much at the airport that he fell asleep. This event caused the company's employees to worry, and the court found the action to have been "quite troublesome" (*soutou no meiwaku*) to the company.

In the end, the court found the firing legal. But a more interesting point is what the plaintiff did following the airport incident: "In September of the same year [2008], the defendant swore never to be intoxicated on company time, signed a written oath in which he agreed to retire if he violated that condition, and quit drinking." The written oath here is key: It is just an oath; it does no legal work, and the court mentioned it only in passing and not as part of its judgment. But the document seems to have placated the firm for a while—until, at least, the plaintiff was asked to stop using his phone during work, once tried to take the company's computer home in the middle of an argument, and presented the company with a doctor's diagnosis of depression as an excuse for missing work. Only then was he fired.[52]

A similar oath-breaking occurred in a 2010 case in which a wife strangled her husband to death with a towel. At the time, he had consumed a large beer and 1.8 liters of shochu. She argued that he had consented to a joint suicide, which carries a lower penalty than that for murder. (Of course she also is admitting that she failed to follow through on her end of the suicide pact, a not uncommon theme in Japanese case law.)[53] The court found that he did not consent and that he had capacity to do so, as he "held his liquor well."

For our purposes, the interesting behavior occurred twelve years before the murder, when the victim swore his oath. He had a "bad alcohol habit," yelled daily at his family, occasionally punched and kicked them, and at least once raped his wife (a legal act in Japan). His wife left him. To get her to return, he got on his knees, bowed to the floor, and swore off alcohol. He was successful in keeping his marriage alive but unsuccessful in stopping his drinking. He soon returned to the usual patterns, eventually his wife strangled him, and the court found her guilty of murder.[54]

The appearance of an abstinence pledge in the facts of an opinion tells us a lot about cultural norms, but pledges in criminal cases arise most frequently in the sentencing process. The pledges here are unique: Unlike in some other crimes, the sentencing factor (not drinking) correlates directly to a factor that actually played a role in the crime (drinking). Sometimes the pledge explicitly references alcoholism in language recommended by attorneys who advocate for "therapeutic justice," but it need not do so.[55]

The role of a pledge is imprecise. In a Kobe District Court case, the defendant had broken into a car in a parking lot and stolen cash and a shoulder bag, with a total value of less than $100. He was intoxicated. He argued that his intoxication was at a level that made him "weak-minded" and that his penalty should be reduced accordingly. The court found otherwise, noting that upon his arrest he was able to tell the police his name, date of birth, address, place of employment, and how much he had had to drink. And yet in sentencing the court noted, "There is no mistaking the fact that this crime was committed while intoxicated after having drunk large amounts of liquor. The defendant says that from this point forward, he wants to begin rehabilitation by abstaining from alcohol and getting a job that will facilitate his return to society." Prosecutors had requested 2.5 years in prison; the court sentenced him to 1.5.[56]

Apart from the legal categories, the court's overall view of drinking in that case cannot be neatly stated. It denied the "weak-minded" intoxication defense, which would have served to reduce the defendant's penalty. But when announcing the defendant's sentence, it explicitly stated that it was taking intoxication into account—and it mentioned, offhand, the pledge.

If that sounds a bit muddled, consider a 2009 rape case in which the defendant had lain in wait at night for his victim. In sentencing, the court examined the defendant's past:

> The defendant has many previous convictions, with a record of imprisonment and recidivism, and the time between his release on parole and the crime in this case is quite short. He has disregard for the law, and many of his previous violent crimes resulted from drinking. At his previous trial, he promised never to drink again, and yet he committed this violent crime while under the influence of alcohol. Defense counsel argues that the influence of alcohol shows that the crime was not planned, but given the defendant's history of violent crime under the influence, that point is not relevant. The crime is severe, the defendant's criminal responsibility is quite heavy, and it is reasonable not to reduce the sentence below the statutory minimum.

The court then explained the positive factors that would decrease the sentence: "Fortunately, the victim's injuries were minor, and although it cannot be said that the defendant has paid a sufficient amount in damages, he has shown that he has developed feelings of remorse and apology, and that he wants to be rehabilitated by pledging abstinence." Prosecutors requested a seven-year sentence; the court sentenced him to six.[57]

The length of the sentence compared to the length requested by prosecutors is roughly the same as in other cases, making the role of the pledge in the algorithm unclear. Nor did the court seem particularly troubled by the defendant's breaking of his previous promise not to drink. The point is that the court mentioned the factor as important—and presumably, with years of experience, prosecutors knew it would, and made their sentencing request accordingly. The words of the oath—even if spoken only in the past, even if unfulfilled, even if disingenuous, as long as not obviously so—seem to matter, at least for the rhetoric of abstinence. The defendant might drink again, and his past suggests that he probably will, but the court took note of the pledge, perhaps to let the defendant know that he had been heard, perhaps as a statement of social aspiration, perhaps for the victim's benefit, or perhaps simply because doing so is part of the sentencing ritual.

Some criminal defendants in drunk-driving cases go further than merely swearing off alcohol. In a Fukuoka case of dangerous driving causing death while under the influence, the court remarked on the defendant's remorse: "Beginning at the investigative stage, the defendant has been frank about his crimes, even admitting that he is a habitual drunk driver. In court, he swore that after his return to society, he would not drink, and resolved to never drive an automobile again. The defendant has clearly shown remorse, has apologized to the victims and the families, and has sworn to spend his entire life atoning." The court sentenced him to three years and eight months. (Prosecutors had requested five years.)[58]

Other defendants state that they will never drive again, leaving alcohol an open question.[59] Some say that they will not drive and even will enlist others to help them stop doing so.[60] Simply getting drunk drivers off the street, when combined with the requisite showing of remorse, is apparently sufficient for sentencing purposes, or at least for a mention. Abstinence from either alcohol or driving would solve the problem of drunk-driving recidivism, and courts seem unconcerned about which mechanism defendants choose.

Support of Others: The Guarantors

Another factor that courts often mention in alcohol-related cases is the unenforceable guarantee by others, usually family, to support the drinker. In Hashimoto's case from the beginning of this chapter, it was his wife and mother who pledged their support (and his mother apologized on his behalf). In a case in which a drunk driver dragged the body of a newspaper delivery boy after hitting him, the court said of the defendant's remorse, "The defendant has apologized to the victims and shown remorse. Moreover, the defendant's father appeared in court and swore that he would guide the defendant when he returned to society. The defendant has no criminal history other than traffic violations, and he works seriously at his carpentry job."[61] Prosecutors requested a sentence of seventeen years; he received thirteen.

In some cases, the role of the family is defined more precisely. In a 2006 DWI case, the court, after noting that it was not the defendant's first drunk-driving offense, stated, "The defendant shows that he is aware of the seriousness of this act, and displays deep remorse. He has no previous history of incarceration. The defendant is the pillar of his family, as he and his common-law wife are raising three children, and his common-law wife has promised to supervise him and maintain strict control of the car keys."[62] Prosecutors had requested eight months' imprisonment, and the court gave only a suspended sentence of one year. Whether the precise discussion of the management of the car keys truly affected that sentence is unclear, but it seems to have mattered to the narrative and might effect change in the defendant's life.

Family support is of course not dispositive. In a case of drunk driving that resulted in death, the defendant received a five-year sentence in district court after prosecutors had requested seven. Prosecutors appealed. The high court settled on a market price of six years, with a lengthy explanation that included the following language:

> The lower court's opinion pointed out that the defendant had no criminal past; lived an ordinary life as a company employee; was only 27 years old; and had suffered social sanctions through, among other things, disciplinary dismissal from his employment; and that he was contrite. According to the evidence this court has investigated, it is clear that his work performance was of such high quality that he received awards. These circumstances should be taken into consideration, but when the seriousness of the incident is taken into account, they do not merit much weight. The defendant did not hesitate to drive drunk while heavily intoxicated, with no sense of guilt. While driving on the expressway, after it was clear that he was unable to drive normally, he continued to drive on the opposite side of the highway, resulting in an accident of great loss, including the loss of two lives and injuries to two persons. The lower court opinion pointed out that the defendant was making amends, and that his father pledged to help him make amends, but given that the above has been made clear, these factors have little value. Accordingly, the trial court's sentence was somewhat light, and must be corrected.[63]

Perhaps more than in other cases, the high court appears to be structuring the factors to justify a heavier sentence. The district court found that the father's words mattered (though they are about making amends and not directly about support), but the high court, after acknowledging them, said specifically that they had "little value." Same behavior, same words, but an additional year in prison from the appellate court.

But note a factor that differs here: The pledge of support came from the father, a man. When men offer support, their role is particularly ambiguous. From a 2003 case of drunk driving that caused the deaths of two middle-school students: "The defendant has visited the relatives of the deceased and apologized, and his father has appeared in court and stated that he will prevent the defendant from drinking and that he also is apologetic."[64] Prosecutors sought seven years and six months; the court gave five years and six months and offered no further detail.

Even more curious are cases in which the gender of supporters is not specified. A 2001 case involved a defendant who had already been found guilty of driving under the influence—twice. After his third incident the court cited as mitigating factors "the fact that he has sworn not to drink again, the fact that although he has two previous convictions for driving under the influence, including a suspended prison sentence, the most recent incident was fifteen years ago, the fact that at age 54 he is already past the halfway point of life, and the fact that his friends from work have appeared in court on his behalf and pledged to support his recovery."[65] Prosecutors requested six months; he received four, and the court said nothing more.

A partial explanation for the apparent ambiguity lies in the quoted language from Borovoy's discussion of Danshukai, the Japanese version of Alcoholics Anonymous: "women recite a 'Family Pledge'" in accordance with "Japanese gender role constructions."[66] That oath includes language like "My husband's/son's affliction is my affliction."[67] "Women," Borovoy observed, "saw it as their job to keep their husbands' drinking from spilling over into public disruption."[68] Given those social dynamics, it is no surprise that women are far more often than men tasked in the case law with the chore of monitoring abstinence.

Consider three cases in which mothers and wives appear in court as cosigners for men who seem to need additional support to receive their reductions of punishment. In the first, the court noted not only remorse but also the significance, again, of mom, finding importance in "the defendant's testimony in court that he swears never to drink again, his youth, and the in-court promise of his mother, with whom he lives, to guide him."[69] In the second, after noting that a seventy-six-year-old defendant pledged to neither drink nor drive again, the court focused on his adult daughter, who appeared in place of his ailing wife and claimed that she wanted him to return soon to her mother's side. The court wrote that the daughter "pledged to turn her attention from her mother (the defendant's wife) to the defendant, supervising him to ensure that he does not drink and drive."[70] In the third example, the wife of the defendant "promised" in court that she would "not allow him to drink."[71]

Courts, then, will allow others to supervise the defendant: Although wives and mothers appear most frequently, friends seem to be acceptable, as is a wife from whom one is separated (perhaps especially because she is female).[72] Defendants simply need some social structure that the court finds trustworthy to help enforce their promises of abstinence—or at least that is the ritual language that courts employ to issue sentences along market price guidelines.

These cases differ markedly from the cases of responsibility for drunken others in the previous chapter. In most of those cases, drunk people were required to take responsibility for themselves. But when sentencing, in an apparent acknowledgment of the admitted fragility of defendants, courts allow others to assume responsibility for them. Of course the legal contexts differ significantly, but taken broadly, courts seem to encourage people to take care of themselves until they cannot, and at that point others—particularly women—are allowed, encouraged, or required to do so.

Finally, consider together two cases, each of which combines oaths of abstinence and family support and represents an extreme on the scale of promise and support. The first case represents the minimum. In a case of arson and underwear stealing (from chapter 2), a "lonely" alcoholic defendant stated that he would follow the guidance of his brother and sister and go to the hospital and "reduce the amount of alcohol he drinks" (*inshuryou o herashi*). That language is noteworthy: the defendant did not pledge abstinence even though he recognized that he was an alcoholic; he merely said he would drink less, which usually counts for little.[73] His brother and sister are mentioned not as guarantors but merely as advisors. Prosecutors requested a three-year sentence; the court predictably gave two years.[74]

The second case, of injury causing death, represents the maximum on the spectrum of oath and support. The defendant had consumed five liters of beer (roughly fourteen cans) at home and at a snack over a six-hour period. He took offense to a remark from a friend and punched him in the face, stomped on him three times, and caused his pancreas to rupture. When his friends asked him what they should do about his victim-friend, he said (in regional dialect), "Just leave him be" (*hottoitaraenya*). The victim died in the street.

The court noted that the defendant had a history of becoming violent when he drank. And as for his good qualities: "The defendant shows remorse, and accepts the seriousness of the fact that he took his friend's life. He has pledged to never take another drink, and has begun a concrete plan including attending Danshukai and taking anti-alcohol medicine. His family has also pledged that when the defendant returns to society they will support him to ensure that he continues his abstinence." Prosecutors requested ten years; he received seven.[75]

The second defendant's belt-and-suspenders pledge seems more restrictive than that of the arsonist, who vowed merely to reduce intake. In the second case, the support comes not from a single person but from the entire family. The defendant not only pledges not to drink but is attending a sobriety group and taking drugs (presumably cyanamide, which increases sensitivity to alcohol, causing hangover-like symptoms), concrete steps, as the court says, to ensure that he will not drink again. No other published drunk-driving case mentions either concrete step. And yet in the end the sentence for the "maximum" promiser was 70 percent of the prosecutor's request, while the sentence for the "minimum" promiser was 66 percent.

* * *

Sentencing decisions in which alcohol plays a role do not deviate significantly from general sentencing patterns: Prosecutors propose a sentence, judges describe the pros and cons of the defendant's case, and the prosecutor's request usually is reduced to a final term of years. The alcohol-related cases might seem, then, to be formulaic, and perhaps necessarily so, as courts strive to achieve equity in sentencing.

Yet that neat conclusion overlooks both the unique factors that separate alcohol-related cases from other cases—including pledges of abstinence and the support of others in achieving that goal—and the differentiation among those cases based on particular facts. Even if oaths of abstinence and the like play no determinative role in sentencing, their mention serves at least to provide a focus on the individual.

These patterns are not necessarily unique to Japan. Remorse, for instance, is the most frequently cited mitigating factor in England and Wales across a wide variety of crimes,[76] and "acceptance of responsibility" is one of the most commonly used provisions of the U.S. Sentencing Guidelines.[77] Inevitably judges at state trial courts hear various claims of remorse but also of the role of alcohol in a defendant's life before, during, and after various crimes. Judges frequently scold drunk drivers.[78] A Michigan judge made national headlines when she did something that would not occur in Japan for a host of reasons both procedural and cultural: She jailed the mother of a drunk driver for laughing as the victim's family read their victim impact statements during sentencing. (Mom apparently matters in the United States too, but in a different way.)[79]

Which suggests significant distinctions between the Japanese and U.S. systems. Among other things, as a procedural matter Japan's official judicial record is publicly available, written, and follows predictable patterns that would be impossible to achieve in the U.S. patchwork court system. But the differences run deeper. As Japanese judges sentence defendants, they unintentionally also provide a rich window into the complexity of Japanese drinking life. Pledges to stop drinking in Japan matter—somehow. Aid from family members, particularly women, in Japan matters—somehow. Would a more precise calculation necessarily be more appropriate?

7

Drunk in Society

Most of the opinions in this book have focused on intoxicated people, their actions, or the actions of people near them. In this chapter I shift the focus away from individuals and toward society. But before turning to specific areas of law to examine the interplay of alcohol and Japanese society, consider four primary expressions of that relation that regularly appear in the case law.

1. *Social Impact.* Courts frequently note the impact that alcohol-related cases have on society. Both the Inoue case (in which the trucker hit a family car and the children burned to death) and the Imabayashi case (in which the municipal official hit a family car and the children drowned) spurred social and legal change. Courts often mention both cases and the resulting media attention as having had an impact on society and on law.[1]
2. *Sense of Society.* As we saw in the insurance cases and will see in cases later in this chapter, courts often make decisions based on the "sense of society" (usually *shakai tsuunen*, but also *shakai gainen* or *shakai kannen*). The concept pervades Japanese judicial opinions as a basis for judgment.[2] The standard is not entirely different from language expressed in U.S. courts, which occasionally look to things like "society's standards" as defined by "objective indicia . . . expressed in legislative enactments and state practice."[3] In Japan, however, courts rarely offer such evidence. They simply *announce* the sense of society.
3. *Social Sanctions.* As we saw in the previous chapter, sometimes courts make explicit reference in the sentencing process to social sanctions. Social sanctions serve to mitigate punishment; when the court mentions them, it purports to substitute some portion of legal punishment with social punishment. The paradigmatic social sanction reference appears in drunk-driving cases, and perhaps no drunk-driving case is more paradigmatic than Imabayashi's. When the district court sentenced Imabayashi to seven and a half years in prison, it noted, "[T]he incident was widely reported in the press, he has lost his position as a public official, and therefore he has

Drunk Japan. Mark D. West, Oxford University Press (2020) © Oxford University Press.
DOI: 10.1093/oso/9780190070847.001.0001

received a certain amount of social sanctions."[4] When prosecutors appealed to the high court, the high court stated, "[E]ven considering . . . the fact that the defendant received social sanctions as he was issued a disciplinary dismissal as a Fukuoka City employee," it was appropriate to raise his sentence to 20 years.[5]

4. *Social Problems.* Courts often mention the "social problems" (*shakai mondai*) that result from alcohol—but usually with little elaboration. For instance, consider an alcohol taxation case from Fukushima in which the court flatly repeated the defendant government's argument:

> Structured sales of alcoholic beverages are socially demanded because of social problems caused by drinking, including accidents, alcoholism, and underage drinking. Therefore, it is widely understood that, unlike the sale of things that are necessities of life, it is necessary to regulate the sale of alcoholic beverages. As a society that tolerates drinking and derives revenue from its taxation, in order to promote thinking about reasonable drinking and prevent alcohol-related problems, we have a duty to foster a healthy drinking culture [*kenzen na sake bunka*].

The court cited that argument but offered no commentary; it simply ruled for the government without editorializing.[6]

The government used an identical argument, again not commented on by the court, in a contemporaneous Urawa case in which the plaintiff claimed that the licensing of liquor sales violated his constitutional right to freedom of occupation: "Structured sales of alcoholic beverages are socially demanded because of social problems caused by drinking, including accidents, alcoholism, and underage drinking."[7] And again in a similar Yokohama case: "Structured supply of alcoholic beverages is required to maintain social order, and the liquor sales licensing law avoids the derivative effects of alcoholic beverages and social problems such as drinking-related accidents, alcoholism, and underage drinking. This not only makes a significant contribution to public health but also stabilizes the price of alcoholic beverages relative to other consumer goods and services."[8]

I'm not certain about the rationale for that last bit about price stabilization, but such editorializing is common. It also brings into question the source of the language. Courts rarely repeat or refer to these particular arguments in the "judgment" section of the opinion that reflects their own reasoning; rather they appear in the section in which the court recounts the government's argument, so I assume they often are taken from the government's briefs.

A Tokyo High Court opinion offers a rare exception, giving a somewhat more academic version of the "drinker's paradise" language in the judgment section of its opinion:

> Across all ages and countries, alcoholic beverages have generally been considered to be a favorite luxury item, and regulation through law of the sales of alcoholic beverages has been socially demanded not only to prevent distribution of inferior products, but also, in recent years, because alcohol-related accidents, alcoholism, and underage drinking have become recognized as social problems. In addition, although the details are not clear in every case, in countries like the United States and Canada, the sales of alcoholic beverages are not freely allowed but are regulated by licensing systems, and in some countries the sale of alcoholic beverages is prohibited for religious reasons.[9]

Two passages leap from the court's text. First, as in the defendant government's arguments, the descriptions of the social problems are passive. The court does not find the problems; society "recognizes" them, and the court merely reports what is presumed to be known fact. Second, the court adds punch to its argument by referring explicitly (though vaguely) to other systems, pointing out that Japan is not alone, for whatever reason, in regulation—though not necessarily in its social problems. Reaching with "religious reasons" to what would seem to be Islamic countries provides further contrast with Japan, where alcohol has no negative connotation. Even across vastly different societies, it seems to be saying, government regulates alcohol.

Each iteration of the argument repeats three social problems, no more and no fewer, caused by alcohol: accidents, alcoholism, and underage drinking. We have examined the first in detail throughout the book. Of course, as a quantitative matter, accidents are less frequent in Japan than in the United States. But as a qualitative matter, because there are so few alcohol-related accidents in Japan, particularly tragic accidents send shock waves through the country via Japan's media, which is dominated by national outlets, giving accidents "social problem" status.

The second problem, alcoholism, is not frequently discussed in the opinions substantively as a social problem, but that is largely due to the nature of court cases. In most instances in which alcohol is raised as a social problem, it occurs in a throwaway sentence, with seemingly little or no connection to the rest of the argument.[10] Still, the mention is sufficient to signal a litany of problems even without elaboration, as alcoholics are viewed as "dirty, selfish, violent, irrational, and without a stable occupation."[11]

Consider in more detail the third prong, underage drinking. The Law Prohibiting Minors from Drinking sets the drinking age at twenty and prohibits both consumption by and provision of alcohol to minors.[12] The law was submitted in 1901 but didn't pass until 1922, in part because debates about the role of ritual sake in weddings gave rise to broader discourse about the regulation of morality—setting the stage, again, for the postwar "drinker's paradise" angst.[13] Those concerns seem to have passed, or at least changed, as around 80 to 90 percent of high school students in Japan report experience with alcohol,[14] a number slightly higher than that in the United States.[15]

Historically vendors paid little attention to underage drinking as long as the consumer looked old enough. But as convenience stores began to replace mom-and-pop liquor stores as the easiest place to buy alcohol, the possibility of liability because of a wayward or inattentive hourly wage clerk increased. Convenience store franchises tightened their age verification procedures not by asking for identification but by installing touch screens that require customers to attest with the press of a finger that they are at least twenty.

Aside from these general references, underage drinking rarely appears in the cases, as it usually is disposed of legally in less formal ways. An exception is a case from 2004 in which the defendant was accused of providing shochu to a sixteen-year-old and a seventeen-year-old, each employees of his painting business, at a snack run by his father. (Readers familiar with Japan should be able to picture these teenagers, in their painting gear, as well as the painting business owner, presumably in his white truck, full of supplies in the back, the social status of all on full display.) The particular provision under which the defendant was charged stated that persons who "act as guardians in place of parents" must stop alcohol consumption by minors if they learn of it (art. 1(2)). In a relatively lengthy opinion, the court found that the defendant had no such duty. But it also agreed with portions of the prosecutor's argument, as it found that the "goal of protection requires the full efforts of society, from the time of the law's establishment through today, and the problem of to what extent people who do not prevent minors from drinking should be punished, and to what extent punishment should be left to ethics and morals, is the same now as at the time of the enactment of the law."[16]

Superfluous commentary has again appeared. The language had nothing to do with whether the defendant stood in the position of a guardian. (He did not, and as such was not guilty.) It does show, however, official recognition of underage drinking as a problem, a recognition that does not often occur in other alcohol-related cases.

Next, consider a case of underage drinking that earned a different kind of social commentary from a court. In a 2013 case a sixteen-year-old (let's call him Kazu; he was never named, even in the media, because he was a minor) stole his father's American Express card and in an eighteen-day period racked up charges of $64,000 at eleven Kyoto cabaret clubs, where the money was spent on alcohol, hostesses, and time charges for the club. His father sued the clubs (a few of which settled) and American Express.

The court provided significant detail. The father, who was forty-three at the time, ran a delivery company. He had married Kazu's mother ten years earlier and had adopted Kazu and his younger sibling. The parents had a third child. Kazu's father worked long hours. Kazu failed the high school entrance examination and went to work in construction as a scaffolder but worked few hours. He didn't talk to his mother much.

I assume that the court is offering some of these details to let readers know why the father was unaware that Kazu had stolen his card out of his wallet. But of course the court, intentionally or otherwise, is doing more than that: It is presenting us with a humanized version of the plaintiff, which it did not do for the defendant cabaret clubs, their workers, or their owners. Even if we didn't know that the credit card was a platinum card with a reported minimum annual income requirement in Japan of $100,000,[17] we have other indications of class and education, and we have a glimpse of household relationships.

Kazu's underage status was the focus of the court's commentary and reasoning. The clubs had argued that Kazu "had been to such clubs before, and he was well-versed in the cabaret club system, including how the bill was calculated. He came to each club with two friends, associated with the hostesses, drank, smoke, bought expensive bottles of alcohol for the hostesses, and did not present [himself] as an underage person." But the court noted that Kazu's father "thought that the clubs were malicious because they served Kazu alcohol without even checking his age, and accordingly they had a duty to pay." Adding its commentary, the court agreed:

> In response to society's request to curtail underage drinking, our nation's Law to Prevent Underage Drinking imposes obligations on those who sell liquor and the restaurant establishment to take certain measures, such as age verification. When those businesses serve alcohol to minors, they commit a crime punishable by a fine of up to $5,000. Due to questions about the effectiveness of the fine, the amount historically was kept low, but in recent years, society has reconfirmed the need to control underage drinking, and Law 134 of 2000 increased the fine [from an unspecified amount left to the judge's discretion] to [the current fine of up to] $5,000. . . . Kazu's facial features make it difficult to tell whether he is of age, but the clubs did not question his age even once. . . . Accordingly, it is appropriate to hold that the contractual arrangement is void pursuant to article 90 of the Civil Code [which makes void acts that are contrary to public order and good morals].

And with that, the court found Kazu's father liable for only $7,600, the amount he had sought from American Express. (The clubs were liable for the remainder.)[18] Underage drinking was not a problem for Kazu, but it was for society.

"Society" is regularly intertwined with alcohol in the cases, often through the concepts of social impact, the sense of society, social sanctions, and social problems. Let us now examine how society and alcohol intertwine in three specific areas of the law: disciplinary dismissals (*choukai menshoku*), divorce, and defamation.

Influence on Society: Fired for Drunken Acts

The national and local governments in Japan may terminate the employment of civil servants as a form of discipline for several reasons, including violation of law.[19] When courts examine the legality of such dismissals, they do so pursuant explicitly to their "sense of society," using factors that include the "influence on society" of the drinker's actions and the dismissal.

At least as recently as the 1970s, local governments rarely dismissed employees, and a drunk-driving conviction was usually seen as insufficient for termination. During that period judges took into account the possibility that a civil servant might be fired when sentencing him for a crime. As one judge stated in a 1978 roundtable discussion about a drunk-driving defendant he had sentenced, "[C]onsidering that the civil servant had a long work history, I thought of his experience and effort, and thought that . . . if I sentenced him to prison with labor he would be fired, but if I gave him less than that, firing would be optional, at least in some municipalities, so I thought I'd just do something or other to keep his punishment lower."[20]

Fukuoka municipal official Imabayashi's 2006 drunk-driving incident changed the norms. The local government was besieged with phone calls from citizens angry with the outcome of the case. The mayor dismissed Imabayashi and announced a no-tolerance policy for any other public employee caught driving drunk. Nationwide, local government policies became stricter and their enforcement more frequent. There are over one hundred published cases of suits brought by civil servants to overturn disciplinary dismissals that come as a result of drunk driving, and each year roughly one hundred people are dismissed for driving-related charges. (The bulk of those charges are for drunk driving.)[21] The stakes in these cases are high, as fired career civil servants often have few career opportunities no matter how they leave their employment, and fewer still if they have a record of drunk driving.

In this section I look at six of those cases to tease out courts' views on when an employee's drunken behavior is sufficiently blameworthy to merit disciplinary dismissal (or similar penalty). Each case is based on the plaintiff's status as a public employee—in each case a respected, stable position. Similar cases can be found for employees at private firms,[22] but they are difficult to compare, even with each other, because of differences in internal employment contracts and rules. Focusing on the relatively standard cases of public employees—the broad outlines of the policy, such as which offenses merit termination, are promulgated by the National Personnel Authority, but local governments have their own rules[23]—allows a more careful examination of social attitudes toward drinking.

The cases fill a space between criminal suits and civil suits. The criminal cases we have seen concerned the punishment of drunk defendants for the harm they caused. The civil suits, such as those in the university and insurance settings, concerned compensation to drunk plaintiffs or their heirs for harm that was done to them. The employment cases in this section require a balancing of the reputational harm that plaintiffs have caused to the profession with their drunken acts and the financial and reputational harm that the profession caused to the plaintiffs when it dismissed them. That balancing usually takes place after a defendant has received criminal punishment, and often civil penalties as well.

The employees in the six cases, presented here in chronological order, come from several different professions: a police officer, a firefighter, a civil engineer, two schoolteachers, and a school vice principal. Each of the professions has relatively high social status. In three cases, courts reversed the dismissal. In two, courts upheld them. And in one case, a lower court found the dismissal proper but was reversed by an appellate court. Each case has a slightly different legal posture, so we might expect a difference in results. The more salient differences lie in the way courts tell the stories.

Police Officer

A Fukuoka police officer worked a twenty-four-hour shift. The next day he dozed until his wife woke him and asked him to take her to play pachinko at 6 p.m. Pachinko is pervasive and legal,[24] but it is a form of gambling: One usually trades in a tray of winning silver balls for a special prize (like a giant candy bar or a special bottle of soy sauce), and then takes that special prize out of the pachinko parlor and around the corner to an ostensibly unaffiliated booth that exchanges the special prize for cash. We have seen pachinko parlors in this book before, but police were summoned there to deal with troublemakers, not to participate. Although it is not uncommon for police officers to play pachinko, it can raise a whiff of corruption in some instances because of their power in day-to-day regulation and the fact that they sometimes accept paid positions in associations and companies related to the industry upon retirement from the force.

After pachinko the officer and his wife went to a sushi bar, where the officer drank two bottles of beer and four *gou* of sake. (The drinking in and of itself is not surprising; one study finds that 97.9 percent of police drink, and both frequency and volume of alcohol consumption have increased over time.)[25] Then came a *yakitori* (chicken skewers) restaurant, and another eight *gou* of cold sake. At this point in the narrative the wife vanishes (the facts here are surprisingly unclear); the officer went alone to the restaurant parking lot at 1:30 a.m. and drove away. He caused an accident, police chased him, and he eventually smashed into a parked truck in the parking lot in front of the Asahi Brewery. He was charged with DWI, fleeing the scene, and negligent driving causing injury. He was successfully sued for $3,000 in a civil case, and the police department fired him.

He sued, arguing that he had little memory of the incident, he did not plan to flee, the resulting damage was minimal, similar cases had not resulted in dismissal, the dismissal process was unfair, and he had worked hard for many years as a police officer. The court discussed the dismissal process in some detail and found it to be fair. The court hardly analyzed the other claims; it simply dismissed them and ended its opinion as follows: "As a local police supervisor, the defendant stands in a position different from the ordinary citizen, and he is expected to follow the instructions of police. Even considering that the plaintiff usually was careful about drunk driving, had no history of discipline, and worked hard as a police officer, according to the sense of society, the disciplinary dismissal was appropriate and not an abuse of discretion."[26] Police, then, are explicitly held to a higher standard than ordinary citizens—and the officer's firing was allowed.

The court did not mention any standard under which the dismissal should be examined. But one exists. The Supreme Court held twenty years earlier in an often-cited ruling that a court in these cases must consider "the cause, motivation, character, circumstances, results, influence and other factors regarding the act, including the attitude of the public employee before and after the incident, as well as the employee's prior disciplinary record and how the chosen disciplinary disposition will *influence* other public employees or *society as a whole*" (emphasis mine).[27] Many of the factors in the Court's standard are subject to multiple translations: "cause" (*gen'in*) can also mean something more akin to "reason"; "motivation" (*douki*) can also mean "motive"; "character" (*seishitsu*) can also mean "quality" or "nature"; "circumstances" (*taiyou*) can also mean "conditions"; and "attitude" (*taido*) can also mean "behavior." In the police officer's case, the exact translation of the terms did not matter, as the court simply did not consider them. It mentioned that the results of the acts were "serious" but did not otherwise meaningfully engage in legal analysis.

If the court had conducted that analysis, the case is unlikely to have been decided differently. "Influence on society," the last factor in the analysis, alone could easily be used to fit the court's thinking. But the court took a different analytical tack: Cops shouldn't act as this one did, and his termination was proper.

Firefighter

With that summary disposition in mind, consider the case of a thirty-year career firefighter who took a seven-day vacation, apparently alone, to Bangkok. (The court subsequently gives considerable detail, but not the reason for his trip. I have my suspicions, but the court, conspicuously, isn't dropping the clues to lead me there.) At 8 p.m. on the night before he was to return to Japan, he had two beers in his hotel room. He had two glasses of champagne on the flight home at 11:45 p.m. We are not told which airline the firefighter flew, but Japanese airlines now routinely inform their passengers, even on short domestic flights, that they should avoid drinking if they are going to drive after deplaning. The Japan Airlines webpage that lists drinks available for in-flight consumption also contains a warning not to drink and drive.[28]

The firefighter landed at Kansai Airport at 5:15 a.m. He had two beers, dozed for two hours, and took the Kobe Bay Shuttle to Kobe port, where his car was parked. He arrived at his car at 7:50. He dozed again, and then drove away at 9:15, attempting to arrive at work before his shift began.

Along the way he rear-ended a car. He was arrested, and the court described his subsequent firing:

> The measure at issue in this case and the standard punishments at issue were revised by the mayor and the chief of the fire department in 2006 following the tragic traffic accident of a Fukuoka municipal employee who was driving drunk. Penalties against drunk driving soon were increased, punishments were revised, and as a result of the movement, an employee who commits driving-under-the-influence will, as a general rule, be dismissed, and only in certain circumstances will the employee be suspended.

The firefighter, the court added, knew of the policy and its strict enforcement. Still, he seems to have done the right thing afterward: On the day of the incident he informed his supervisor and apologized profusely. He swore in a written oath never to drink again. He apologized to the other driver and to the owner of the driver's car.

The court examined the evidence of drunk driving. It doubted the firefighter's claim about the amount he drank. It dismissed his claim that his measured breath alcohol level was inaccurate. It even used his excellent driving record against him: "Because he had an excellent driving record for approximately 30 years, and this accident occurred only on the day when he was driving under the influence, it is natural to think that this incident was influenced by the alcohol he drank the previous day, and that the impairments to his sense of care were not minor."

Before we get to the verdict, a bit of background: Claims that one has sobered up after drinking usually fail. In a 2013 dismissal case, a postal delivery worker drank potato shochu from 10 p.m. until 4 a.m. on a Saturday night while watching DVDs; he woke up three hours later to take his son to high school, then went to pick him up again at noon. While adjusting the car audio on that noon trip, six hours after he had stopped drinking, he smashed his right fender. He took the car in for repairs immediately, but someone had seen the accident and had called it in. He was arrested for DUI and fired. The court, noting that the postal service warned its workers not to drive for at least four hours after drinking a single beer, that the defendant had not reported the accident, and that the defendant's job required him to drive a car, found the dismissal appropriate.[29] The high court affirmed, noting further that local post office customers who learned of the incident from the press had declined their stamped, pre-ordered New Year's cards from his employer, Japan Post, in protest of his actions.[30] Similar cases abound,[31] and I can find only one similarly situated case in which a drunk driver prevailed. In that case, the drunk driver—despite blowing a 0.20, like the firefighter—lost at the trial court but prevailed on appeal, in part because of evidence that he had not drunk for fifteen hours, and in part because it was he who suggested after an accident that the police be involved.[32]

The firefighter's case does not look promising, as the court noted that he had had two beers that very morning. The court did not dwell on this fact, which is quite good for him. There are five cases in which a court has noted in the facts that the defendant had "hair of the dog" (*mukaezake,* a drink the next morning to prevent the effects of a hangover). Every one of those cases is a criminal case that involves a murder conviction.[33] It appears that the firefighter at least has avoided the most negative of implications of his morning drinking.

Despite those morning beers, the court ruled in the firefighter's favor, finding only that his "impairments" were "not minor." Unlike the court in the police officer's case, this court explicitly quoted the Supreme Court and listed the factors used for judging such cases; "cause, motivation, character, circumstances, results, influence and other factors regarding the act, including the attitude of the public employee before and after the incident, as well as the employees' prior disciplinary record and how the chosen disciplinary disposition will influence other public employees or society as a whole."

Unlike the police officer's case, the court in this case conducted a thorough analysis of those factors. The cause and motive of the firefighter's acts were not "shameful"; he simply still had alcohol in his body from the previous night, apparently a condition that does not cause shame. Character, circumstances, and results, the court said, were not terribly problematic, as the firefighter was attempting to get to work on time and his breath alcohol level was quite low. Influence on society was minimal, as the incident did not attract great public attention—again note the role, or lack thereof, of the media here—and as such did not cause great distrust of public employees.

The employee's "attitude before and after the incident" was in his favor: He had immediately apologized and had sworn in writing to never drink again. He had no prior record. The court understood, it said, the decision of the fire chief to dismiss the firefighter, as "many tragedies occurred because of drunk driving," "the criticism of drunk driving by society as a whole has increased," and "public employees, as persons in service of society, must of course guard against drunk driving."[34] But in this case, considering that the firefighter, who had worked hard for thirty years, would lose his job, his salary, and his retirement pay, the penalty was too harsh. Even after getting in a few jabs after following the factor-based reasoning, the court ordered that he be reinstated.

The firefighter's actions might seem less blameworthy than those of the police officer, but the court's sudden switch in tone was unexpected. It acknowledged the Fukuoka crash and let readers know that it understood the seriousness of drunk driving. And yet the court reinstated the firefighter after its analysis, which could easily have gone the other way had it wished, especially by focusing on "influence on society." Perhaps his actions simply were not so bad, or perhaps the judges could imagine being in his fender-bending position more easily than that of the fleeing police officer who landed in the Asahi Brewery.

Civil Engineer

A civil engineer and his friend went to an izakaya from 6 to 8 p.m., where they drank three or four beers and four or five shochu mixed with water. The predictable pattern followed: snack, driving, accident at 10:34, arrest, firing, lawsuit.

The court began by citing the Supreme Court factors for dismissal. It then postponed the analytical step of applying the factors to the facts, and instead first considered broader social factors and how they meshed with the particular applicable standard in this case:

> It is certainly true that the evils of drunk driving have become a social problem . . . and it is reasonable to punish an employee heavily for drunk driving. However, the standard in this case for discipline, in which drunk driving cases result in disciplinary dismissals uniformly

> for all public employees if there is a personal injury accident, or an accident involving property damage, or a self-injury accident, or a violation of traffic laws, with the only exception being a case of hangover, is very rigid.

Lurking in the last dozen words or so is potential good news for the engineer. Yes, drunk driving is a social problem, the court says. But there is an exception, which this court calls the "hangover exception." As we saw a few pages back, time-lapse drunkenness cases usually fail, and "I'm merely hung over" usually is not helpful. But the ordinance regarding dismissals in Kochi prefecture, where these events occurred, does, in fact, contain a hangover exception: Authorities have the discretion to suspend instead of dismiss drunk drivers whose intoxication is based on a hangover unless an accident causing death occurs.[35] At least two other prefectures have similar provisions: Tottori prefecture is virtually identical, and Kanagawa prefecture allows suspension if the drinking occurred the previous day and there was no accident.[36] The National Personnel Authority provisions contain no such exception.[37]

The court goes no further than noting that the hangover exception exists, and it's not clear if the result would have been different if the accident occurred two hours later, past midnight, and therefore the next day. But the court seems, at least, to be hinting that there are other possible, more lenient outcomes, that the engineer was plausibly near one of them, and that maybe, accordingly, this is a time for leniency as well.

The court then returned to a factor-based analysis. The engineer's blood alcohol level was high; he caused property damage; and the character, circumstances, and results of the acts were considerably blameworthy. His motivation was problematic, as he had refused to be fingerprinted by the police. But the court then changed tone on the question of influence: He was not even a manager, and as such the damage to trust of public officials was negligible. (The media hardly noticed.) He had only minor traffic violations. He was remorseful. And yes, "criticism of drunk driving has increased," but given the facts in the plaintiff's favor, dismissal in this case was too severe.[38]

The civil engineer's employer, the defendant prefecture, appealed to the high court, arguing that "the penalties against drunk driving have increased drastically after the August 2006 incident in which three children were killed as a result of the drunk driving of a Fukuoka city employee." From 2006 until 2009, it noted, every single case of DWI in Japan resulted in a disciplinary dismissal. Even in cases of DUI, 63 of 131 cases resulted in dismissal, including 24 of 39 cases of property damage. Accordingly it had not abused its discretion when it fired the engineer.

Like the lower court, the high court began by describing the background in which the case arose: Drunk driving had become a social problem. It then turned to the specifics of the engineer's case, hitting each damaging fact squarely to press specifically on questions of influence and results:

> On April 28, 2009, beginning at 6 p.m., the appellee began to drink. He had three or four beers, four or five shochu mixed with water, and then, at a snack, despite the fact that he was staggering, slurring his words, and drunk, he drank beer, but he did not think he was very drunk, and instead of calling a taxi or a driving agency . . . [he drove drunk and caused an accident]. The accident did not result in injuries, and only a traffic signal pole was damaged. . . . Considering that the accident occurred immediately in front of an intersection on a two-lane national highway, in an area surrounded by homes and businesses, looking only at the period from 10:47 to 11:42, approximately twenty cars and two pedestrians passed the scene every five minutes. It is fortuitous that there were no personal injuries, and the situation could easily have been much more dangerous. . . . The appellee's drunk driving has resulted in a tremendous loss of faith in public employees.[39]

The high court allowed the dismissal, and it did so by criticizing the engineer's actions at every turn. The lower court glossed over the facts, but the high court framed them negatively. The lower court did not consider the fact that the engineer had other options; the high court scolded him for not thinking of taking a taxi. And where the lower court found a relatively benign accident, the high court reached for counterfactuals and found that the results of his actions could have been much worse. Because neither court tells us much about the engineer, providing little of the individualized justice to which we have become accustomed and focusing more on society, the reasons for the differences are unclear. If we knew a bit more about him, perhaps the case might make more sense.

Schoolteachers

Let's compare two cases of drunk-driving schoolteachers in which we learn even more about the individuals, or at least about one of them in particular. In the first, a high school teacher drank shochu at home, dozing on and off as he did so. And then the pattern began: driving, accident, arrest, firing, lawsuit.

The court made quick work of the Supreme Court factors. The character and circumstances of his acts were evidenced by all the factors for which he was arrested: the blood level, the objective physical appearance, and so on. The result was a crash, with a head injury to the other driver. The teacher's attitude and behavior after the incident were evidenced by his failure to contact his school, which learned of his actions only when informed by the administrative board that dismissed him.

At this point in the opinion the court has reached its decision: Pursuant to the Supreme Court standard, the teacher can be dismissed. But it continued to discuss additional arguments. The teacher urged the court to consider his circumstances: He was undergoing treatment for alcoholism, was depressed, and after telling his principal about these issues, he was not asked to take a leave. The school, he argued, should have considered his condition and the fact that the accident occurred because he was doing everything he could to get to work on time. The court disagreed, ignoring the blame-shifting argument and finding that "even though the plaintiff knew he could not drive safely," he did not contact the school, call a taxi, or think of any other way of getting to work besides drunk driving.

But, the teacher pressed, in cases in which teachers had sexually harassed students while drunk, or in cases of drunk driving resulting in injury involving prefectural employees who weren't teachers, the employees received only suspensions and pay reductions. Why should he be singled out for dismissal? The court countered:

> Even if drunk driving is compared to those incidents of obscene acts and other situations, considering the great danger to human life and possibility for injury, and considering that drunk driving has become a social issue, in a case such as this involving not only driving under the influence but drunk driving, it is appropriate for the personnel department to institute measures that allow disciplinary dismissal. Given the difference in roles between a teacher, who guides students, and other school employees, even if compared to other cases, according to the sense of society, the dismissal is entirely appropriate.[40]

The teacher lost on both counts. He did not try other ways of getting to school. It was irrelevant that other employees, even school employees, had received different forms of discipline. He was a teacher, and in that particular profession the dismissal was appropriate, especially when he tried to avoid telling the school of his misdeeds in the first place.[41]

That seems easy. But what results if we muddy both the facts and the law a bit? On Saturday, April 11, 2009, the plaintiff teacher went drinking. The plaintiff, the court tells us, is a Nagano prefecture middle-school English teacher of eighteen years and the assistant lead teacher of the seventh grade. Perhaps you can already sense a difference here, as the court is giving extraneous facts that point to the plaintiff's authority and experience.

But it's not quite that simple. I'm purposely going to distort a detail here so that you will read the case as I initially did, and I will correct that detail later. The court tells us that the teacher, with a friend, drank seven or eight glasses of shochu mixed with water between 6:30 and 11:30 p.m. He walked home and arrived around midnight. He had a habit, the court says, of placing items on his car's cowl—that place on the outside of the car, above the top of the hood and below the wiper blades—whenever he returned home, and that's where he placed his wallet. He usually slept about five hours a night and usually woke up without an alarm. This night he woke up at six. (The court reports with assurance that he felt well rested.) He looked for his wallet in his shoe and around his home but couldn't find it. He then called his friend, who suggested he call the credit card company to place a hold on his card. He got in his car, drove to his friend's house, and retraced his steps. Because he was still unable to find the wallet, he decided to file a lost property report at the local police substation (*kouban*). Filing such a report is what one does in Japan when one loses one's wallet. (And as I've shown elsewhere, the legal system ensures that there is a very good chance that it will be recovered.)[42]

As the teacher was filling out the report, the police officer smelled alcohol on his breath from the previous night. (Only seven hours or so had passed.) Although the teacher showed no other signs of intoxication (the police reported as normal his speech, gait, facial color, eye condition, and so on), he had a breath alcohol level over the limit, at 0.30. He was arrested for drunk driving and eventually fined. To get home he called a driving agent service, which arrived with two drivers and one car. The driver who drove his car home for him found the wallet precisely where he had left it: just underneath the windshield wipers of the car that he had driven to report the wallet lost. The prefecture fired him, and he sued to get his job back, hoping for a mere suspension.

Three things seem important for understanding this case, including the detail that I changed. Let's start with that. The opinion does not name the plaintiff, and the Japanese language often doesn't need gender-specific pronouns. Accordingly one can occasionally read through an opinion like this one, which offers no gender clues, and assume that the drunk person is male, as most parties in such cases are. But a little research shows that the plaintiff here is in fact female. The press reported her name as Tsuboi Kayo, and she was not remotely private in her actions after her dismissal; a petition to the court to be signed by supporters remains on a law firm website,[43] and she gave televised interviews.[44] So now change all of those male pronouns to female. Is the outcome of the case becoming clearer?

Second, the bit about the plaintiff's habit of placing objects on top of what we now know to be *her* car, below the wipers? For the first time in this book, I will say it: I don't believe it. Perhaps that's neither here nor there, as the court is the one telling the story and deciding the case, but (a) I don't think people normally do this and (b) if the plaintiff knew that she normally placed objects there, surely that would have been a good place to look for the lost wallet before driving around town Sunday morning. The irony of being in possession of the thing you think you've lost and getting fired for going to report it lost makes for a good story, but I think the court is being too charitable in accepting a reading of the facts that most favors the plaintiff. I believe a more likely scenario is that the plaintiff drunkenly put it in an odd place that she had never used before and had no memory of doing so the next morning. But of course I could be wrong.

Third and finally, Nagano prefecture has an odd ordinance that gives officials even more discretion than the prefectures with hangover exception ordinances. In the absence of an accident, Nagano can suspend instead of terminating employment if the drunk driving happens after "considerable time has passed after drinking" (*inshugo soutou no jikan keikago ni untenshita baai*). The language essentially allows the officials, and by extension judges, to bypass the seemingly hard data of breathalyzer results and the like and use their own soft concepts of intoxication to determine the seriousness of the drunken offense. We have seen courts do so in many other contexts; the statute here just makes it easy.

The outcome of the case now seems obvious. The defendant prefecture argued that strict penalties were necessary after national drunk-driving tragedies, but the court did not agree that such penalties were necessary in this case. Without analyzing the factors, it held that the prefecture had abused its discretion.[45]

The prefecture appealed. The Tokyo High Court again did not mention gender and again did not discuss the factors, but this court did not mention the wallet's placement. (Perhaps the judges agreed with my assessment, or perhaps they thought the detail unnecessary.) It considerably individualized the case and placed some moral weight on the prefecture, saying, "Alcohol metabolism varies among individuals, and it is not dependent on any single physical characteristic. The general public normally is not well informed about the time required for alcohol to metabolize, and the appellant [prefecture] has not been active in raising such awareness for its staff."[46] The plaintiff, then, unlike the other schoolteacher, was reinstated, in part because her employer didn't give her sufficient information about the rates at which people sober up. Her postverdict press statement: "I'm looking forward to returning to my work as a teacher."[47]

We can of course find many distinctions between the two cases, especially given the stark differences in the prefectural ordinances. But even setting aside the ordinances, or even if we applied the Nagano "considerable time" rule in both cases, the court, administering individual justice, has let us know what kind of facts matter in determining culpability.

Vice Principal

Perhaps the second teacher's case is the exception, and the first teacher's case is the rule. If so, the outcome does not look favorable for our final plaintiff, a middle school vice principal, who, one assumes, would be held to a very high standard of conduct, surely higher than a teacher or a firefighter. The court began by noting that the educator was loved by students, worked late at night, developed materials for new teachers, supervised the basketball club, and was recognized by the Ministry of Education as being of such high caliber that he was made part of a trip to Australia. He had never been disciplined and had never had an automobile accident.

Rarely do opinions in this area of the law begin like this. Sometimes courts begin opinions with a description of a litigant's background, but it is odd for a court to heap such praise on a plaintiff before getting to the facts of the case. Of course the words are not accidental.

When the court reached the facts that related directly to the incident, it presented them in a way that made the vice principal an even more sympathetic figure. It began the narrative twenty-three years before the incident: "The plaintiff married in 1987." That might seem like an odd point in time to begin the story, but again, words matter, and the court knows what it is doing. It proceeds to explain:

> His wife became a teacher at an elementary school, and they worked together in education as instructors. But beginning a few years ago, his wife increasingly did not come home at night, and when he asked her why, she simply said that she slept at the elementary school or in the car. He began to suspect infidelity. When his wife did not return home at all beginning April 11, 2010, he confirmed his suspicions, and decided to divorce. On the sixteenth, he emailed his wife, "I have something important to talk about. When can we meet?" She did not respond.

Now we have a rationale for the court's extensive narrative; it wants to let us know that there is more to this situation than meets the eye. And then:

> Just after noon on the seventeenth (Saturday), to distract himself, he started drinking whisky at his home in Kyoto prefecture, Uji City. He drank one-third of a 700-milliliter bottle of whisky, straight, with an

> alcohol content of 40 percent. At three in the afternoon, he received an email [response] from his wife that said, "I don't know."

The court again seems to be attempting to paint a portrait of someone undeserving of punishment. His wife left him. He drank "in order to distract himself"—another reason to drink to add to our list. He drank the whisky straight, when almost every other person in the cases mixes it with water (and rarely drinks it at home). And his wife was completely unresponsive to his needs. The court continued with facts that differ considerably from the previous cases:

> The plaintiff impulsively decided to go to the school where his wife worked to search for her. With the bottle of whisky in his hand, he got in the car. His wife had been transferred on the first day of the month, but because the plaintiff did not know to which school she had been transferred, he went to the school where she had been employed through March. He did not see her car in the area. He stopped his car, drank whisky, and thought about what to do next. Thinking that he had a good guess about which school employed his wife, he decided to go there. He drove in that direction, but he could not find the school, and he ended up in Osaka prefecture. He realized that he had driven too far, and turned back toward Kyoto. He stopped at a convenience store parking lot. Regardless of whether the car was stopped or moving, he continued to drive and drink whisky.
>
> As he was driving, lost and confused, at around 7:45 p.m., in Hirakata City, Osaka prefecture, and as he was attempting to put out a cigarette in the ashtray, he absent-mindedly lost focus. He did not notice a car stopped at a red traffic light at the upcoming intersection. He had no time to brake, and caused the accident. The driver in the stopped car incurred damages but was not injured.

The picture is now becoming clear. Instead of reminding readers of the children who drowned in Hakata Bay, or even focusing on the extreme nature of a man driving around with whisky bottle in hand, the court turned the whisky bottle into a pitifully stereotypical prop, an indication of how distraught the vice principal was over his wife's bad behavior. Even the accident that he clearly caused is immediately framed as minor, and it occurred after he "lost focus," with no mention of whisky's contribution to that state.

The plaintiff was arrested for driving under the influence. His breath alcohol level was 0.70. He paid a fine of $5,000. The Kyoto Board of Education issued a disciplinary dismissal and took away his retirement pay. The plaintiff accepted the dismissal and protested only the loss of his retirement pay. There is thus a significant legal difference from the other cases, but the underlying conduct—drinking and driving—is still the same, and as such it would not be unreasonable to think that even if the court reaches a different legal result, the narrative might at least be similar.

And yet it wasn't, and the court proceeded as one might expect. It first noted that the plaintiff's job "as a middle school vice principal was to teach students the difference between right and wrong" and that accordingly the influence of his acts on his profession was quite large. However:

> On the other hand, the plaintiff had served as a teacher for 27 years, and as seen above, he has served as a homeroom teacher, a curricular advisor, and in other capacities, and has zealously become involved in matters pertaining to student guidance. He has been commended many times by the board of education, and has made large contributions to school education. He has no history of disciplinary dismissals. The illegal act, though dangerous, was driving under the influence and not driving while intoxicated, and was an aspect of private life that had no direct relation to his work duties. . . . The accident fortunately resulted only in property damage, and a negotiated settlement has been reached with the victim.[48]

This language is practically a petition for sainthood in this area of the law, even more laudatory than the mention of the English teacher's eighteen years of service. The court found the board's action to be extremely inappropriate according to the sense of society and ruled in favor or the vice principal. And what of the Supreme Court factors? The court touched on a few along the way; the "cause" and "motivation" were unease over his wife, the "circumstances" were the lesser crime of driving under the influence, and the "results" were the absence of injury, but there was no systematic analysis, and each factor worked squarely in the plaintiff's favor. The court glossed over "influence on society" despite noting early in the opinion that the events were made public in the local newspaper.

Perhaps the court's analysis should not be directly compared with the other cases. Again the issue was merely retirement pay, on which the court had additional guidance from a Cabinet Office policy. But the court did not discuss that policy. Given that the vice principal had accepted the dismissal, it is interesting that the court examined his acts less than it did his character, which it presented in a positive light.

It is impossible to say precisely what caused this court's apparent sympathy. Perhaps it viewed the plaintiff's condition at the time in the same way that it might view a "weak-minded" defendant in a criminal case. Perhaps it simply was reacting to the fact that the defendant seemed to be such an upstanding member of the community, a fact that in other cases might have worked against the plaintiff, as courts measure the influence of acts. Perhaps the facts just didn't fit the usual patterns. Perhaps, as with our angry nonnative Japanese speaker in chapter 3 who stabbed his father's girlfriend to death after she insulted his language ability, the court is excusing emotional behavior.

Or here is another possibility that might help the outcome make sense: Perhaps the all-male bench in the case could identify with the vice principal's emotional anguish over his wife. Consciously or otherwise, the judges might have been telling the husband that his behavior was an understandable reaction to the wife's conduct. Whether the outcome would have differed if the vice principal had been a woman reacting to actions of her husband is impossible to know.

If this is indeed what's going on, it is not the first time in a Japanese court that a wife has been at the root of a defendant's understandable behavior; the bed-burning arsonist from chapter 2 is but one example. Although it is possible to extrapolate too much, there is at least a case to be made that women in the case law have amazing powers to affect male behavior, a characterization that might also help explain the power of women in the sentencing narrative.

In any event, the court kept society out of the lesson and tailored the facts into a personalized story. Even when expressing its own views of the case, the court's criticism was extraordinarily light. It almost made the sight of a vice principal driving with a whisky bottle in hand sound like no big deal.

* * *

How should we view these cases? They are not easily reconciled. Despite the similarity of the cases, and despite the fact that every person drove drunk, courts express no unified, precise theory of how people think about—or should think about—acts committed while intoxicated. But the personalized stories they tell suggest that other factors are at play.

The Sense of Society: Divorced for Being a Drunk

For many wives of alcoholics in Japan, divorce is made especially difficult not only by financial issues but also because of the codependency that develops as they care for their husbands.[49] From a purely legal standpoint, however, divorcing in Japan is easy if both spouses agree to do so—they just submit a form to a local government office to make the divorce official. Ninety percent of divorces occur in this manner; another 9 percent are settled through mediation. If negotiation and mediation fail, the parties go to court. Courts may grant—or refuse to grant—a divorce based on several grounds, the relevant one in cases involving alcohol being the catchall "grave reason that makes continuing the marriage difficult" (Civil Code art. 770(1)(5)).[50] The Supreme Court has ruled that there is "grave reason" only "when the marital relationship is so completely destroyed that the efforts required for a spouse to continue it would be too severe, in the sense of society."[51] Courts' views in the cases in this section thus are explicitly intended to express the sense of society regarding alcohol.

Spouses who file for a divorce in court in Japan check a box on a form that asks their motivation for filing. Among the choices: personality clash, abnormal personality, adultery, violence, psychological abuse, problems over money, sexual dissatisfaction, and "drinks too much." In 2018 courts recorded 46,756 responses for wives (multiple responses are allowed) and 17,146 responses for husbands who filed for divorce. (That ratio of filers is stable over the years.) In 2,752 cases, or about 5.9 percent, wives claimed drinking as the motivating for filing; for husbands, the number was 384, or about 2.2 percent.[52] These numbers significantly trail issues like personality clash and adultery, but the fact that the government includes "drinks too much" as a proper motivation gives some indication as to how drinking is conceptualized as a factor in a relationship.

Advice columns paint a similar picture. *Yomiuri Shinbun,* the most widely circulated newspaper in the world, runs a column in its evening edition that roughly translates to "Small Town Talk." The online version contains many requests for help by wives who dislike their husbands when they drink—and they often say not that they dislike the behavior but that they dislike their husbands in that state. Among many, in 2014 a woman claimed that her "giant" husband's playful violence after every year-end party, beginning-of-the-year party, and other workplace gatherings was causing her pain and stress: "I love my husband, but I don't like my drunk husband." The advice (from several readers): "Take a video of him drunk and show it to him when he's sober" and "Make him clean up his own vomit."[53] And from 2019: "When we first married a year and a half ago, every day I felt loved . . . but now my husband drinks every night [*banshaku*], and he drinks a lot, and he'll take a little thing I say and get angry and completely turn into a different person several times a month." The responses: "Maybe he just has a bad alcohol habit"; "Maybe this is just stress"; and "Maybe you should start thinking about a divorce."[54] Drunk wives exist, but the only one I can find in this forum is a self-complaint: "I'm a mother raising a one-year-old. My husband works hard at his job and doesn't help with the child-rearing." She explains that she has begun to drink and asks whether she is a "bad wife." The responses: "Why not drink together with your husband?"; "It's fine for a housewife to drink every once in a while"; and "Can you not find some other form of stress relief besides alcohol?"[55]

Despite these complaints I can find no case in which drinking too much, with nothing more, was the legal reason to grant a judicial divorce. Instead drinking arises in more subtle and complicated ways. In each case in this section, alcohol is one in a progressively longer list of factors that lead courts to a determination of whether the couple has a "grave reason that makes continuing the marriage difficult" according to their "sense of society."

An early warning: We might not learn quite as much about drinking in Japan in the divorce cases, as courts tend to focus more on the general concept of drinking, or patterns of drinking. Marriages degrade over time and usually not as the result of particular drinking incidents, and therefore the facts might be less colorful. But courts can at least tell us the extent to which alcohol is a problem in marriages that reach the courts, and the answer—"not much"—is informative nonetheless.

Let's begin with a case that does not involve alcohol to understand how courts normally editorialize in divorce cases and to see how litigants and courts speak about the *absence* of alcohol. The case involves a couple that had been married for nearly forty years. The wife sought a divorce. The husband contested, so the case went to court.

The wife painted a picture of her husband as unkind. He was unsympathetic to her numerous health issues. He expected her to prepare his bath and his dinner every night. The couple communicated mostly through notes. She felt exhausted. The court refused to grant the divorce, mostly because the husband truly wanted to stay in the marriage, and the couple's adult children supported them. The court argued along the way that a marriage like theirs, even if "lacking in sympathy and kindness," was "ordinary," and encouraged them to "strive to create a harmonious marriage." That kind of editorializing from a personal standpoint, as opposed to sweeping language about social views, abounds in divorce cases.[56]

I want to focus more narrowly on a statement from the husband's brief that the court repeated: The husband "does not gamble, does not commit adultery, has never been violent, and is a serious, scholarly, hard-working person." Set aside the husband's good points and look at the specific vices he *lacks* but which courts often cite as a group:[57] gambling, adultery, and violence. Drinking in this case is not listed among the vices, suggesting that the court did not think it a flaw equal to the other three.[58]

Perhaps I am placing too much emphasis here on the omission. But interestingly, when courts list vices that men lack, it is usually these three—gambling, adultery, violence—and not drinking. Drinking is mentioned as a vice that men lack in marriage in sources like prewar Japanese fiction,[59] but not in the case law, suggesting, however subtly, that it is a lesser vice at worst.

Still, although courts do not group drinking with other vices when it is *lacking*, they do so when it is present. In a 2003 case, for instance, the wife sued for divorce and custody of the couple's two children. The husband, according to the wife's brief, had three problems. First, he was terrible with money; he had racked up $85,000 in debt that required repayment of $4,000 per month, and he put his wife's name on the loans in the process. The second and third problems were related: "Despite [the money issues], the defendant uses his own salary to drink, play pachinko, and gamble on the horses every day, with no financial planning whatsoever. On top of that, when he drinks, his personality changes completely; he becomes violent if the plaintiff does not do his will, and even in front of the children, he uses words like 'prostitute,' 'whore,' and 'villain' [*gedou*], inflicting psychological abuse on the plaintiff."

When the court issued its judgment, finding for the wife and granting the divorce and awarding her custody of the children, it copied the language from her brief almost verbatim and added its own views. The defendant husband "left no money for daily expenses after the loans were paid, used his own salary to drink and gamble away their money . . . and since fall 2002, when the defendant drank, he would become rude, and if the plaintiff did not do his will, he would become violent. . . . He paid no attention to the children's upbringing, and never discussed the children's education or occupations. . . . He has a selfish personality." Again notice the court's penchant for editorializing. But the more interesting piece, which stands in contrast to the first case, is the court's grouping of drinking together with other vices. The drinking in and of itself might not have been blameworthy, but at least when coupled with the money that his drinking took from the family, the fact that it caused the husband to become violent, or both, it was a vice. It was not the deciding factor in the divorce, but it clearly played a role in the narrative, suggesting at least that drinking with certain attendant consequences is unacceptable.[60]

In a 2004 case, however, alcohol appears throughout the opinion but seems to have had little impact on the outcome. In this case the husband sought the divorce. He argued that his wife "had an alcohol habit, continued to drink throughout her pregnancy, and when she drank she slapped the plaintiff in the face, cut the shirt he was wearing into shreds with scissors, threw the telephone on the furniture, and committed other violent acts. Moreover, the defendant, while drinking, in front of the two oldest children, with no resistance from the plaintiff, stabbed the husband ten times in the abdomen and wrapped a towel around his neck to strangle him." The wife countered, "The defendant drinks, but not after she became pregnant. The plaintiff is a fourth degree black belt in judo, and when they fought, he used judo moves, so she had to protect herself with a knife and scissors."

The court found that the wife "liked [*suki*] to drink," a phrase similar to the husband's phrase that she "had an alcohol habit [*sakeguse*]." She "had a custom of drinking a few beers, and the plaintiff, who did not drink, would become uneasy when she drank, became drunk, and acted strangely." Once, the court noted, "the defendant, who had been drinking, slapped the plaintiff, the plaintiff hit her back, and she cut herself below her eye with her glasses, which led to a large loss of blood and required them to call an ambulance."

Clearly the marriage had serious problems; besides the violence, the court mentions money issues and arguments over the wife's policy of raising their children in a gender-neutral environment. The court focused more on those issues than the drinking. It flatly rejected the husband's claim that the wife's drinking interfered with her ability to do housework and take care of the children. The court simply found in a conclusory way that the "grave reason" standard was met because the couple "appeared to be headed toward bankruptcy and felt great friction because of their different values [*kachikan*] and daily habits." It granted the divorce, awarded the wife custody of the children, distributed the assets, and ordered child support with no moral commentary about the state of affairs that appeared to be interwoven with alcohol use.[61]

A similar treatment of alcohol as a minor factor among others in divorce arose in a case from 2005. The wife sued her husband for divorce, arguing that he had been unfaithful (he received a letter from a woman telling him that she wanted him to return to Osaka to be with her), that he pulled a knife on her when she was slow to answer the door, that he had money problems, and that he was selfish and short-tempered. Moreover, "[t]he defendant has a bad alcohol habit [*sakeguse ga waruku*]. In spring 1977, while viewing cherry blossoms at Ueno Park, he was arrested for performing a lewd act toward a woman. He apologized to the victim, and the charges were dropped, but as he continued to return to view cherry blossoms, he turned it into a joke. Clearly he did not have genuine remorse."

The incident appears to have been isolated, but the plaintiff used it against the defendant, pointing specifically to his drinking. The wife thus turns his drinking from an excuse for his behavior into a problem for the marriage. The husband responded, "A woman who happened to pass by while we were cherry blossom viewing was insulted by one of the defendant's colleagues, and in order to stop that, the defendant got into some trouble with the man she was with. The police were called, but he was never arrested and there were no charges to drop." The court reconciled the two accounts by finding that when the husband "went to view cherry blossoms with his work colleagues, he caused a scene when, while he was drunk, a woman said he tried to touch her, and the police were called. The plaintiff went to the victim's house and offered an apology and compensation, and the next day, the defendant got on his knees and bowed to his wife."

The court has confirmed that the cherry blossom viewing incident occurred and that alcohol was involved. But that incident played only a small role in the opinion. The court focused more on financial issues, and its other reference to alcohol simply showed differing ideas on marital roles: "From the beginning of the marriage . . . the wife took care of the housework, childrearing, and cooking, while the husband said things like 'it's a tough world out there for a man' [*otoko wa soto ni dereba 7nin no teki ga iru,* literally, 'seven enemies await every man who ventures out'] and worked long hours diligently at his job, and he had many nights of drinking parties while he did not take care of the housework or the childrearing." The drinking merited no further mention. The rest of the opinion was entirely alcohol-free, focusing largely on financial difficulties, violence, infidelity, fights over their adult daughter's proposed marriage, and other reasons why the marriage fell apart. The court granted the divorce.[62]

The opinion featured two mentions of drinking-related behavior on which the court *could* have commented but didn't. It spent far more time discussing why the husband did not attend his daughter's wedding and the father-daughter rift. The workplace drinking parties were, it seems, just part of life. And the drunken incident that led to police action and a bow to the floor—a story that the court could easily have utilized as the wife did—was given no analytical weight.

The theme continues in a 2002 case in which the court *refused* to grant a divorce. An additional family law principle arises in this case: Absent special circumstances, courts in Japan do not grant a divorce to a spouse who is responsible for the breakdown of the marriage. The refusal to grant a judicial divorce in such situations forces the party who wishes to divorce into a situation in which he (and it is usually he) must negotiate a settlement with the spouse who does not want the divorce, and the deck is thus stacked in the contesting spouse's favor.

In this case it was the husband who was suing for divorce. Both husband and wife were born and raised in Japan, but of Korean descent (his family was from South Korea and hers from North Korea). These facts are of questionable relevance to the story, but they are revealed to us nonetheless, presumably to let us know to expect something different. The husband was a judo wrestler in high school and weighed over 100 kilograms (220 pounds); query how this morsel of information will matter. After graduating he went to work in the pachinko business at which his mother was a corporate director. The court mentions that he trained to work at a pachinko parlor in Nakagami named Amusement Venus on Tokyo's far western edge.

The couple dated for six months before they married. Before the marriage, the husband dated, and briefly lived with, "a Korean woman named E." After the spouses began dating, the wife-to-be found another woman's underwear in the husband-to-be's apartment. He claimed that the underwear belonged to a woman with whom he used to live, who had come from Korea to work in a restaurant, but who had since returned home. "The defendant," the court deadpanned, "believed the plaintiff's words."

Obviously we have learned a lot about the status of the parties, but the court is just getting started. The court tells us that the couple held their wedding party at Shinjuku's Keio Plaza Hotel. That seemingly innocuous statement is loaded with information. The hotel was built in 1971 and is still generally considered to be a four-star upscale establishment, in part because of its size, but the top Tokyo hotels have become more lavish since. The average cost of a wedding there in 2019 was $25,000. That might sound expensive, but it is below the cost of an average wedding party ($31,600), and less than half the cost of a party at higher end hotels like the Conrad Tokyo or the Grand Hyatt Tokyo.[63] Moreover, it is common practice in Japan for guests to gift envelopes of cash to the bride and groom at a wedding; $300 is common.[64] The average wedding party at the Keio Plaza in 2019 had sixty-one guests,[65] which equates to roughly $400 spent per guest by the bride and groom. Even if the wedding cost $25,000, then, the couple would be responsible for only about a quarter of the bill. In other words, the wedding might seem lavish, but in fact it is squarely middle class. Of course Japanese readers do not need to calculate so precisely; many will instinctively and subconsciously link the hotel to social class.

At the wedding after-party the husband got drunk with his friends before returning to the hotel room, where his bride was waiting. She was worried about his condition, so she helped him to the toilet. When she did so, the drunken husband mistook her for "E," and said "E, why did you come back?" The couple fought. The husband was so drunk that he "mistook the bed for the toilet and urinated there, causing an uproar."

The couple initially planned to honeymoon in Hawaii, but instead opted for two nights and three days in Miyazaki, in southern Japan. After returning from the honeymoon, the husband began to drink almost every night. The following sentence comes directly on the heels of that one: "Around December 25th, the plaintiff and the defendant argued about a trifling matter, and the plaintiff was flung down." The court does not explicitly link the two factors—drinking and violence—but the prose suggests it. (Recall also the romance that surrounds December 24 in Japan.)

At the wife's urging, the husband came home early on her birthday. He then went drinking with his friends and did not return until the following morning. The couple fought again, and the husband hit and kicked the wife, making relevant the earlier mention of his weight and judo skills. Around the same time, the wife discovered that the husband was still in communication with E.

One May evening the husband stayed out late drinking. He returned drunk at two in the morning. He woke the wife, yelled at her, and hit and kicked her. He threw her out of the house in her pajamas. A pattern then developed: drink, become violent, apologize, swear to "never touch alcohol or the defendant again," repeat.

The husband sued for divorce, and the court ruled:

> As seen above, the plaintiff continued to have feelings for E, with whom he previously had a relationship, even after the marriage began. He continued to contact her, and his love and sympathy for the defendant was insufficient. Despite the fact that they were newlyweds, he was cold, she felt unease, she was psychologically abused, and the plaintiff had an alcohol habit that went beyond moderation. He would become drunk, lose his sense of reason, become violent, and repeat the pattern again. The defendant occasionally had to return to her parents' home in Osaka, leading to long times of separation, which led to the destruction of the marriage, but considering the above points, the fault for the marriage's demise was the plaintiff's, and it is clear that the defendant's return to her parents' home in Osaka does not constitute malicious abandonment.
>
> Although it is clear that when the couple fought, the defendant often exhibited hysteric behavior toward the plaintiff, considering the plaintiff's attitude, this response from the defendant was somewhat necessary, and cannot be said to be the fault of the defendant. Accordingly, the cause of the marital breakdown was the plaintiff, and his request for divorce is denied.[66]

The request so denied, the wife has renewed bargaining power to negotiate a favorable out-of-court financial settlement from her divorce-seeking husband.

Again the alcohol clearly mattered to the court's ruling, and it played a prominent role in the facts. Still, I suspect that the result would not have been much different without it, as adultery and violence likely would have been sufficient to disallow the divorce. Alcohol adds something, but the court did not use it as a primary factor. It commented on "hysteric behavior," a direct translation (*hisuterikku*), but not on the alcohol, except to say that its use went beyond moderation.

The takeaway from these divorce cases is not succinct. Drinking to excess might not be a vice of the same caliber as gambling, adultery, or violence. Drinking can be bad if combined with other things, and it can lead to violence, but on its own, even in large amounts, it is not the stuff on which divorces are based. Drinking while pregnant might be bad, and drinking too much outside the home might be bad, at least according to the parties' portrayal of the facts, but courts comment little on these behaviors. In fact there is little commentary in the cases on drinking or alcohol at all, an absence that stands in stark contrast to courts' willingness to editorialize about marriage and divorce. Ultimately the role in married life of drinking, as depicted in court cases, without some additional accompanying negative factor that clearly results from the drinking, seems small, but how small depends on the particular facts of a particular couple's case before a particular court.[67]

Social Standing: The Defamatory Accusation of Drunkenness

Defamation cases are common in Japan, far more common as a percentage of civil litigation than in the United States. In this section I examine cases in which plaintiffs allege that they have been defamed by statements regarding their use of alcohol.[68] If there is a place in the case law in which courts could easily make a strong statement on alcohol's role in society, or as seen by society, along the lines of the "drinker's paradise" case, this might be it.

Two provisions in the Civil Code govern civil suits for defamation. First, article 709 provides that "a person who violates . . . the right of another" is entitled to compensation. That basic tort provision encompasses a broad range of behavior; it is the same one that is used if a neighbor's tree falls on another neighbor's yard. The second provision, article 723, is more specific; a party who "has injured the honor of another" must "take suitable measures for the restoration of the latter's honor either in lieu of or together with compensation for damages."[69]

A statement is defamatory if an ordinary person, using ordinary care, would find that the statement lowers a person's social standing.[70] The precise question in the alcohol-related cases in this section is when statements regarding alcohol or its use lower a person's social standing.

In Japanese law, unlike in U.S. law, the fact that the plaintiff is a public figure is not relevant; the law differs based on characterization of the *matter* as public or private.[71] Still, as in the disciplinary dismissal cases of public officials, the public or private nature of the plaintiff might affect how the court views damage to their social standing. I briefly examine two cases in which alcohol plays a prominent role. In each case the court does not give the names of the parties, but it gives sufficient clues as to their identities that I was able to gather names and additional facts from press accounts.

The first case was brought against a tabloid by Hirosue Ryoko, an actress, singer, and model who starred in the 2008 film *Departures*, which won the Academy Award for Best Foreign Language Film. In this case there can be no doubt whatsoever about the plaintiff's status: She's a star, and has been since she was fifteen. Hirosue made headlines in Japan in 2004 when she suddenly married at age twenty-four and gave birth three months later. She was criticized in the tabloids when she planned to return to acting four months after the child's birth. She succumbed to the criticism and stayed home.

That is only the beginning of Hirosue's story. In 2005 the popular tabloid *Shuukan Gendai* published a story about her over which she sued its publisher in Tokyo District Court. The article in question (and the advertising for that issue in subway posters and in the newspaper *Yomiuri Shinbun*) appeared under the headline "Hirosue Ryoko Dead Drunk [*Deisui*] in Host Club, Abandoning Her Child."

Hirosue summarizes some of the relevant allegations in her brief, as recited by the court:

> [The article] states that the plaintiff "was so drunk in a Kabukicho host club that customers around her whispered "Her child is so young" and "Isn't she neglecting her child?" This article leaves readers with the impression that the plaintiff is an irresponsible person who stays out late getting drunk and neglecting her child soon after giving birth, and as such it lowered her social standing. The plaintiff has never been to a host club, and since giving birth in April 2004 has never been out drinking at night or become drunk. The defendant's quoted statements of witnesses are fabricated, and the article is completely false and malicious.
>
> The defendant claims that because [another article it published] quoted a friend, the first article did not leave readers with the impression that she abandoned her child. But this article strengthened the impression that the defendant abandoned her child while drunk at a host club, and did nothing to counteract the first article.

The defendant publisher responded, first, about the article's general legality. It "was simply information about the plaintiff's words and behavior while drinking, and it did not lower her social standing in an illegal way." It then turned to the host club allegation specifically: The articles simply stated what other people had said about Hirosue, and as such it did not lower her social standing. And as for the drinking: "The term 'dead drunk' [*deisui*] is nothing more than a direct word used to show that a person had had more than a reasonable amount to drink, and such an expression does not lower a person's social standing." Whether genuine or merely strategic, the publisher argued that being drunk is no big deal, even for a well-known actress. If the court addresses that argument directly, we will learn something important about drunk Japan.

But first, it matters—again—that Hirosue is female. We have seen instances throughout the book in which men and women seem to be treated differently (either by courts or others), and given the "social status" aspect of defamation law, we should explore the social context for those differences briefly here. Evidence from outside the case law suggests other ways in which people view drunk men and women differently. Popular web magazines contain scores of surveys that purport to represent opinions regarding drunk men and women—separately. I am unsure of the rigor of the methodology, but they largely correlate with each other, and even if they were invented out of whole cloth (and they are not), the fact that they are so pervasive is meaningful.

Consider drunk men first. One survey of 150 female participants from 2015 finds that only 10 percent of women like drunk men; 90 percent dislike them. Among the reasons for liking drunk men: They are open to conversation, they are cute, and drinking together is fun. Among the reasons to dislike them: They're weak, their personalities change, they brag, they are a pain to deal with, and they become hypersexual.[72] A 2016 survey of 358 working women between the ages of twenty-two and thirty-four found the top worst drunken behaviors of men to be, in order of increasing unpleasantness, getting involved with strangers, leaving the woman unable to go home because she must care for the man, anger, sexual harassment, vomiting "all over the place," and violence.[73]

The complaints about drunk women focus more on social behavior. A 2016 survey of working men between the ages of twenty-two and thirty-six listed the worst behaviors of drunk women: repeating the same stories, becoming too drunk to control oneself, seeming angry, and becoming overly dramatic.[74] Another 2016 survey of one hundred men found the worst behaviors to be "becoming difficult to deal with others while drinking," vomiting, needing to go to the bathroom frequently, falling asleep, and becoming bad at sex.[75] A 2014 survey took a different tack: It asked 433 single *women* in their teens and twenties what the worst behavior was of drunk *women*. Among the top answers: women who say things like "Hey, stop it!" disingenuously while touching a man flirtatiously, begging a man to sing karaoke duets, saying "Oh, I'm soooo drunk" in a feminine way to get a man's attention, making sexual conversation, and encouraging more drinking at second and third parties.[76] And finally a 2017 advice article lists the top five drunken behaviors of women that men consider "cute" and the top five that are "turnoffs." Among the cute: becoming cheerful and expressing amorous feelings. Among the turnoffs: being rude toward superiors and vomiting.[77]

It is in that gendered social context that the court weighed the arguments of Hirosue and the publisher. The court found that the tabloid articles had indeed lowered Hirosue's social standing. It awarded her $4,400, an amount that seems appropriate considering the low damages traditionally awarded in other defamation cases. From the standpoint of analyzing drinking life, a more interesting question is how the court examined "dead drunk." In the excerpts I cited, the court was merely quoting the parties, who used the word twenty-three times.

When it analyzed the issue independently, it used the word seven times. Three of those mentions were exact quotes of the article headline: "Ryoko Hirosue Dead Drunk in Host Club." A fourth mention was from the tabloid's quoting a bystander: "Isn't she dead drunk?"

The court, then, mentioned "dead drunk" only three times in its own voice. All three times, the court noted that the article lowered Hirosue's social standing. But, crucially, unlike the defendant tabloid's brief, none of the three mentions disentangled "dead drunk" from "host club." The first mention stated that it could be considered "abnormal" for "a mother or an adult to visit a host club and became dead drunk while taking care of a child." The second stated, "Generally, getting dead drunk in a host club and abandoning a child is seen as abnormal, irresponsible behavior." The third stated that "taking the entire article into account, the fact that the plaintiff left the child with someone else, went to a host club, and became dead drunk can leave readers with the impression that she is irresponsible and behaves abnormally."[78]

The court's opinion tells us a lot about visiting a host club, getting dead drunk, and leaving a child behind, especially for a mother, but it tells us little about the stand-alone act of getting dead drunk. Of course it was not analytically necessary for the court to separate the concept, but the point is that it chose not to, leaving us with the possibility that being called dead drunk, in and of itself, does not lower a person's social standing.[79]

The second defamation case concerned a person who is less famous but arguably more "public," if public is defined as politically or civically engaged. Kitabayashi Yoshinori, the plaintiff, is the representative director of the funeral services company Houonsha, but he is better known for his close association with the religious group Soka Gakkai, a Buddhist sect with strong political ties. Kitabayashi was one of several people convicted of election law violations in a widely known 1968 incident.

The defendant is Yamasaki Masatomo, a former attorney ten years Kitabayashi's senior who rose to the rank of inside counsel and vice chairperson of Soka Gakkai before he left the organization in 1980. After his departure he began a highly critical, sustained campaign against the organization not unlike those of critics of the Church of Scientology in the United States. In a 2001 book that attempted to expose senior Soka Gakkai officials' improper activities, Yamasaki leveled various allegations against Kitabayashi.[80] Kitabayashi sued.

The defendant took particular offense to the following phrases from the book, as repeated verbatim in the opinion. (I am sufficiently prudish to feel discomfort as I translate them accurately; I am unsure of the court's feelings.)

> The defendant has very bad habits with drinking and with women. When he gets drunk, he becomes sadistic.

> Once when the defendant got drunk he told his wife, "You're eating for free around here, but the service is bad. A woman at a soapland will do anything for $100. You should study up." She cried and he forced her to perform fellatio and stimulate him manually. He ejaculated to the ceiling and it fell on his face on the way down. He told his wife, "You can't do anything right. That happened because you didn't have your hand up, you idiot," and he hit her.
>
> When the defendant drinks at parties [*sake no seki*; in the "drinking seats"], he gets drunk and brags about himself.

The plaintiff argued that the book defamed him and violated his right to privacy. Although the Soka Gakkai organization does not prohibit its members from drinking alcohol, the allegations of violence and the comparison of the member's wife to a soapland worker (a female sex worker who washes a man's body with her own) are not claims with which most ordinary persons would be pleased. But what of the drunkenness?

As in Hirosue's case, the court found for the plaintiff and ordered the defendant to pay $8,000. And as in Hirosue's case, the court did not disentangle the drunkenness from the other allegations. The court found that "the allegation that the defendant became drunk and ordered his wife to perform as a soapland woman, insulting her, then used violence toward her, as well as the allegation that he is the kind of person who became arrogant toward others when at a party, when seen from the perspective of a general reader, is such that it lowered the plaintiff's social standing and as such was defamatory." Despite the fact that each allegation specifically mentioned drunkenness, the court did not separate that issue, telling us little about how it views drunkenness, even when it is alleged to lead to very unseemly behavior. The words lowered his social standing, but apparently only when taken altogether.[81]

There are many more cases to examine, but the results are uniform.[82] Alcohol-related defamation cases *could* give us a window at least into courts' views on how alcohol consumption lowers social standing, but they offer incomplete information at best. Does being dead drunk, with no other additional factors, lower one's social standing? Does becoming "sadistic" toward women lower one's social standing by itself, or does the alcohol make it worse? How much worse? The fact that these questions remain despite courts' obvious penchant for editorializing in other cases raises the possibility that such statements about alcohol consumption and intoxication, with nothing more, are inconsequential.

* * *

In several different contexts in this chapter, we have seen courts discuss drinking in their narratives but make relatively little analytical use of it. In disciplinary dismissal narratives, drinking seems less important than courts' thoughts about plaintiffs' positions and circumstances. In divorce stories, drinking again merits mention, but something additional is needed for it to affect the outcome of a case. The same is true of defamation: The courts' language suggests that an allegation of intoxication, with nothing more, might not be enough to lower one's social status.

Even without explicit comment, however, the courts provide vivid descriptions, through highly particularized facts, of various aspects of Japanese drinking life. For some, that includes drinking very carefully if one is a public official, drinking while viewing cherry blossoms, and drinking to the point of being "dead drunk" in a host club. Each carries cultural weight in Japan in ways that differ significantly from the United States.

This chapter's vision of the law remains consistent with that seen in the rest of this book, as even the society-focused cases provide an astonishing level of detail about people, their relationships, and their place in the world. Yes, Japanese drinking patterns are different. But the larger point is that the role of alcohol in Japanese society is far more complex than it appears at first glance. How do people in Japan feel about public officials who are dismissed for drunk driving, spouses who drink to excess, and famous people drunk in various situations? Judges, even as they proclaim the "sense of society" on those issues, are less than clear. Of course it's not their role to express a universal vision, but the lack of thematic consistency is telling nonetheless.

8

Conclusion: One for the Road

Let us step back from the accumulation of Japanese case law to consider briefly the following 2011 case that comes from a different place: Maryland, USA.

> Kirchoff first tried to play beer pong, but the tables were occupied, and there was a list of people waiting to play. Then he sat down by the fire to talk to one of the friends with whom he had come to the party. While sitting there, he noticed a man he did not know yelling at him from across the fire. This person turned out to be Defendant Justin Abbey. Abbey approached Kirchoff in a threatening manner and "invaded Kirchoff's personal space." . . . When Kirchoff was almost to his friend's car, Abbey struck him on the side of the head with an empty vodka bottle and Kirchoff fell to the ground.[1]

As with the Appletinis from chapter 1, some of these facts are unlikely to appear in a Japanese case. Let's start with beer pong. The game is not unheard of in Japanese (*biiru pon* or *bia pon*), but the case law never mentions it. Also out of place in the Japanese context is "personal space," which of course exists in Japan but never appears in the case law. Finally, the empty vodka bottle is odd; in the Japanese case law, bottles are rarely empty, and rarely does a bottle contain vodka (unless it is used for poisoning).

Another comparative taste comes from a 2011 homicide case in California:

> Pauline Baldiviez was Olivia Baldiviez's daughter and Cindy's sister. On September 18, 2005, she and her boyfriend Joe Cruz, Cindy and [Petitioner], and Joe's sister Christina Cruz and her boyfriend Daniel Nanez, left Olivia's house around 7:00 or 8:00 a.m. to go to an Oakland Raiders football game. They traveled in a van. Joe drove. [Petitioner] had a couple of beers and Daniel also was drinking. Although the game did not start until 5:30 p.m., they left early to make sure they had plenty of time, as they planned to tailgate before the game.

Drunk Japan. Mark D. West, Oxford University Press (2020) © Oxford University Press.
DOI: 10.1093/oso/9780190070847.001.0001

The court then tells us that there was an argument: "This type of misunderstanding occurred a lot when [Petitioner] was drinking: he would get a little jealous of Cindy or not be quite sure what was going on. [Petitioner] tended to act very inappropriately toward Cindy when he drank, and he frequently cursed at her." Cindy was shot and killed after the game, and before that the court tells us that the group had "two or three cases of beer," that Joe described the group as "wasted," and that there was testimony that Petitioner was not "falling-down drunk" but had "probably had a good six-pack."[2]

If this book were the cultural reverse—a book from a Japanese legal perspective about American drinking life—there would be much to digest in the court's words. The framing actually feels somewhat Japanese. But some of the drinking terms would require some explanation in Japanese, as "tailgating" and a "good six pack" don't translate easily.

Contrast those cases with one final case from Japan that displays many of the Japanese themes that have resonated throughout this book. On April 15, 2009, thirty-four-year-old Suzuki Yoshihiro (a pseudonym) had a few beers. He was taking allergy medication, which might have increased the effects of those beers. The Osaka District Court's 2012 opinion tells us the circumstances of the drinking that preceded his death:

> On the day of the accident (a Wednesday), from around 6:30 p.m. until 8:00 p.m., the deceased attended the first party for a workplace get-together at an izakaya near Station B. He drank four or five narrow, medium-size mugs of beer. He then attended the second party at a darts bar, where he had two small bottles of beer. This amount of alcohol was no more that the deceased usually drank, and at both the first party and the second party, he chattered cheerfully and did not seem abnormal. The deceased planned to take the next morning's 7 a.m. bullet train from Kyoto Station to Tokyo on a business trip, and these were not circumstances in which he would drink any more than usual.

In that brief description the court has given much information not only about drinking in Japan but about Suzuki. Suzuki's get-together was an office function; even without the explicit reference to his workplace in the text, the Japanese word for the gathering used here, *konshinkai*, implies it. The event was held in the middle of the week, immediately after work.

As for Suzuki himself, we know that he is neither upper nor lower class; he is neither a person of considerable means nor a person with tattoos, a person who can't hold down a job, or a person whose favorite drink is One Cup sake. Suzuki is a salaryman, perhaps even a manager, who takes the bullet train on business trips. With a bit more information, we might be able to guess his wedding party venue.

Note also that Suzuki attends two parties, as is often the norm. The second party is held at a darts bar, a Japanese trend at the time and another place where he can drink and interact with his work-based colleagues. Bad people don't go to darts bars. (There are only ten other cases that mention darts bars, and in only one does someone get hurt as a result of action there—a pedestrian who was hit in a crosswalk after having one drink at a darts bar on the heels of five drinks consumed at izakaya and a bar.[3] A more typical activity that occurs in a darts bar is a discussion of whether to violate intellectual property laws.[4]) We know this case will end in death because the court refers to Suzuki as "the deceased," but it is already clear that the death is not going to come from a barroom brawl as it did in the case with which this book began.

Suzuki's six or seven beers, the court notes, were his usual amount. This sort of drinking is expected for a person like Suzuki. He was taking the early-morning train and that was the reason why he did not drink more. (Under other circumstances, the court implies, he might have had reason to drink "more than usual.") The court explains what happened after he drank:

> The party broke up at around 10:30 p.m., and the deceased, along with his workmate Yamamoto (who at the time of the accident was 24 years old), boarded a 10:39 rapid express train from Station B on Track F. The deceased planned to get off at Station C, and Yamamoto planned to get off at Station G, three stops further....
>
> Until he boarded the rapid express train, the deceased talked cheerfully, but after two or three minutes on the train he began to speak less, and he gripped the strap with both hands, looking sleepy. At 10:54 p.m., when the train arrived at Station E [one stop before Suzuki's planned exit], he tried to stagger off the train, and Yamamoto said, "It's still only Station E." Suzuki got off the train, saying "I'm changing trains," and Yamamoto stepped off the train with him. Suzuki leaned against one of the poles on the platform, then squatted down, not moving. Yamamoto watched over him for a bit, then said "Let's go home," and he and Suzuki boarded the 10:58 local express, which stopped at stations A, F, and C.
>
> After the deceased boarded the local express train, he seemed somewhat refreshed, and he stood near the door. But at around 11 p.m., when the train arrived at Station A, he again tried to exit. As Yamamoto was trying to decide whether to stop the deceased or let him go, the deceased withdrew his hand, waved him off, exited the train, and Yamamoto left Station A on the local express train.

> From that time until 11:29, six trains passed through or stopped at the platform, and at approximately 11:38, the deceased, who was on the train tracks, was run over.

Let's examine those facts. Suzuki and Yamamoto are not drinking and driving; a sophisticated public transportation network of rapid express, local express, and bullet trains handles all of their travel. Suzuki did not sit on the 10:39 train (he merely holds the strap), perhaps because there are no open seats or perhaps because that is simply what inebriated passengers do. The scene of Yamamoto standing over his colleague, crouched motionless on the platform, urging him to get back on the train, is a common one that apparently attracts no attention from passersby. And all of this action occurs not on a special occasion, not after a sporting event, and not even on a weekend—but after a two-stage midweek work party.

For readers who know Japan, the scene feels familiar. Suzuki probably is wearing a white shirt and dark pants with a dark tie. The posters that regularly appear in Tokyo rail and subway stations that warn passengers "[B]e careful on the days you drink too much" feature men in precisely that uniform, but occasionally minus the tie.[5] The same character—briefcase in hand, blue suit, intoxicated—appears in Japan Railways' 2019 safety promotion materials, in which the company explains that it is changing the angle of benches on the platform from parallel to perpendicular to the tracks, so as to reduce the chances that drunken men will stand up in a stupor and stumble in a direct path to the tracks.[6]

Suzuki's tale, then, is unfortunately not at all unusual. Government data show that roughly three thousand people accidentally fall onto the tracks each year and roughly two hundred are hit by a train, though numbers have fallen in recent years. Those data explicitly carve out a subcategory for those who fall or are hit while intoxicated (roughly two-thirds of both the falls and the train contacts).[7]

Suzuki, lying on the tracks, did not go completely unnoticed. A few minutes before the accident, a female college student (the court supplied the gender) saw his body. She alerted a station worker, but she was unable to make herself understood before the train, horn blaring, ran over Suzuki. The college student "felt that he looked like he was sleeping deeply, feeling drunk, with his necktie undone and his body in the shape of [the *kanji*, or Japanese-adopted Chinese character, that means 'large' and that resembles Leonardo's Vitruvian Man, with arms horizontal and legs stretched apart]." Notice that the student did not say that Suzuki looked unconscious, ill, or otherwise disabled. Her characterization, described by the court, of a man sprawled on the train tracks, necktie undone, was that he looked as if he was drunk and sleeping deeply. *That* description, including "drunk," was the one that resonated.

Subsequent investigation found that Suzuki had left his shoes on the platform and had vomited three times in the space between the platform and the tracks, a space with a radius of approximately one meter. The vomiting further suggests overdrinking; the shoes suggest disorientation, as it is not uncommon to see intoxicated men passed out on the street after removing their shoes, perhaps because they think they have arrived home for the night.[8] The court passes over those details, but their mention breeds familiarity.

The legal issue at stake: Suzuki's family—his wife and three young children, one of whom was not yet born at the time of the incident—sued the railway company, arguing that it breached the duty it owed to its passengers by failing to notice Suzuki's body or construct a platform barricade and door system. (The doors that block the platform in such systems open only when the train comes to a full stop.)[9] The court found that the station, through which (it stated) 22,938 people passed every day in the previous year, was not particularly dangerous, that the station workers did not neglect their duties, and that platform doors were not required—though many have been constructed. The court dismissed the family's claims.

But that's not all. As part of the same action before the court, the railway company sued the family as it would in a suicide-by-train case. Suicide-by-train is common in Japan. It is usually referred to euphemistically, whether in law, on platform monitors, or in station announcements, as *jinshin jiko*, literally "human accident"[10] (translated occasionally by railway operators into English as "passenger injury," but referred to far less tactfully by railroad personnel as *maguro*, or "tuna," because the victims resemble the red-fleshed fish at market[11]).

The difficulty of determining motive in such incidents means that estimates of suicide-by-train events vary widely. In the leading book on the topic, the freelance journalist Satou Yuuichi finds that 55 percent of the 4,013 railway deaths and injuries from 2002 to 2009 were suicide attempts, but those data are now dated (though the existence of the book, which details every single incident over the period down to the speed of the train and the number of minutes of delay caused by each incident, is itself remarkable).[12] An annual report produced by the Ministry of Land, Infrastructure, Transport, and Tourism shows roughly 700 to 800 train-related deaths per year (including 670 in 2017), but the report makes clear that it does not purport to determine how many of those deaths are suicides.[13] A recent Information Disclosure Act request to the ministry produced data that show slightly fewer than 600 suicide-by-train *attempts* per year.[14] Journalists and researchers place the number of suicides-by-train at roughly 300 to 400 per year, or at least once a day, mostly on Tokyo rail lines,[15] an astounding figure, but far short of the 1,000 per year reported in the early twentieth century, when suicide by train was a "fad."[16] By comparison, in New York City in 2017 there were said to be forty-three suicides or attempted suicides in the subways, though officials there note that "it is often difficult to determine what motivates people."[17] Suffice it to say that although estimates are inexact, death by train, whether through suicide, stumbling, alcohol, or some combination, is a recognizable problem in Japan that occurs with relative frequency.

Railway companies in Japan routinely seek damages from the heirs of people who commit suicide by train—damages that in 2019 averaged between $10,000 and $30,000.[18] In this case the company sought compensation from Suzuki's family for worker overtime payments, customer taxi fares home from the station (the trains had stopped running for the night), and damage to the train. The court does not specify the station at which the accident occurred, calling it only "station a" (and noting its daily passenger load), but I was able to determine that the accident occurred at the Kouzenji Station on the Keihan line in Osaka, a station not known for suicide attempts. (Suzuki's was the only incident to occur there between 2002 and 2009; by comparison, Tokyo's busy Shinjuku Station had twenty-six incidents in the same period.)[19]

Based on this evidence, and perhaps using unstated knowledge about the station, the court found that unlike a true suicide case or a case in which a person falls onto the tracks when trying to retrieve an object, Suzuki lacked mental capacity. Under those circumstances the court applied comparative negligence principles, stating, "[A]ccording to the sense of society, in this incident, it would not be fair to assign all the damages to the deceased." Citing the railway company's "absolute, highest" duty to passengers, the court required the company to pay half of the damages it incurred, leaving Suzuki's family with a bill of approximately $2,800 for the remaining half.[20]

Although Suzuki's drunkenness was a partial excuse (as it might have been in the criminal context as well), also underlying the court's decision is an understanding that some of the costs of drunken behavior fall on the intoxicated. The family received nothing from the railway company, and it also was required to bear some of the cost of cleaning up the drunken man's remains. In some societies that might seem harsh, but Japan has taken the view that, according to the sense of society, in this context heirs are responsible for damages caused by the behavior of their deceased, intoxicated family members.

And none of this is surprising, not only because of the cases we have reviewed but also because the court has humanized Suzuki. Familiarity with the victim helps make the outcome understandable—even if the facts themselves, with shoes on the platform and drinking that the court did not find unusual, leave a few details unclear.

Suzuki's case is one of the more intriguing I have read. Not because of the horrific events, of course; I feel sympathy for Suzuki, his family, onlookers, his coworkers, railway personnel—no person in this tragic narrative is to be envied. The intriguing aspect of the case is the degree to which the judges tell us so much about a deceased stranger without directly describing him in detail. That their writing is informative would be true no matter the audience, but it is particularly fascinating for readers who look beyond the legal rules, as it's loaded with cultural information that paints a vivid portrait of drunk Japan.

It's so loaded, in fact, that when combined with the information from all the other fact-loaded cases in this book, the collective weight can be a bit heavy. So let us take a step back from the extraordinary level of detail that courts have provided to assess the broader landscape.

In the cases that we have seen, across a wide variety of legal fields, we have often encountered similar narratives or similar sets of fact patterns that transcend the legal issues at stake. It's not just that people get drunk; it's how they get drunk, where they get drunk, what they do after they're pulled over, or how their families react. In some sections of the book I gave several examples of cases to show uniformity in fact patterns, legal reasoning, or outcomes. I also sometimes discussed multiple cases to convey the depth of the available information; in many instances there are hundreds of officially documented examples of a phenomenon that until now was evidenced largely by anecdote.

The similarity of the stories in the opinions suggests a clear picture of some aspects of Japanese drinking life that differ, if only by degree, from that of other countries. Social drinking in Japan is largely a male activity. It often is workplace-based. Drinking at home, with or without family members around, is also common—as are liver-rest days. Norms against drunk driving, and drunk driving by public employees in particular, have strengthened. Courts hold intoxicated people accountable for certain behavior, especially in high-profile cases. Those cases can generate legislative reform and social change, especially if the people involved are public officials, who are held to a higher standard of behavior. Bad behavior requires a showing of remorse, however contrived, and swearing off alcohol, especially with the help of others, doesn't hurt.

We know all of these things because of the surprising level of detail in the opinions. Although the level of detail in the facts of the opinions in Japan and the United States is not dissimilar, that level of detail is unexpected in Japan. Japan is a civil law country, with judges who have standardized training and who are said to be out of touch with society. Japan's rules of opinion writing are more rigid than in the United States, but Japanese judges delve into extraordinary detail and express differing opinions explicitly and implicitly.

This combination of patterned facts and extreme detail leads to a surprising outcome: In the midst of the uniformity of the opinions lies extraordinarily personalized justice, at least in the presentation of the facts, if not always in the outcome. Sometimes courts send both thinly and not so thinly veiled hints about social status and class through references to work—Suzuki, for instance, is clearly a company worker, even if the court had not said so explicitly—or the type of alcohol consumed. Determinations of intoxication are highly personalized and courts freely shift their emphasis from arguably objective or scientific evidence (breathalyzer data and psychiatric evaluations) to subjective evidence (the sense of society, or perhaps just assumptions) and back again, with little or no explanation. Courts know drunkenness when they see it, and if they don't, they rely on Binder drinking tests to attempt to determine precisely how each defendant responds to specific types and amounts of alcohol (a precision that seems artificial at best).

This decision-making style is unexpected from a judiciary that is said to be "nameless" and "faceless" in order to render uniform opinions.[21] It is not the "standardized, homogenized justice" that is said to describe the Japanese legal system.[22] Nor was it my initial hypothesis. When I began reading alcohol-related cases, I incorrectly assumed that there would be more uniformity in the cases and a more uniformly strict view of drinking, or at least on drinking to excess. The degree to which judges discuss factors that are seemingly insignificant, at least at first glance, is surprising.

The high level of detail raises a host of questions both interesting and troubling: If judgments in these cases are so heterogeneous, how uniform can we expect them to be in others? Is judicial decision-making tied to differences in class and status, or are those markers just a feature of the literary genre in which they are writing? If the former, what, if anything, can be done? If the latter, should anything change?

Some readers might prefer that I tie things up a bit more tightly here, or that I offer some directions from the Japanese experience for other countries. But all of this—law, society, alcohol—is incredibly messy stuff, and I fear that turning the data into a set of neat statements that describe drunk Japan will result in little more than fancy stereotypes. I'm also confident that it makes little sense to extrapolate large scale from Japan anything as interconnected with society as we have seen alcohol to be (though I do like the concept in chapter 2 of wrapping up dangerous intoxicated folk into plastic sheets for safety reasons). One thing of which I am certain, however, is that this kind of analysis, not just in Japan, but throughout comparative legal studies, is critical to understanding both the law and various social phenomena. I hope that I have shown, even if in a small way, that a deep reading of a broad range of cases beyond their narrow legal holdings can create valuable knowledge.

A final question remains: Given this detailed picture of law and alcohol in Japanese society, does Japan still seem to be the "drinker's paradise" that the midcentury court so loudly bemoaned at the beginning of the book? The answer is complex and depends in part on what you've done. Intoxicated crimes can result, remarkably, in a lack of culpability, but drunk driving is dealt with harshly—sometimes. The answer also might turn on who you are and the specifics of your case—including not only hints of class and social status but also how well your specific body holds your specific type of liquor in front of a psychiatrist, unless, of course, the court chooses to ignore that. As for your particular punishment, or at least the way the court discusses it, whether Japan is a paradise depends in part on the extent to which you walk the ritual path of remorse, pledge abstinence, have the support of a woman, and are socially shamed.

But there is another way to look at the "drinker's paradise" label besides simply looking at the results of the cases, or even the ways courts talk about the parties to a case. If we disentangle the rich facts from the narratives that courts create in the cases, we might find a drinker's paradise in the form of a variety of beverages and places in which to drink them, perfectly acceptable and indeed encouraged home drinking, highly ritualized workplace drinking with a built-in social circle, and singing and dancing with hosts and hostesses, even if underage and courtesy of your dad's credit card. If that's what you're looking for, you've found paradise.

Then again, we have seen another aspect of Japanese drinking life. The other side of paradise includes the loss of your pension or your job (unless the court understands you; perhaps because your spouse was unfaithful), divorce (if some additional bad behavior is involved), vomiting (but as the boss said, if you can throw it up, you can keep drinking), and death—death by pocketed dagger (your killer goes free), death of your children by fire (after which the drunk driver visits you), death of your children by drowning (which becomes a public spectacle), death after drinking shots (which are part of your compensation package at a girls bar or are forced on you in your job at a host club), or death while splayed on the train tracks (the tab for the cleanup of which will be paid by your family).

Cheers.

NOTES

Chapter 1

1. Penelope Francks, The Japanese Consumer: An Alternative Economic History of Modern Japan 58 (2009).
2. Chiba District Court, 593 Hanrei Times 41, Mar. 26, 1986.
3. Tokyo High Court, 39(4) Koutou Saibansho Keiji Hanreishuu 357, Sept. 29, 1986, *aff'd*, Supreme Court, 718 Hanrei Times 65, Dec. 14, 1989.
4. Kyoto District Court, 83 Hanrei Jihou 6, July 5, 1956.
5. See, e.g., John W. Dower, Embracing Defeat 107 (1999).
6. See, e.g., Edward Seidensticker, Tokyo Rising: The City Since the Great Earthquake 189–90 (1990).
7. See, e.g., Jeffrey W. Alexander, Drinking Bomb and Shooting Meth: Alcohol and Drug Use in Japan 102–10 (2018); Miriam Kingsberg, Methamphetamine Solution: Drugs and the Reconstruction of Nation in Postwar Japan, 72(1) Journal of Asian Studies 141 (2013).
8. See, e.g., Matsujirou Tobita and Morio Shimano, Shin Biiru wa Dokoga Katta? [Who Won the Beer Wars?] 9 (1997).
9. Kanako Takayama, Comment on Kenjirou Asami, Inshu Meitei to Chuudoku Joutai Shita ni Okeru Hanzai to Ryoukei [Crime and Sentencing under the Influence of Alcohol and Drugs], in Oosaka Keiji Kitsumu Kenkyuukai ed., 2 Ryoukei Jitsumu Taikei [A Treatise on Sentencing Law and Practice] 238, 240 (2011).
10. Preface note to Kyoto District Court, 83 Hanrei Jihou 6, July 5, 1956.
11. Dai 28kai Kokkai Sangiin Houmu Iinkai Giroku Dai 7gou [Proceedings of the Judicial Affairs Committee of the House of Councillors of the 28th Diet Session], Feb. 18, 1958, available at http://kokkai.ndl.go.jp/SENTAKU/sangiin/028/0488/02802180488007a.html.
12. Kazuhiko Nishimura, Meiteisha ni Taisuru Rippou Sochi, Sono San [Part 3, Legislative Measure regarding Intoxicated Persons] in Meitei to Keiji Sekinin [Intoxication and Criminal Responsibility], Vol. 9, Joint Issue 3–4 Keihou Zasshi [Journal of Criminal Law] 1, 134, 135 (1959).
13. The first White Paper on Crime, issued annually by the Ministry of Justice, was published in 1961 and quoted the court's language. See Shouwa 35nen Hanzai Hakusho [1960 White Paper on Crime] (1961), available at http://hakusyo1.moj.go.jp/jp/1/nfm/n_1_2_1_2_3_3.html.
14. Parola v. Commercial Net Lease Realty, Inc., 2011 N.J. Super. Unpub. LEXIS 2494 (App. Div. Oct. 3, 2011).
15. Chris Bunting, Drinking Japan 6, 9 (2011); see also Drinking Culture in Japan, Japan Visitor, available at http://www.japanvisitor.com/japanese-culture/drinking-in-Japan ("drinker's paradise"); Kimiko Fukutake, Bengoshi no Me Onna no Me [Eyes of a Lawyer, Eyes of a Woman] 56 (1992) ("yopparai tengoku" (drunk's paradise)); Takeya Yamasaki, Sake o Ajiwau, Sake o Tanoshimu [Tasting and Enjoying Alcohol] 128 (2002) (same).

16. The first were installed in 2015. See West Japan Railways, News Release, Aug. 12, 2015, available at http://www.westjr.co.jp/press/article/2015/08/page_7489.html.
17. For instance, Sangaria's *kodomo no nomimono* ("children's drink"), a drink the company advertises not only as a way of allowing children to join in the toast, but also for its ability to leave a beer-like foam moustache. See Sangaria, Kodomo no Nomimono, http://www.sangaria.co.jp/kodomo/; see also television commercial at Kodomo no Nomimono, YouTube video, https://www.youtube.com/watch?v=pHaBzxHsJuU.
18. Amy Chavez, Amy's Guide to Best Behavior in Japan 102 (2018).
19. Arukooru Kenkou Shougai Taisaku Kihon Hou [Basic Law on Measures against Alcohol-Related Health Problems], Law no. 109 of 2013.
20. Ministry of Justice, Inshu (Arukooru) no Mondai o Yuusuru Hanzaisha no Shoguu ni Kansuru Sougouteki Kenkyuu [Comprehensive Analysis of the Treatment of Criminals with Alcohol Problems, Report #43 (2011) at 1, available at http://www.moj.go.jp/housouken/housouken03_00055.html.
21. See, e.g., John P. Dawson, The Oracles of the Law 381 (1968) (describing French system in which "every effort was made ... to strip down the logic tc its bare essentials, to minimize the contributions that the judges were making, and to trace a path through whereas clauses directly to some governing text").
22. Daniel H. Foote, Namonai Kaomonai Shihou [Nameless Faceless Justice] 13 (2007).
23. J. Mark Ramseyer, Second-Best Justice: The Virtues of Japanese Private Law 6 (2015).
24. J. Mark Ramseyer, Second-Best Justice: The Virtues of Japanese Private Law 239, 241 (2015).
25. Takao Tanase, The Management of Disputes: Automobile Accident Compensation in Japan, 24(3) Law and Society Review 651, 667 (1990).
26. See, e.g., Robert A. Ferguson, The Judicial Opinion as Literary Genre, 2 Yale Journal of Law and Humanities 201, 207 (1990) ("The only thing the judge never admits in the moment of decision is a freedom of choice. [The opinion] must instead appear as if forced to the inevitable conclusion.").
27. Mark D. West, Lovesick Japan: Sex, Marriage, Romance, Law (2011).
28. See J. Mark Ramseyer and Eric B. Rasmusen, Outcaste Politics and Organized Crime in Japan: The Effect of Terminating Ethnic Subsidies, 15(1) Journal of Empirical Legal Studies 192 (2018).
29. These findings have some support in the quantitative literature. For instance, Holger Spamann and Lars Klöhn found in an experimental setting that it was more likely than not that U.S. federal judges placed more weight on legally irrelevant characteristics of defendants than on weak precedents in the outcome of a case. In their written decisions, however, those same judges focused on the precedent and disregarded the individual characteristics. Holger Spamann and Lars Klöhn, Justice Is Less Blind, and Less Legalistic, Than We Thought: Evidence from an Experiment with Real Judges, 45 Journal of Legal Studies 255 (2016).
30. Amy Beth Borovoy, The Too-Good Wife: Alcohol, Codependency, and the Politics of Nurturance in Postwar Japan 45–46 (2005).
31. Yakudoshi Kitousai (Yakubarai Koi No Ryuu) [Bad Luck Year Ceremony (Carp-Releasing Exorcism], Tourism Information in Toyama, https://www.info-toyama.com/event/40043/.
32. Stephen Richard Smith, Drinking and Sobriety in Japan, Ph. D. Dissertation, Columbia University (1988).
33. Amy Beth Borovoy, The Too-Good Wife: Alcohol, Codependency, and the Politics of Nurturance in Postwar Japan (2005).
34. Paul Christensen, Japan, Alcoholism, and Masculinity: Suffering Sobriety in Tokyo (2015). Christensen has also written perceptively about changes over time, including the relation of alcohol to masculinity; see Paul Christensen, Real Men Don't Hold Their Liquor: The Complexity of Drunkenness and Sobriety in a Tokyo Bar, 15(2) Social Science Japan Journal 239 (2012); and about the development of "connoisseur culture" among young people; see Paul A. Christensen, Connoisseurship and Drunkenness in Tokyo, 25(4) International Journal of Drug Policy 804 (2014).
35. Shin'ichi Nakamoto, Arukooru Izon Shakai [The Alcoholism Society] (2004).
36. Kenji Miki, Saibankan ni Naru ni wa [Becoming a Judge] 124 (2009).

37. Takao Kokubo and Hiroyuki Nakagawa, Saibankan toshite no Ikigai to Seikatsu [Judges' Passions and Daily Lives], in Shintarou Katou ed., Zeminaaru Saibankanron [Seminar: Theory of Judges] 121, 135 (2004).
38. Yukio Mishima, Runaway Horses 3 (1970, Michael Gallagher trans. 1973).
39. Masahito Monguchi, Hanjiho no Minasan e [To the Assistant Judges], 2147 Hanrei Jihou 3, 3–4 (2012).
40. Kouseiroudoushou, Heisei 29nen Kokumun Seikatsu Kiso Chousa [2017 National Livelihood Survey], available at https://www.mhlw.go.jp/toukei/list/dl/kanichousa_h29.pdf. Each figure includes taxes and social security income; take-home pay is lower.
41. See Saibankan no Houshuu nado ni kansuru Houritsu [Law concerning Judicial Compensation], Law no. 74 of 1948, art. 2 and attached chart.
42. United States Courts, Judicial Compensation, 2019, available at https://www.uscourts.gov/judges-judgeships/judicial-compensation.
43. The Organization for Economic Cooperation and Development defines middle class as 200 percent percent of median household income. See OECD, Under Pressure: The Squeezed Middle Class (2019).
44. In civil cases the written judgment must state "the main text, the facts, the reasons, the date of conclusion of oral argument, the parties and their statutory agents, and the name of the court." The statement of facts must clarify the claim and indicate allegations necessary to show that the main text is "justifiable." Code of Civil Procedure arts. 253–54. In criminal cases the law requires the court to "render a judgment" in every case, and in sentencing it must give "the facts constituting the crime, the list of evidence and the application of laws and regulations." Code of Criminal Procedure arts. 333–35.
45. Naohide Iehara, Minji Hanketsusho no Arikata ni Tsuite [About Civil Judicial Opinions], 10 Toukyou Daigaku Houkadaigakuin Roo Rebyuu [University of Tokyo Law Review] 63 (2015), available at http://www.sllr.j.u-tokyo.ac.jp/10/papers/v10part05(iehara).pdf.
46. See, e.g., Tokyo Chisai, Osaka Chisai Keiji Hanketsusho Kentou Guruupu, Keiji Hanketsusho no Minaoshi ni Tsuite [Regarding the Revision of Criminal Opinions], 755 Hanrei Times 10 (1991); Toukyoukou/Chisai Minji Hanketsusho Kaizen Iinkai and Osakakou/Chisai Minji Hanketsusho Kaizen Iinkai, Minji Hanketsusho no Atarashii Youshiki ni Tsuite [Regarding the New Form of Civil Opinions] 715 Hanrei Times 4 (1990).
47. See, e.g., Shihou Kenshuujo ed., Keiji Hankestusho Kian no Tebiki [A Guide to Drafting Criminal Opinions] (2007); Shihou Kenshuujo ed., Minji Hankestusho Kian no Tebiki [A Guide to Drafting Civil Opinions] (2006).
48. Hanjiho no Shokken no Tokurei nado ni Kansuru Houritsu [Law concerning the Special Authority of Assistant Judges], Law no. 146 of 1948.
49. See, e.g., Manabu Yamasaki, Keiji Soshou ni okeru Saibankan no Yakuwari [The Role of the Judge in a Criminal Case] in Shintarou Katou ed., Zeminaaru Saibankanron [Seminar: Theory of Judges] 193, 231–38 (2004).
50. See, e.g., Jirou Nomura, Nihon no Saibankan [Japanese Judges] 78 (1992).
51. Shin'ichi Yoshikawa, Minji Soshou ni okeru Saibankan no Yakuwari [The Role of the Judge in a Civil Case], in Shintarou Katou ed., Zeminaaru Saibankanron [Seminar: Theory of Judges] at 147, 191 (2004) ("the highest function of an opinion is to inform the parties as to the content of the judgment and to give them an opportunity to consider whether to appeal").
52. See, e.g., Arthur L. Goodhart, Determining the Ratio Decidendi of a Case, 40 Yale Law Journal 161 (1930); J. L. Montrose, Ratio Decidendi and the House of Lords, 20 Modern Law Review 124 (1957); A. W. B. Simpson, The Ratio Decidendi of a Case, 21 Modern Law Review 155 (1958); A. L. Goodhart, The Ratio Decidendi of a Case, 22 Modern Law Review 117 (1959) (weighing in on the Montrose-Simpson debates).
53. See, e.g., Tsugio Nakano, Hanrei no Riyu no Dono Bubun ga "Hanrei" nanoka [What Part of the Holding Can Be Considered "Precedent"]? in Tsugio Nakano et al. eds., Hanrei to Sono Yomikata [Judicial Precedents and How to Read Them] 29, 42–4 (3d ed. 2009).
54. A. W. Brian Simpson, Reflections on *The Concept of Law* 8 (2011).
55. Tokyo District Court, 622 Hanrei Times 149, July 12, 1986.
56. Thomas S. Kuhn, The Essential Tension: Selected Studies in Scientific Tradition and Change xii (1977).

Chapter 2

1. Yokohama District Court, Heisei 27 (wa) 281, Nov. 16, 2015.
2. Osaka High Court, Heisei 26 (u) 1301, Mar. 10, 2015.
3. Tokyo District Court, Heisei 15 (wa) 7325, Mar. 20, 2006.
4. Kyoto District Court, Heisei 17 (wa) 1841, Apr. 27, 2007.
5. Kagoshima District Court, Heisei 23 (wa) 25, Nov. 18, 2011.
6. Mito District Court, Heisei 9 (wa) 53, Feb. 26, 2009.
7. Nagasaki District Court, Heisei 17 (wa) 390, Sept. 22, 2006.
8. Tokyo District Court, Heisei 18 (wa) 11183, July 10, 2007.
9. Sendai District Court, 1183 Hanrei Times 263, Mar. 14, 2002
10. Yokohama District Court, 916 Roudou Hanrei 56, July 8, 2005.
11. Tokyo District Court, 1471 Hanrei Jihou 127, Oct. 27, 1992.
12. Tokyo District Court, Heisei 18 (wa) 21158, May 31, 2007.
13. Tokyo High Court, Heisei 5 (ne) 824, Feb. 24, 1999.
14. Sapporo District Court, 937 Roudou Hanrei 165, Mar. 29, 2006.
15. Tokyo District Court, 768 Roudou Hanrei 62, Apr. 19, 1999.
16. Yokohama District Court, Heisei 21 (wa) 2363, July 15, 2010.
17. Supreme Court, 1330 Hanrei Times 81, July 22, 2010.
18. World Health Organization, Global Status Report on Alcohol and Health 2018 (2018), available at https://apps.who.int/iris/bitstream/handle/10665/274603/9789241565639-eng.pdf. On the complexity of accurate measurement and comparison, see Kim Bloomfield et al., International Comparisons of Alcohol Consumption, National Institute on Alcohol Abuse and Alcoholism, National Institutes of Health, National Institute on Alcohol Abuse and Alcoholism, Dec. 2003, available at https://pubs.niaaa.nih.gov/publications/arh27-1/95-109.htm.
19. World Health Organization, Global Status Report on Alcohol and Health 2018 (2018), available at https://apps.who.int/iris/bitstream/handle/10665/274603/9789241565639-eng.pdf.
20. Susumu Higuchi et al., Japan: Alcohol Today, 102 Addiction 1849, 1853 (2007). There is no standard East Asian drinking pattern. A higher percentage of people in Japan drink than in China: 9.1 percent of people in Japan (and 9.2 percent in the United States) are lifetime abstainers, far less than in China (42.1 percent), but more than in South Korea (7.1 percent). Japan has roughly the same percentage of male binge drinkers as China (52.9) but lower than Korea (62.2), and Korea has far more male alcohol use disorders (21.2 percent) than Japan (5.7 percent) or China (8.4 percent). World Health Organization, Global Status Report on Alcohol and Health 2018 (2018), available at https://apps.who.int/iris/bitstream/handle/10665/274603/9789241565639-eng.pdf.
21. See Pew Research Center, Global Views on Morality, 2017, available at http://www.pewglobal.org/2014/04/15/global-morality/table/alcohol-use/.
22. Harry H. L. Kitano et al., Norms and Alcohol Consumption: Japanese in Japan, Hawaii and California, 53(1) Journal of Studies on Alcohol 33, 38 (1992).
23. Tooru Tsunoda et al., The Effect of Acculturation on Drinking Attitudes among Japanese in Japan and Japanese Americans in Hawaii and California, 53(4) Journal of Studies on Alcohol 369, 374 (1992).
24. Ministry of Health, Labor, and Welfare, Arukooru Izonshou [Alcoholism] (2011), available at http://www.mhlw.go.jp/kokoro/speciality/detail_alcohol.html; Naikakufuu Saisaku Toukatsukan, Joushuu Inshu Untensha no Inshu Unten Koudou Yokushi ni Kansuru Chousa Kenkyuu [Investigative Research regarding the Deterrence of Drunk Driving Behavior by Habitual Drunk Drivers] (2010), available at http://www8.cao.go.jp/koutu/chou-ken/h21/houkoku.html.
25. Yoneatsu Osaki et al., Waga Kuni no Seijin Inshu Koudou oyobi Arukoorushou ni Kansuru Zenkoku Chousa [National Study of Alcoholism and Drinking among Japanese Adults], 40(5) Nihon Arukooru Yakubutsu Igakkai Zasshi [Japanese Journal of Alcohol Studies and Drug Dependence] 455 (2005).
26. Ministry of Justice, Inshu (Arukooru) no Mondai o Yuusuru Hanzaisha no Shoguu ni Kansuru Sougouteki Kenkyuu [Comprehensive Analysis of the Treatment of Criminals with

Alcohol Problems], Report #43 (2011) at 20, available at http://www.moj.go.jp/housouken/housouken03_00055.html.

27. Shurui Sougou Kenkyuujo ed., Sake no Shouhin Chishiki [Liquor Product Knowledge] 286–87 (3d ed. 2018).
28. Charles W. Bamforth, Food, Fermentation and Micro-organisms 143 (2005).
29. Christopher Pellegrini, The Shochu Handbook 9 (2014).
30. Penelope Francks, The Japanese Consumer: An Alternative Economic History of Modern Japan 58, 95n.46, 196 (2009).
31. James E. Roberson, Book Review of Paul Christensen, Japan, Alcoholism, and Masculinity: Suffering Sobriety in Tokyo, 42(2) Journal of Japanese Studies 362, 365 (2016).
32. Edward Fowler, San'ya Blues: Laboring Life in Contemporary Tokyo (1996).
33. See, e.g., Hajime Nakano, Daisanji Honkaku Shouchuu Buumu to Sanchikan Kyousou no Hen'you [The Shouchuu Boom and the Transformation of Production Competition], 25 Kumamoto Gakuen Daigaku Sangyou Keiei Kenkyuu [Kumamoto Gakuen University Economics and Business Research] 15 (2006), available at http://www3.kumagaku.ac.jp/eb/achievement/documents/25-2.pdf; Bank of Japan Miyazaki Office, Shouchuu Gyoukai no Genjou to Kadai [Current Status and Issues Regarding the Shochu Industry], Mar. 12, 2014, available at http://www3.boj.or.jp/miyazaki/miyazakinote/data/note29.pdf.
34. See Nicola Caruthers, Higher-abv Iichiko Saiten for Bartenders Lands in the US, The Spirits Business, Mar. 27, 2019, available at https://www.thespiritsbusiness.com/2019/03/higher-abv-iichiko-saiten-for-bartenders-lands-in-the-us/.
35. Shouchuu Shouhiryou (2016-nen Daiichii Kagoshimaken) Todoufuken Toukei to Rankingu de Miru Kenminsei [Shouchuu Consumption (2016 Number One Kagoshima Prefecture): Examining Prefectural Characteristics through Rankings], Todo-Ran, Nov. 15, 2017, available at http://todo-ran.com/t/kiji/14525.
36. Arukooru Shouhiryou (2016-nen Daiichii Kagoshimaken) Todoufuken Toukei to Rankingu de Miru Kenminsei [Alcohol Consumption (2016 Number One Kagoshima Prefecture): Examining Prefectural Characteristics through Rankings], Todo-Ran, Nov. 16, 2017, available at http://todo-ran.com/t/kiji/14569.
37. Jeffrey W. Alexander, Brewed in Japan 12–16 (2013); see also Japan Brewers Association, Biiru no Rekishi [The History of Beer], http://www.brewers.or.jp/tips/histry.html.
38. Jeffrey W. Alexander, Brewed in Japan 9 (2013).
39. Penelope Francks, Inconspicuous Consumption: Sake, Beer, and the Birth of the Consumer in Japan, 68(1) Journal of Asian Studies 135, 156–59 (2009).
40. World Health Organization, Global Status Report on Alcohol and Health 2018 (2018), available at https://apps.who.int/iris/bitstream/handle/10665/274603/9789241565639-eng.pdf.
41. Supreme Court, 1051 Hanrei Times 279, Nov. 20, 2000.
42. Tsu District Court, 1074 Roudou Hanrei 5, Mar. 28, 2013.
43. Wan Kappu ni Gentei Dezain [Limited Edition One Cup Design], Asahi Shinbun Digital, Feb. 28, 2017, available at http://www.asahi.com/articles/ASK2R4SJ6K2RPLFA00G.html.
44. Tom Gill, Failed Manhood on the Streets of Urban Japan: The Meanings of Self-Reliance for Homeless Men, 10(1) Asia-Pacific Journal 1, 14 (Dec. 2011), available at http://apjjf.org/2012/10/1/Tom-Gill/3671/article.html.
45. Poster available online at Ministry of Health, Labor, and Welfare, http://www.mhlw.go.jp/file/06-Seisakujouhou-12200000-Shakaiengokyokushougaihokenfukushibu/poster_13.pdf.
46. Yasushi Nishiyama, Otona no Utanetto Supesharu Intabyuu: Yoshi Ikuzou, [Special Interview: Yoshi Ikuzou], Mar. 9, 2010, available at http://www.uta-net.com/user/otona/otona_interview/1005yoshi1.html.
47. Yokohama District Court Kawasaki Branch, Heisei 20 (wa) 332, May 25, 2009; Osaka District Court, Heisei 17 (wa) 3529, Mar. 24, 2008; Saga District Court, 1947 Hanrei Jihou 3, May 10, 2005; Saga District Court, Heisei 14 (wa) 194, Sept. 16, 2004; Tokyo District Court, Heisei 14 (gou wa) 64, Nov. 11, 2002; Urawa District Court, 1064 Hanrei Times 67, Mar. 21, 2001; Tokyo High Court, 1013 Hanrei Times 245, Apr. 28, 1999; Kofu District Court, 1249 Hanrei Jihou 132, July 6, 1987.
48. Tokyo District Court Hachiouji Branch, 1118 Hanrei Times 299, Oct. 29, 2002.
49. Kyoto District Court, Heisei 26 (wa) 859, Mar. 27, 2015.

50. Kyoto District Court, Heisei 25 (wa) 1317, Sept. 19, 2014.
51. Hiroshima High Court, Heisei 27 (u) 78, Apr. 13, 2016; Yokohama District Court, 25 (wa) 731, July 3, 2014; Fukui District Court, 21 (wa) 28, Sept. 1, 2010; Osaka District Court, Heisei 19 (wa) 3706, Aug. 8, 2008; Osaka District Court, Shouwa 57 (wa) 1048, July 9, 1982.
52. Kobe District Court, Heisei 16 (wa) 733, June 13, 2005; Sapporo District Court, 873 Hanrei Times 288, Feb. 7, 1994.
53. Tokyo High Court, Heisei 25 (u) 78, Mar. 38, 2013.
54. Osaka High Court, 1404 Hanrei Jihou 128, June 13, 1991.
55. Osaka Summary Court, 1204 Hanrei Jihou 161, Dec. 11, 1985.
56. Okayama District Court, Heisei 19 (wa) 82, Apr. 23, 2002.
57. Osaka District Court, Heisei 18 (wa) 1704, Nov. 30, 2006.
58. Tokyo High Court, 1164 Hanrei Times 188, May 8, 2013; Tokyo District Court Hachiouji Branch, 1164 Hanrei Times 188, May 8, 2003; Chiba District Court, 489 Roudou Hanrei 18, Dec. 26, 1986.
59. Wakayama District Court, 1056 Hanrei Times 196, Nov. 21, 2000; Nagoya High Court, 716 Roudou Hanrei 62, Mar. 28, 1997; Nagoya District Court, 691 Roudou Hanrei 29, Jan. 26, 1996.
60. Urawa District Court, 1076 Hanrei Times 286, Mar. 30, 2001.
61. Supreme Court, 603 Hanrei Times 48, Mar. 25, 1986; Osaka High Court, 498 Hanrei Times 219, June 29, 1983.
62. Osaka High Court, 986 Hanrei Times 289, May 22, 1998.
63. Hiroshima High Court, Heisei 27 (u) 78, Apr. 13, 2016.
64. Aya Kinjo et al., Different Socioeconomic Backgrounds between Hazardous Drinking and Heavy Episodic Drinking: Prevalence by Sociodemographic Factors in a Japanese General Sample, 193 Drug and Alcohol Dependence 55 (2018).
65. See, e.g., Nagoya High Court, Heisei 25 (o) 7, May 28, 2014; Nagoya High Court, Heisei 22 (ke) 2, May 25, 2012.
66. Tokyo High Court, 1303 Hanrei Times 57, Dec. 16, 2008.
67. Yokohama District Court, 553 Hanrei Times 251, Feb. 8, 1985. In a 2018 case, vodka appears on a list of things, along with tomatoes and wheat, for which the plaintiff was tested at a hospital to determine allergic reactions. Kyoto District Court, Heisei 24 (wa) 1230, Feb. 20, 2018. The other two exceptions are from a copyright infringement case. Osaka High Court, Heisei 14 (ne) 28, Sept. 18, 2002; Kyoto District Court, Heisei 11 (wa) 111, Dec. 20, 2001.
68. Mito District Court, Heisei 19 (wa) 53, Heisei 18 (wa) 820, Heisei 19 (wa) 93, Feb. 21, 2006; see also Tokyo District Court, Heisei 19 (wa) 53, June 30, 2009, *aff'd*, Tokyo High Court, Heisei 21 (u) 1403, Mar. 17, 2010.
69. Saitama District Court, Heisei 12 (wa) 529, Dec. 1, 2002.
70. Mito District Court, Heisei 19 (wa) 53, Feb. 26, 2009, *aff'd*, Tokyo High Court, Heisei 21 (u) 1403, Mar. 17, 2010, Tokyo High Court, Heisei 21 (u) 566, Aug. 24, 2009, Tokyo High Court, Heisei 23 (u) 1477, Nov. 27, 2012.
71. Tokyo District Court, Heisei 21 (kei wa) 640, Heisei 21 (kei wa 945), Heisei 21 (kei wa) 223, Heisei 21 (gou wa) 151, Mar. 29, 2010.
72. Tokyo High Court, Heisei 23 (u) 1477, Nov. 27, 2012.
73. Tokyo District Court, 1168 Hanrei Times 99, Nov. 2, 2004.
74. See Shurui Sougou Kenkyuujo ed., Sake no Shouhin Chishiki [Liquor Product Knowledge] 429 (3d ed. 2018).
75. Wakabayashi District Court, 1122 Hanrei Times 64, Dec. 11, 2002.
76. Osaka District Court, Heisei 26 (wa) 6333, Nov. 21, 2016.
77. Ministry of Health, Labor, and Welfare, Seijin no Inshu Jittai to Kanren Mondai no Yobou ni Tuite [The Prevention of Drinking and Related Problems in Adults] (2006), available at http://www.mhlw.go.jp/topics/tobacco/houkoku/061122b.html.
78. See, e.g., Toshiyuki Miyaba ed., Kaisei Shuzeihou Tou no Tebiki [Handbook for Revised Alcohol Taxation Law] (2018).
79. Brewers Association of Japan, Nihon no Biiru, Happoushuu Shin Janru to Zei [Japanese Beer, Happoushuu, and New Genre Beer and Tax] (2016), available at http://www.brewers.or.jp/contents/factbook.html, at 12.

80. National Tax Agency, Sake no Shiori [Statistics on Alcoholic Beverages] (2012), available at http://www.nta.go.jp/shiraberu/senmonjoho/sake/shiori-gaikyo/shiori/2012/pdf/003.pdf, at 13.
81. See, e.g., Yoshihei Nakamura, Kirin Biiru no Daigyakushu [Kirin Beer's Counterattack] (1999); Keigifurou Seimaru, Bia Uoozu: Suupaa Dorai vs. Happoushu [Beer Wars: Super Dry vs. Happoushu] (1999).
82. Chris Bunting, Drinking Japan 141–42 (2011).
83. National Tax Agency, Sake no Shiori [Statistics on Alcoholic Beverages] (2018), available at http://www.nta.go.jp/taxes/sake/shiori-gaikyo/shiori/2018/pdf/100.pdf, at 17.
84. National Tax Agency, Sake no Shiori [Statistics on Alcoholic Beverages] (2018), available at http://www.nta.go.jp/taxes/sake/shiori-gaikyo/shiori/2018/pdf/100.pdf, at 17.
85. Japan Franchise Association, Konbiniensu Sutoa Toukei Deeta [Convenience Store Statistics] (Feb. 2019), available at http://www.jfa-fc.or.jp/particle/320.html.
86. See, e.g., Biiru: Kouri Kakaku ga Joushou Shuzeihou Kaisei de Yasuuri Kisei Kyouka [Beer: Retail Prices Increase as Revised Liquor Tax Law Strengthens Regulation of Bargain Pricing], Mainichi Shinbun, June 8, 2017, available at https://mainichi.jp/articles/20170609/k00/00m/020/074000c.
87. Susumu Higuchi et al., Drinking Practices, Alcohol Policy and Prevention Programmes in Japan, 17 International Journal of Drug Policy 358 (2006).
88. Jeffrey W. Alexander, Brewed in Japan 188–89 (2013).
89. See National Tax Agency, Sakerui Jidou Hanbaiki no Settchi Joukyou [The Establishment of Alcohol Vending Machines], Sept. 21, 2018, available at https://www.nta.go.jp/taxes/sake/miseinen/jihanki2018/01.htm.
90. Brewers Association of Japan, Nihon no Biiru, Happoushuu Shin Janru to Zei [Japanese Beer, Happoushuu, and New Genre Beer and Tax] (2016), available at http://www.brewers.or.jp/contents/factbook.html, at 10.
91. Ienomi wa Suki Desuka? [Do You Enjoy Drinking at Home?], Weekly Survey, Asahi Holdings, June 27, 2018, available at https://www.asahigroup-holdings.com/company/research/hapiken/maian/201806/00682/; see also Hitoshi Utsunomiya and Katsumi Hashizume, Seishuu, Biiru, Uisukii no Inshuu Douki ni Kansuru Chousa [Survey regarding Motivations for Drinking Sake, Beer, and Whisky] (2007) at 80–1, available at http://www.nrib.go.jp/data/pdf/syutyo0201.pdf (earlier survey with similar results).
92. Supreme Court, 1425 Hanrei Times 126, Mar. 1, 2016.
93. Sumio Imada, Isato Furumitsu, and Hanae Izu, Development of a Five Factor Drinking Motive Questionnaire for Japanese (DMQ-J), 57(2) Studies in the Humanities and Sciences 153, 154 (2017), available at http://doi.org/10.15097/00002413.
94. Keiko Kato, Dysfunction of Functional Drinking: Voices of Japanese Alcoholics' Wives, Ph.D. Dissertation, Washington State University, 465 (2004).
95. Keiko Kato, Dysfunction of Functional Drinking: Voices of Japanese Alcoholics' Wives, Ph.D. Dissertation, Washington State University, 277 (2004).
96. See, e.g., Tomomi Marugame et al., Patterns of Alcohol Drinking and All-Cause Mortality: Results from a Large-Scale Population-Based Cohort Study in Japan, 165(9) American Journal of Epidemiology 1039 (Mar. 2007).
97. See, e.g., Fukuoka District Court, 2157 Hanrei Jihou 68, Mar. 24, 2012; Tokyo District Court, Heisei 18 (gyou u) 397, Jan. 29, 2008.
98. Akita District Court, 1379 Hanrei Times 109, Mar. 23, 2012.
99. Morioka District Court, 810 Roudou Hanrei 56, Feb. 23, 2001.
100. Tokyo District Court, Heisei 25 (gyou u) 794, July 14, 2016.
101. Osaka High Court, 2121 Hanrei Jihou 134, Feb. 23, 2011.
102. Tokyo District Court, Heisei 16 (gyou u) 455, Mar. 20, 2007.
103. Tokyo District Court, Heisei 16 (gyou u) 518, Feb. 1, 2007.
104. Fukuoka District Court, 916 Roudou Hanrei 20, Apr. 12, 2006.
105. Sendai District Court, Heisei 18 (wa) 172, Dec. 27, 2007.
106. Tokyo District Court, Heisei 16 (ta) 86, Aug. 26, 2004.
107. Yoshitaka Kaneita et al., Use of Alcohol and Hypnotic Medication as Aids to Sleep among the Japanese General Population, 8 Sleep Medicine 723 (2007).

108. Constantin R. Soldatos, How Do Individuals Sleep around the World? Results from a Single-Day Survey in Ten Countries, 6 Sleep Medicine 5 (2005).
109. See Kazaki Yamashita, Tokyo "Shinjuku Gourudengai" de "Dasai Kyaku" ni Narazu ni Tanhoshiku Nomu Houhou [How to Drink Like a Pro in Tokyo's Shinjuku Golden Gai], Nippon.com, Sept. 3, 2018, available at https://www.nippon.com/ja/guide-to-japan/gu900051/.
110. Tokyo District Court, 1513 Hanrei Jihou 179, July 29, 1993.
111. See, e.g., Harumi Befu, An Ethnography of Dinner Entertainment in Japan, 11 Arctic Anthropology 196 (1974) (Supplement Festschrift Issue in Honor of Chester S. Chard) (*ryoutei* are preferred to Western restaurants for entertaining because customers sit on the floor and always have a private room, workers interact with the guests, the host orders food in advance, everyone eats the same thing, and sake flows liberally).
112. Elizabeth Andoh, In Tokyo's Ryotei, the Art of Service, New York Times, Apr. 20, 1997, available at http://www.nytimes.com/1997/04/20/travel/in-tokyo-s-ryotei-the-art-of-service.html.
113. Fukuoka High Court, 1327 Hanrei Times 95, Sept. 1, 2001. See also Hiroshima District Court, Heisei 14 (u) 2, July 29, 2003 (Hiroshima governor); Tokyo High Court, Heisei 19 (gyou ko) 50, Sept. 26, 2007 (Tokyo governor).
114. See Mark D. West, Lovesick Japan: Sex, Marriage, Romance, Law 166–68 (2011).
115. Tokyo District Court, 1411 Hanrei Times 312, Apr. 14, 2014.
116. Yamazoe v. Itagaki, Supreme Court, 908 Hanrei Times 284, Mar. 26, 1996.
117. Legal commentary had suggested that an alienation of affections action could not be brought against a soapland worker (in a soapland, a female sex worker washes a man's body with her own, which is legal) who was having sex with customers only to receive compensation from her employer. See Itsumi Hino, Furin no Riigaru Ressun [Legal Lessons: Adultery] 70 (2003). Courts have avoided discussions of whether soapland visits constitute adultery (as grounds for divorce). See Tokyo District Court, Heisei 15 (ta) 600, Heisei 15 (ta) 603, June 24, 2005. Media and scholarly commentary afterward were abundant nonetheless, as the case opens the door to larger questions about what kinds of adultery are actionable. See, e.g., Untitled Comment, 1411 Hanrei Times 312 (May 25, 2015); "Makura Eigyou" wa Furin de wa nai? [Pillow Sales Tactics Aren't Adultery?], Sankei News, June 17, 2015, available at http://www.sankei.com/premium/news/150617/prm1506170004-n1.html.
118. Osaka District Court, Heisei 26 (yo) 10062, Apr. 30, 2015.
119. Osaka District Court, 1269 Hanrei Times 203, Jan. 30, 2008.
120. Tokyo District Court, Heisei 15 (wa) 1978, Sept. 5, 2003.
121. Intellectual Property High Court, 2170 Hanrei Jihou 107, May 31, 2012.
122. Mark Robinson, Izakaya: The Japanese Pub Cookbook 8 (2008).
123. Intage, Shigoto Kaeri no Sotonomi Jijou 2012 [2012 Survey of Drinking on the Way Home from Work], available at http://www.intage.co.jp/chikara/02_topics/629/.
124. Asahikawa District Court, Heisei 27 (wa) 100, Nov. 25, 2015.
125. Saitama District Court, Heisei 28 (ro) 11, Oct. 17, 2016.
126. Fukuoka High Court, Heisei 23 (u) 222, May 16, 2012.
127. Yokohama District Court, Heisei 22 (wa) 164, Mar. 10, 2011.
128. Kiyoko Kawaida et al., The Use of All-You-Can-Drink System, Nomihodai, Is Associated with the Increased Alcohol Consumption among College Students: A Cross-Sectional Study in Japan, 245 Tohoku Journal of Experimental Medicine 263 (2018), available at https://doi.org/10.1620/tjem.
129. Number of Establishments in the Bars, Taverns and Nightclubs Industry in the United States from 2003 to 2017, Statista, https://www.statista.com/statistics/281713/us-bars-taverns-und-nightclubs-industry-establishments/.
130. Kouichi Taniguchi, Sunakku Kenkyuu Kotohajime [Beginning to Research Snacks], in Kouichi Taniguchi ed., Nihon no Yoru no Koukyouken: Sunakku Kenkyuu Josetsu [Japan's Nighttime Public Sphere: An Introduction to Snack Research] 7, 16 (2017). McDonald's data from Kaisha Gaiyou [Company Profile], McDonald's Japan, http://www.mcdonalds.co.jp/company/outline/gaiyo.html andhttp://corporate.mcdonalds.com/mcd/investors.html. Starbucks data from Kaisha Gaiyou [Company Profile], Starbucks Japan http://

www.starbucks.co.jp/company/summary/ and https://www.starbucks.com/about-us/company-information/starbucks-company-profile.

131. Jasmin Sun, Here Are the States with the Most Bars per Capita, Eater, May 29, 2013, available at https://www.eater.com/2013/5/29/6428463/here-are-the-states-with-the-most-bars-per-capita.
132. Yokohama District Court, Heisei 21 (wa) 1908, June 17, 2011.
133. Kiichirou Arai, Sunakku no Chii to Kinou [The Location and Function of Snacks], in Kouichi Taniguchi ed., Nihon no Yoru no Koukyouken: Sunakku Kenkyuu Josetsu [Japan's Nighttime Public Sphere: An Introduction to Snack Research] 187, 198–201 (2017).
134. Tokyo District Court, Heisei 22 (gyou u) 444, Nov. 10, 2011.
135. See Lieba Faier, Filipina Migrants in Rural Japan and Their Professions of Love, 34(1) American Ethnologist 148 (Feb. 2007).
136. Tokyo High Court, Heisei 22 (u) 1672, Feb. 15, 2011; Tokyo High Court, Heisei 22 (u) 516, Oct. 8, 2010.
137. See, e.g., "Honnin ga Jibun de Sashita" Mune ni Houchou ga Sasatta Dansei . . . Doukyo Onna ga Taiho [Man Stabbed with Knife "Stabbed Himself"; Woman Living with Him Arrested], Naver Matome, June 18, 2013, available at https://matome.naver.jp/odai/2137151554232679901.
138. Gifu District Court, Heisei 25 (wa) 297, Dec. 17, 2014.
139. See, e.g., Kobe District Court Himeji Branch, Heisei 14 (wa) 374, Dec. 11, 2002 (woman sexually assaulted according to plan after she became intoxicated; no analysis of degree of intoxication or amount of alcohol ingested).
140. Tokyo District Court, Heisei 15 (wa) 7582, Dec. 20, 2004. A growing body of case law makes clear that the sexual assault of intoxicated women is "evil." See, e.g., Osaka District Court, Heisei 25 (wa) 3381, Feb. 7, 2014 (coworkers after year-end party); Tokyo District Court, Heisei 23 (gou) 293, Feb. 1, 2013 (judo instructor with student). Still, a 2019 decision found a lack of criminal liability when a suspect had sex with an unconscious drunk woman because the court decided that he might have believed that she had consented. The rarity of the decision is reflected in the public outcry that resulted. See, e.g., Satoshi Sugita, "Jungoukan" Jiken, Fukuoka Chisai: Muzai Hanketsu no Hijoushiki ["Quasi-Rape" Incident and the Fukuoka District Court: The Nonsensical Not Guilty Verdict], Asahi Ronza, Mar. 22, 2019, available at https://webronza.asahi.com/culture/articles/2019032000006.html.
141. See, e.g., Ruth Weissenborn and Theodora Duka, State-Dependent Effects of Alcohol on Explicit Memory: The Role of Semantic Associations, 149 Psychopharmacology 98 (2007).
142. See, e.g., Millan v. Hedgpeth, 2008 U.S. Dist. LEXIS 118298 (E.D. Cal. Oct. 31, 2008).
143. Akiko Takeyama, Staged Seduction: Selling Dreams in a Tokyo Host Club 49 (2016).
144. Yoshimasa Kijima, "Otokorashisa" no Souchaku [The Creation of "Masculinity"] in Shinji Miyadai, Izumi Tsuji, and Takayuki Okai, eds., "Otokorashisa" no Kairaku [The Pleasure of "Masculinity"] 137, 153, 162–66 (2009).
145. Akiko Takeyama, Commodified Romance in a Tokyo Host Club, in Mark McLelland and Romit Dasgupta eds., Genders, Transgenders and Sexualities in Japan 200 (2005).
146. Nagoya High Court, 271 Hanrei Times 286, Aug. 8, 1971.
147. Akiko Takeyama, Commodified Romance in a Tokyo Host Club, in Mark McLelland and Romit Dasgupta eds., Genders, Transgenders and Sexualities in Japan 200, 204 (2005).
148. Kobe District Court, Heisei 20 (wa) 287, Nov. 11, 2008.
149. See, e.g., Yoneatsu Osaki et al., Prevalence and Trends in Alcohol Dependence and Alcohol Use Disorders in Japanese Adults; Results from Periodical Nationwide Surveys, 51(4) Alcohol & Alcoholism 465 (July/Aug. 2016); Susumu Higuchi et al., Japan: Alcohol Today, 102 Addiction 1849, 1853 (2007); Susumu Higuchi et al., Drinking Practices, Alcohol Policy and Prevention Programmes in Japan, 17 International Journal of Drug Policy 358, 360 (2006).
150. Jeffrey W. Alexander, Brewed in Japan 227 (2013).
151. Anne Allison, Nightwork: Sexuality, Pleasure, and Corporate Masculinity in a Tokyo Hostess Club 45 (1994).
152. See, e.g., Osake no Nomisugite Yatte Shimatta Rankingu [Ranking of Worst Things to Happen While Drunk], Zexy, May 24, 2018, available at https://zexy.net/contents/lovenews/

article.php?d=20180524 (vomiting number one in 2018 survey of 184 women); Osake de Shippai Shita Koto ga Aru Hito wa 3nin ni 2nin & Gutaitekina Shippai Rankingu [Ranking of Alcohol-Related Failures; Two Out of Three Have Experienced], Nifty News, July 20, 2012, available at https://news.nifty.com/article/item/neta/12225-120719000743/ (vomiting number one in 2012 survey of 4,271 participants).

153. https://www.instagram.com/shibuyameltdown. This kind of photography seems to have become its own genre. See Kenji Kawamoto, Yopparai Tengoku (Drunkards' Heaven), photography series, available at https://www.lensculture.com/articles/kenji-kawamoto-yopparai-tengoku-drunkards-heaven as well as Simon Bowcock, Legless Japanese Businessmen: The Photographer Who Caught a Tokyo Epidemic, The Guardian, Oct. 12, 2018, available at https://www.theguardian.com/artanddesign/2018/oct/12/legless-japanese-businessmen-the-photographer-who-shoots-street-sleepers-pawel-jaszczuk-high-fashion (discussing the work of Pawel Jaszcuk) and the work of Lee Chapman; see Lee Chapman, The Drunk, available at https://leechapman.photos/the-drunk.
154. Yokohama District Court, Heisei 23 (wa) 1583, Oct. 19, 2012.
155. See, e.g., Natsuko Kasai, Man'in Densha de "Kusai Ojisan" ni Nattenai? [Have You Ever Been a "Smelly Middle-Aged Man" on a Packed Train?], Diamond Online, June 10, 2013, available at http://diamond.jp/articles/-/37125.
156. Sake ni Yotte Koushuu ni Meiwaku o kakeru Koui no Boushi nado ni Kansuru Houritsu, Law no. 103 of 1961. The law is often abbreviated to Yopparai Boushihou (Drunk Law) or Meitei Kiseihou (Intoxication Rules Law).
157. See Yukari Satou, "Yopparai Boushihou" no Saihyouka to Sono Genkai [The Limits and a Reevaluation of the "Drunk Law"], 14 Kokuritsu Josei Kyouikukan Kenkyuu Jaanaru [Journal of the National Women's Education Center] 80 (Mar. 2010).
158. Kazuhiko Nishimura, Meiteisha ni Taisuru Rippou Sochi, Sono San [Part 3, Legislative Measure regarding Intoxicated Persons] in Meitei to Keiji Sekinin [Intoxication and Criminal Responsibility], Vol. 9, Joint Issue 3–4 Keihou Zasshi 1, 134, 135 (1959).
159. Keisatsukan Shokumu Shikou Hou [Police Duties Execution Act], Law no. 136 of 1948, art. 3(1).
160. Keisatsu Jitsumu Kenkyuukai, Chiiki Keisatsukan no tame no Keibi Hanzai no Sochi Youryou [Guidelines for Minor Crimes for Local Police] 104 (2010).
161. Keisatsu Jitsumu Kenkyuukai, Chiiki Keisatsukan no tame no Keibi Hanzai no Sochi Youryou [Guidelines for Minor Crimes for Local Police] 103 (2010).
162. Keisatsu Jitsumu Kenkyuukai, Chiiki Keisatsukan no tame no Keibi Hanzai no Sochi Youryou [Guidelines for Minor Crimes for Local Police] 105 (2010).
163. "Meitei" to "Deisui" no Imi to Tsukaikata no Chigai [The Difference between "Drunk" and "Dead Drunk"], Tap-biz, July 4, 2018, available at https://tap-biz.jp/lifestyle/word-meaning/1033494.
164. Keisatsuchou, Nenjibetsu Hogo Toriatsukai Joukyou [Annual Protective Custody Overview], 2018, available at https://www.npa.go.jp/toukei/soubunkan/h29/pdf/H29_27.pdf.
165. 1994 Keisatsu Hakusho [Annual Police White Paper] (1995), available at https://www.npa.go.jp/hakusyo/h05/h050400.html.
166. 2017 Keisichou no Toukei [Tokyo Police Statistics] 251–52 (2018), available at https://www.keishicho.metro.tokyo.jp/about_mpd/jokyo_tokei/tokei/k_tokei29.files/ktd119.pdf and https://www.keishicho.metro.tokyo.jp/about_mpd/jokyo_tokei/tokei/k_tokei29.files/ktd120.pdf.
167. See, e.g., Ministry of Justice, 2015 Kensatsu Toukei Nenpou [2015 Annual Report of Statistics on Prosecution] 60, 78 (2016).
168. David H. Bayley, Forces of Order: Policing Modern Japan 100 (1991).
169. See, e.g., Tokyo District Court, 1134 Hanrei Times 199, Nov. 11, 2002.
170. See, e.g., Doujouron ga Wakiokotta SMAP Kusanagi Tsuyoshi no "Zenhadaka Deisui" Soudou [Outpouring of Sympathy over Kusanagi Tsuyoshi's "Naked Dead Drunk" Disturbance, Nikkan Gendai, Sept. 5, 2014 (famed boy band member allegedly carted off in protective sheet).

171. See, e.g., Bangkok55bar, Keisatukan ga Kyouakuhan o Fukurozume ni suru Shunkan [The Moment Police Wrap Up a Thug], YouTube video, Nov. 10, 2013, available at https://www.youtube.com/watch?v=QfC6pVOsbt4 (video of sheet in use).
172. Kouno v. Mie Prefecture, Tsu District Court, 2228 Hanrei Jihou 64, Feb. 20, 2014.
173. Sumio Imada, Isato Furumitsu, and Hanae Izu, Development of a Five Factor Drinking Motive Questionnaire for Japanese (DMQ-J), 57(2) Studies in the Humanities and Sciences 153–62 (2017).
174. Sumio Imada, Isato Furumitsu, and Hanae Izu, Development of a Five Factor Drinking Motive Questionnaire for Japanese (DMQ-J), 57(2) Studies in the Humanities and Sciences 153–62 (2017).
175. Katsuhiro Oono, Keisatsukan no Inshu Joutai ni kansuru Kenkyuu [Police Drinking Patterns], 30(3) Arukooru Kenkyuu to Yakubutsu Izon [Alcohol Studies and Drug Dependence] 97 (1995).
176. Hitoshi Utsunomiya and Katsumi Hashizume, Seishuu, Biiru, Uisukii no Inshuu Douki ni Kansuru Chousa [Survey regarding Motivations for Drinking Sake, Beer, and Whisky] (2007) at 92, available at http://www.nrib.go.jp/data/pdf/syutyo0201.pdf.
177. Hitoshi Utsunomiya and Katsumi Hashizume, Seishuu, Biiru, Uisukii no Inshuu Douki ni Kansuru Chousa [Survey regarding Motivations for Drinking Sake, Beer, and Whisky] (2007) at 86, available at http://www.nrib.go.jp/data/pdf/syutyo0201.pdf.
178. See Fukushima District Court, Heisei 23 (wa) 86, Jan. 27, 2012 (victim drunk after attending *nomikai*); Tokyo High Court, 1822 Hanrei Jihou 153, Apr. 22, 2002 (defendant attends *nomikai* twice monthly, including a precrime *bounenkai*).
179. See, e.g., Kumamoto District Court, 1638 Hanrei Jihou 135, June 25, 1997.
180. See, e.g., Tokyo District Court, Heisei 15 (ta) 535, Mar. 22, 2004.
181. Tokyo District Court, Heisei 17 (wa) 16420, Nov. 9, 2006.
182. Tokyo District Court, Heisei 16 (wa) 11434, July 20, 2005.
183. Okayama District Court, 2114 Hanrei Jihou 119, Feb. 22, 2011.
184. Yukio Mishima, Runaway Horses 3 (1970, Michael Gallagher trans. 1973).
185. Tokyo Kaijou Nichidou Risuki Konsorutingu, Shokuba no Pawaa Harasumento ni Kansuru Jittai Chousa Houkokusho [Report on Empirical Study of Workplace Power Harassment], Dec. 12, 2012, available at http://www.mhlw.go.jp/stf/houdou/2r9852000002qx6t-att/2r9852000002qx9f.pdf.
186. Tokyo District Court, Heisei 22 (wa) 11853, Mar. 9, 2012.
187. Intage, Shigotokaeri no Sotonomi Jijou 2012 [2012 Survey of Drinking on the Way Home from Work], available at http://www.intage.co.jp/chikara/02_topics/629/.
188. Intage, Shigotokaeri no Sotonomi Jijou 2012 [2012 Survey of Drinking on the Way Home from Work], available at http://www.intage.co.jp/chikara/02_topics/629/.
189. David Milne, Alcohol Consumption in Japan: Different Culture, Different Rules, 167(4) Canadian Medical Association Journal 388 (Aug. 20, 2002).
190. Tokyo District Court, 906 Hanrei Times 163, Mar. 28, 1996.
191. Shizuoka District Court, 773 Hanrei Times 247, Nov. 15, 1991.
192. Osaka District Court, 2382 Hanrei Jihou 60, Mar. 1, 2018.
193. Nagoya District Court, Heisei 20 (gyou u) 51, Apr. 21, 2010.
194. Fukuoka High Court, 1633 Hanrei Jihou 147, Dec. 4, 1997.
195. Chiba District Court, 1214 Hanrei Times 315, Feb. 14, 2006.
196. Ministry of Justice, Inshu (Arukooru) no Mondai o Yuusuru Hanzaisha no Shoguu ni Kansuru Sougouteki Kenkyuu [Comprehensive Analysis of the Treatment of Criminals with Alcohol Problems], Report #43 (2011) at 30, available at http://www.moj.go.jp/housouken/housouken03_00055.html.
197. Ministry of Justice, Inshu (Arukooru) no Mondai o Yuusuru Hanzaisha no Shoguu ni Kansuru Sougouteki Kenkyuu [Comprehensive Analysis of the Treatment of Criminals with Alcohol Problems, Report #43 (2011) at 11, available at http://www.moj.go.jp/housouken/housouken03_00055.html.
198. Tokyo High Court, 1822 Hanrei Jihou 153, Apr. 22, 2002.
199. Oita District Court, Heisei 14 (wa) 407, May 16, 2005.

200. Jeffrey W. Alexander, Drinking Bomb and Shooting Meth: Alcohol and Drug Use in Japan 86 (2018).
201. Shizuoka District Court Hamamatsu Branch, Heisei 20 (wa) 361, July 11, 2011.
202. Aomori District Court, Heisei 18 (wa) 123, Sept. 25, 2006.
203. Osaka Family Court, 36(11) Katei Saiban Geppou, Apr. 25, 1984.
204. Fukuoka High Court, Heisei 24 (u) 104, Sept. 6, 2012.
205. Matsuyama District Court, 1113 Hanrei Times 231, Oct. 29, 2001.
206. Tokyo District Court, Heisei 13 (ta) 746, Heisei 13 (ta) 933, June 27, 2003.
207. Kobe District Court, Heisei 15 (wa) 502, Sept. 29, 2003.
208. Saitama District Court, Heisei 21 (wa) 59, May 27, 2009.
209. Tokyo District Court, Heisei 14 (u) 14726, Dec. 16, 2003.
210. See Paul Christensen, Scripting Addiction, Constructing Recovery: Alcoholism and Ideology in Japan, 37(3) Japanese Studies 371 (2017); Richard Chenhall and Tomofumi Oka, "The Way of Abstinence": Stigma and Spirituality in Danshukai, a Japanese Self-Help Organisation for Alcoholics, 36(1) Japanese Studies (2016).

Chapter 3

1. Ministry of Justice, Inshu (Arukooru) no Mondai o Yuusuru Hanzaisha no Shoguu ni Kansuru Sougouteki Kenkyuu [Comprehensive Analysis of the Treatment of Criminals with Alcohol Problems] Report #43, at 20 (2011), available at http://www.moj.go.jp/housouken/housouken03_00055.html.
2. Great Court of Cassation, 10 Keishuu 682 (Dec. 3, 1931).
3. Supreme Court, 535 Hanrei Times 204 (July 30, 1984); see Kazushige Asada, Keiji Sekinin Nouryoku no Kenkyuu [A Study of Criminal Capacity] 310–17 (1999).
4. Keiji Tanaka, Meitei to Keiji Sekinin [Intoxication and Criminal Responsibility] 8, 49–114 (1985). See also Yoshio Suzuki Mohan Keihou oyobi Nyuu Yooku Shinkeihou ni okeru Sekinin Nouryoku no Kijun [The Standards of Responsibility in the Model Penal Code and the New York Penal Code], 37(6) Keisatsu Kenkyuu 63, 79 (1966) (noting general lack of emphasis on volitional prong in Japanese law).
5. Montana v. Egelhoff, 518 U.S. 37, 56 (1996).
6. See, e.g., Mitchell Keiter, Just Say No Excuse: The Rise and Fall of the Intoxication Defense, 87 Journal of Criminal Law and Criminology 482 (1997); Douglas B. Marlowe, Jennifer B. Lambert, and Robert G. Thompson, Voluntary Intoxication and Criminal Responsibility, 17 Behavioral Sciences and the Law 195 (1999).
7. People v. Chapman, 418 N.W. 2d 658 (Mich. Ct. App. 1987); see Lawrence Taylor and Steven Oberman, Drunk Driving Defense 212 (8th ed. 2015).
8. The intoxication defense is limited by a doctrine from the German legal tradition called *actio libera in causa* (*gen'in ni oite jiyuu na koui*) that essentially holds that a defendant cannot create the conditions of his own defense. The doctrine has no systematic equivalent in U.S. law but manifests throughout (for instance, cases that invoke defenses based in the lesser evils and self-defense justifications or the duress excuse). See Paul H. Robinson, Causing the Conditions of One's Own Defense: A Study in the Limits of Theory in Criminal Law Doctrine, 71 Virginia Law Review (1985). Strategic intoxication is a prime example of the principle: People may not deliberately drink themselves into a state in which they would not be blameworthy in order to commit a crime. The hypothetical situation is prominent in Japanese treatises, but actual examples in the case law are rare. See, e.g., Osaka District Court, 516 Hanrei Times 186, June 6, 1983 (denying applicability of doctrine in arson case because defendant, who knew of his pathological intoxication, did not intend to put others in danger). See also Shizuoka District Court, 825 Hanrei Times 189, Mar. 26, 1993 (applying a similar civil law principle to reduce damages to a murder victim pursuant to Civil Code art. 713: "A person who has, while in a state of mental unsoundness, caused damage to another is not liable in compensation for damages; however, this shall not apply if he has brought upon himself a temporary mental unsoundness either intentionally or by his own negligence").

9. See, e.g., Osamu Nakata, Waga Seishin Kantei Rei [Examples of My Psychiatric Evaluations] (2014); Kiyoshi Oomagari, Ankoku to no Taiwa: Seishin Kantei Jirei Shuu [Conversations with Darkness: A Collection of Psychiatric Evaluations] (2019).
10. Hans Binder, Über Alkoholische Rauschzustände [On the Condition of Alcoholic Intoxication], Scheiz Archiv fur Neurologie, Neurochirurgie und Psychiatrie 25: 209–28, 36: 17–51 (1935).
11. See, e.g., Jinsuke Kageyama, Arukooru Hanzai Kenkyuu [A Study of Alcohol and Crime] 140–54 (1992).
12. See, e.g., Osaka High Court, 5(5) Keiji Saiban Geppou 899, May 9, 1973 (earliest high court case in database); Fukui District Court, 691 Hanrei Jihou 102, Nov. 30, 1972 (earliest district court case in database).
13. Tokyo District Court, 560 Hanrei Times 255, Apr. 24, 1985; see also, e.g., Takashi Hara, Arukooru Seishin Shougai [Alcohol Psychiatric Failures] in Masaaki Matsushita ed., 2 Keiji Jiken to Seishin Kantei [Criminal Incidents and Psychiatric Evaluations, Vol. 2] 159–66 (2006) (comparing Binder with other measures).
14. Tokyo District Court, 560 Hanrei Times 255 (Apr. 24, 1985).
15. See, e.g., Keiji Tanaka, Meitei to Keiji Sekinin [Intoxication and Criminal Responsibility] 60 (1985).
16. Kanazawa District Court, Heisei 27 (wa) 18, Nov. 27, 2015.
17. Kobe District Court, 2259 Hanrei Jihou 48, Aug. 20, 2014, *aff'd*, Osaka High Court, 2014 (ne) 2565, Feb. 27, 2015.
18. Tokyo High Court, 2013 (u) 78, Mar. 28, 2013.
19. In each drinking test case, the evaluator determines a Binder category at the time of the drinking test and attempts to extrapolate from that evidence the Binder category that the defendant experienced at the time of the crime. Evaluations can be mixed: For an example of a defendant who was found to have been "simply" intoxicated at the time of the crime although his intoxication at his evaluation was "complex," see Osamu Nakata, Waga Seishin Kantei Rei [Examples of My Psychiatric Evaluations] 342–49 (2014). One study finds that the two measures—experimental Binder and extrapolated Binder—correlate in 80 percent of free drinking tests; in other words, in 20 percent of the cases psychiatrists are not able to accurately extrapolate the defendant's drinking category at the time of the crime from the experimental data. Isamu Aoki and Masahi Nasu, Inshu Shiken [Drinking Tests], in Youko Shibata and Naokata Arai eds., Meitei Hanzai no Seishin Kantei [Psychiatric Evaluations for Intoxication-Related Crimes] 237, 251 (1985).
20. Jinsuke Kageyama, Inshuu Oyobi Yakuzai ni yoru Hanzai no Seishin Kantei [Psychiatric Evaluation of Crimes Committed While Intoxicated or under the Influence of Drugs], 125(9) Nihon Ishikai Zasshi [Journal of the Japan Medical Association] 1421 (2001); Takashi Hara, Arukooru Kanren Shougai [Alcohol-Related Failures] in Yoshito Igarashi ed., Keiji Seishin Kantei no Subete [A Compendium of Criminal Psychiatric Evaluations] 113–24 (2008).
21. One study by two psychiatrists examined thirty-five of their own cases to describe the use of free-drinking tests to determine intoxication levels. In the thirteen cases in which the defendant's intoxication was diagnosed as simple, six drank sake, one drank beer, one drank whisky, and five drank a combination of two of the three. In the sixteen cases of complex intoxication, five drank sake, one drank beer, one drank whisky, one drank shochu, six drank more than two kinds of alcohol, and two drank more than three kinds. In the seven cases of pathological intoxication, two drank whisky, three drank more than two kinds of alcohol, and one drank more than three kinds of alcohol. Most of the crimes, they concluded, are conducted by people who simply had too much to drink, regardless of the type of alcohol consumed. Isamu Aoki and Masahi Nasu, Inshu Shiken [Drinking Tests], in Youko Shibata and Naokata Arai eds., Meitei Hanzai no Seishin Kantei [Psychiatric Evaluations for Intoxication-Related Crimes] 237, 250 (1985).
22. Shibata Youko writes that she conducted fifty-three drinking tests over a fourteen-year period for court cases. Of these, the results of twenty-one tests were simple, twenty-three were complex, and nine were pathological. Roughly 90 percent of the evaluations were conducted for cases of murder or other violent crimes. Youko Shibata, Gaisetsu [Outline], in Youko

Shibata and Naokata Arai eds., Meitei Hanzai no Seishin Kantei [Psychiatric Evaluations for Intoxication-Related Crimes] 13 (1985).

23. See Ministry of Health, Labor, and Welfare, Arukooru Meitei [Alcohol Intoxication], available at https://www.e-healthnet.mhlw.go.jp/information/dictionary/alcohol/ya-020.html.
24. Kazuya Kondou, Meitei Bunseki to Sekinin Nouryoku [Intoxication Analysis and Capacity], 19(2) Teikyou Hougaku [Teikyou Law Review] 241, 246 (Jan. 1994).
25. Kazuya Kondou, Meitei Bunseki to Sekinin Nouryoku [Intoxication Analysis and Capacity], 19(2) Teikyou Hougaku [Teikyou Law Review] 241, 247–49 (Jan. 1994).
26. See, e.g., Akihiro Shiina, Mihisa Fujisaki, and Masaomi Iyo, Beyond Binder: Determination of Criminal Responsibility While in a State of Drunkenness by Japanese Courts, S11 Journal of Forensic Research 5 (2013).
27. Jinsuke Kageyama, Arukooru Hanzai Kenkyuu [A Study of Alcohol and Crime] 221–36 (1992).
28. Jinsuke Kageyama, Arukooru Hanzai Kenkyuu [A Study of Alcohol and Crime] 236–51 (1992). For similar examples, see, e.g., Akira Nishiyama, Keiji Seishin Kantei no Jissai [The Practice of Criminal Psychiatric Evaluations] 81–110 (2004); Takashi Hara, Arukooru Kanren Shougai [Alcohol-Related Failures] in Yoshito Igarashi ed., Keiji Seishin Kantei no Subete [A Compendium of Criminal Psychiatric Evaluations] 113–24 (2008).
29. Masashi Nasu, Satsujin, Satsujin Misui Jiken Hikoko S.T. [The Murder and Attempted Murder Case of S.T.] in Youko Shibata and Naokata Arai eds., Meitei Hanzai no Seishin Kantei [Psychiatric Evaluations for Intoxication-Related Crimes] 126–39 (1985).
30. Fukuoka District Court, 277 Hanrei Times 372 (Feb. 16, 1972).
31. Sapporo High Court, Heisei 18 (u) 34, May 30, 2006.
32. Osaka District Court, Heisei 17 (wa) 3529, Mar. 24, 2008.
33. See, e.g., Akira Fukushima, Seishin Kantei [Psychiatric Evaluations] 64 (1985); Kazuya Kondou, Meitei Bunseki to Sekinin Nouryoku [Intoxication Analysis and Capacity], 19(2) Teikyou Hougaku [Teikyo Law Review] 241, 247 (Jan. 1994).
34. Ministry of Justice, Saiban'in Seido ni Kansuru Kentoukai (Dai 7kai) Gijiroku, [Records of the Seventh Meeting of the Investigative Committee on the Lay Judge System] 15–6 (2011), available at http://www.moj.go.jp/content/000082680.pdf.
35. Prosecutors make independent decisions as to whether a defendant's claim of lack of capacity will hold up in court if they decide to prosecute. Nationwide, prosecutors request approximately two thousand psychiatric evaluations per year. Psychiatrists have three basic options for concluding those evaluations: full capacity, limited capacity, and no capacity. In roughly half of the cases that psychiatrists reviewed, they found that the suspect had full capacity. The other half were roughly split between limited and no capacity. In roughly three-quarters of cases in which psychiatrists found full capacity, prosecutors went to court. Toyoaki Hirata, Kisomae Kan'i Kantei no Genjou to Mondaiten [Problems and the Current State of Pre-Indictment Summary Evaluations], in Masaaki Matsushita ed., Shihou Seishin Igaku 5—Shihou Seishin Iryou [Forensic Psychiatry 5: Forensic Psychiatric Services] 11 (2006); see also Youji Nakatani, Sekinin Nouryoku no Genzai [The Current State of Mental Capacity] 75 (2006).
36. Keiji Tanaka, Meitei to Keiji Sekinin [Intoxication and Criminal Responsibility] 72–3 (1985); see also Keiji Tanaka and Tetsuo Jou, Iwayuru Ijou Meitei to Keiji Sekinin Nouryoku ["Abnormal" Intoxication and Criminal Liability], Kagoshima Daigaku Hougaku Ronshuu [Kagoshima University Law Review] 11(2), 103 (1976) and 12(2), 39 (1977) (listing similar and additional factors).
37. Chiba District Court, 9(6) Kakeishuu 825, June 1, 1967.
38. Fukuoka High Court, Heisei 22 (u) 258, Sept. 7, 2011.
39. See, e.g., Hikoku Sekken Eizou, Houteinai de Jouei: Toukyou Chisai no Saiban'in Saiban [Defendant Interview Video Screened in Tokyo District Court Lay Judge Trial], Nihon Keizai Shinbun, Sept. 29, 2010, available at https://www.nikkei.com/article/DGXNASDG2805N_Z20C10A9CC0000/.
40. Tokyo District Court, Heisei 21 (wa) 437, Oct. 5, 2010.
41. See Chichi no Kousai Aite Shisatsu no Otoko Shichinen [Seven Years' Imprisonment for Man Who Murdered Father's Girlfriend], Yomiuri Shinbun, Oct. 6, 2010, available at https://blog.goo.ne.jp/lqawxdg/e/5afbae58e3413c6743a7a34197b86419.

42. Gifu District Court, 8(9) Kakeishuu 1273, Sept. 21, 1966.
43. Shizuoka District Court, 1125 Hanrei Jihou 169, Oct. 27, 1980.
44. Tokyo High Court, 1125 Hanrei Jihou 166, Jan. 25, 1984.
45. Fukuoka District Court, 1544 Hanrei Jihou 132, May 19, 1995.
46. Fukuoka High Court, 998 Hanrei Times 267, Sept. 9, 1998.
47. See J. Mark Ramseyer and Eric B. Rasmusen, Outcaste Politics and Organized Crime in Japan: The Effect of Terminating Ethnic Subsidies, 15(1) Journal of Empirical Legal Studies 192 (2018).
48. Because the court has provided such detail, here is the song, for the curious: Kishidan, Kenka Joutou, YouTube video, https://www.youtube.com/watch?v=wWpDMCOGLIY.
49. Kanazawa District Court, Heisei 27 (wa) 18, Nov. 27, 2015.

Chapter 4

1. Supreme Court, 219 Hanrei Times 136, Feb. 27, 1968 (intoxication not a defense if defendants know they are driving drunk); see also Supreme Court, 272 Hanrei Times 298, Dec. 23, 1971 (defendants must know that they are driving drunk); Tokyo District Court, Heisei 27 (wa) 88, July 10, 2013 (defendant lacked capacity when she hit and killed sixty-five-year-old driver while under the influence of a combination of prescription drugs and alcohol consumed at a host club).
2. A standard shot in the U.S. is 1.5 ounces. A standard shot in the U.K. varies in part depending on the type of drink but tends to be about 1 ounce. See, e.g., How Many Ounces in a Shot Glass, Beverage Society, available at https://beveragesociety.com/how-many-ounces-in-a-shot-glass/.
3. Tokyo District Court, 1718 Hanrei Jihou 176, June 8, 2000.
4. Tokyo High Court, 1064 Hanrei Times 218, Jan. 12, 2001.
5. Tokyo District Court, 1135 Hanrei Times 184, July 24, 2003.
6. Douro Koutsuu Hou Shikourei [Road Traffic Law Enforcement Order], Law no. 270 of 1960, art. 44(3). Higher penalties attach at the 0.25 (breath) and 0.50 (blood) levels, in the form of increased points on a license; see chart 2. First-time offenders usually receive a summary trial, a fine, and license suspension. A person who refuses a breathalyzer test may be fined $500 (art. 120(1)), a provision that Japan's Supreme Court has held does not violate the Constitution's confrontation clause. Supreme Court, 931 Hanrei Times 131, Jan. 30, 1997.
7. California Vehicle Code Section 23142(b).
8. Blood alcohol levels and breath alcohol levels do not necessarily correlate precisely for every individual; see Alan Wayne Jones, The Relationship between Blood Alcohol Concentration (BAC) and Breath Alcohol Concentration (BrAC): A Review of the Evidence, Department for Transport Road Safety Web Publication No. 15 (June 2010), available at http://assets.dft.gov.uk/publications/research-and-statistical-reports/report15.pdf. The Japanese statute bases its BrAC to BAC formula of 2000:1 (0.15/1000 x 2000 = 0.30), while the state of Michigan, which provides both BrAC and BAC levels (as well as urine), uses a formula of 2100:1 (0.08 grams per 100 milliliters of blood or per 210 liters of breath); see Michigan Vehicle Code Section 257.625 (1)(b).
9. California Vehicle Code Section 23142(a).
10. Miyazaki District Court, 1300 Hanrei Jihou 157, Dec. 8, 1988.
11. Kagoshima District Court, 726 Hanrei Times 244, Jan. 26, 1990.
12. Tokyo High Court, 1106 Hanrei Jihou 161, June 1, 1983.
13. See, e.g., Fukuoka High Court, Shouwa 58 (u) 44, June 11, 1986. Relatively few of the cases concern the standard challenges to methodology that are the mainstay of U.S. drunk driving defense. See, e.g., Lawrence Taylor and Steven Oberman, Drunk Driving Defense 315–948 (8th ed. 2016) (more than six hundred pages, or about a third of the book, devoted to field evidence and blood, urine, and breath analysis). And yet there are at least two cases of police forging evidence in drunk driving cases. See Nagano District Court, Heisei 26 (wa) 196, Dec. 9, 2014 (after breathalyzer tube cracked after positive results, officers pretended it didn't and attempted to forge evidence to obtain conviction); Osaka District Court, Heisei 24 (wa) 1431, Jan. 23, 2013 (recording false breathalyzer results).

14. See, e.g., Naikakufuu Saisaku Toukatsukan, Joushuu Inshu Untensha no Inshu Unten Koudou Yokushi ni Kansuru Chousa Kenkyuu [Investigative Research regarding the Deterrence of Drunk Driving Behavior by Habitual Drunk Drivers] 20 (2010), available at http://www8.cao.go.jp/koutu/chou-ken/h21/houkoku.html. Technically a person can be charged with DWI (but not driving DUI, due to a statutory exception) even if the vehicle being driven is a bicycle, but enforcement is rare. Bicycles are "light vehicles" under the Road Traffic Law, art. 2(11), but are excused from driving under the influence charges by article 117-4(3).
15. U.S. Department of Justice, Federal Bureau of Investigation, Crime in the United States, Table 29, available at http://www.fbi.gov/about-us/cjis/ucr/crime-in-the-u.s/2010/crime-in-the-u.s.-2010/tables/10tbl29.xls.
16. Keisatsuchou Koutsuukyoku, Heisei 30nen no Koutsuu Jiko no Hassei Joukyou [2018 Automobile Accidents] 21 (2019), available at https://www.e-stat.go.jp/stat-search/files?page=1&layout=datalist&lid=000001227249.
17. Inshu Unten, Shibouritsu wa Ta Jiko no 8-bai [Drunk Driving Mortality Rate Eight Times That of Other Accidents], Nihon Keizai Shinbun, Feb. 23, 2017, available at http://www.nikkei.com/article/DGXLASDG22HAK_T20C17A2CR0000/.
18. National Highway Traffic Safety Administration, Alcohol-Impaired Driving, DOT HS 812 630 (2018), available at https://crashstats.nhtsa.dot.gov/Api/Public/ViewPublication/812630.
19. On Japan, see, e.g., "Aori Unten" Shakan Kyori Ihan 1.8 Bai ["Road Rage" Caught: Tailgating Violations Increase 180 percent], Asahi Shinbun, May 23, 2019, at 1, also available at https://www.asahi.com/articles/DA3S14025808.html. On the U.S., see National Highway Traffic Safety Administration, Aggressive Driving, available at https://one.nhtsa.gov/people/injury/research/aggdrivingenf/pages/Introduction.html.
20. The United States has 214 million drivers and 252 million vehicles; seeFederal Highway Administration, Highway Statistics 2014, Licensed Drivers, Vehicle Registrations, and Resident Population, available at https://www.fhwa.dot.gov/policyinformation/statistics/2014/dv1c.cfm. Japan has 82 million licensed drivers, according to Keisatsuchou Koutsuukyoku Unten Menkyoka, Unten Menkyo Toukei Heisei 28nenban [2016 Statistics on Licensed Drivers] (2017), available at https://www.npa.go.jp/toukei/menkyo/pdf/h28_main.pdf, and 81 million cars, according to Jidousha Kensa Touroku Jouhou Kyoukai, Jidoousha Hoyuu Daisuu [Number of Vehicles] (2017), available at https://www.airia.or.jp/publish/statistics/ub83el00000000wo-att/01.pdf.
21. The U.S. Department of Transportation Federal Highway Administration, Annual Automobile Vehicle Miles of Travel (VMT) per Capita and Number of Automobiles Per Capita 1997, available at https://www.fhwa.dot.gov/ohim/onh00/bar4.htm, reports that U.S. vehicles travel five times the number of miles annually as Japanese vehicles and that per capita miles differ by a factor of roughly 2.5; see Our Nation's Highways 8 (2000), available at https://www.fhwa.dot.gov/ohim/onh00/our_ntns_hwys.pdf. The same authority states that Americans drive an average of 13,476 miles per driver annually (Average Annual Miles per Driver by Age Group, available at https://www.fhwa.dot.gov/ohim/onh00/bar8.htm), while Japanese government data show that the average noncommercial driver drives 6,571 miles (10,575 kilometers) (Kokudou Koutsushou Jidousha Koutsukyoku, Heisei 15 Nendo Jidousha no Kensa, Tenken Seibi ni Kansuru Kiso Chousa Kentou Kekka Houkokusho [2004 Basic Investigative Report on Automobile Inspection and Maintenance] (2005), available at http://www.mlit.go.jp/jidosha/iinkai/seibi/6houkokusyo.pdf), and private Japanese survey data similarly cluster around 10,000 kilometers annually (6,214 miles) (Kuniaki Yabe et al., Ankeeto Kekka ni Motozuku Hi Soukou Kyori Bunpu to PHEV no CO2 Sakugen Kouka [The Distribution of Daily Drive Length and CO2 Reduction Effect by PHEVs], 32 (4) Journal the Japan Society of Energy and Resources 18 (2011), available at http://www.jser.gr.jp/journal/journal_pdf/2011/journal201107_3.pdf).
22. Koutsuu Jiko Sougou Bunseki Sentaa, Heisei 28nenban Koutsuu Jiko Toukei Nenpou [2016 Automobile Accident Statistical Annual] 316 (2017).
23. See Sannomiya Eki de Densha no Doa ni Shgamitsuku Jiken: "Shuuden ni Noritakatta" [Incident of Gripping the Train Door at Sannomiya Station: "I Wanted to Ride the Last Train"], Breaking News Japan, Apr. 3, 2018, available at https://breaking-news.jp/2018/04/03/039230.

24. Traditionally the profession was unregulated, and it was often run by specialty companies, not taxi companies, often with funds from organized crime firms. But along with the new rules on drunk driving that followed the Inoue crash came a new law that regulated the business, requiring licensing of such services at the local level and effectively removing organized crime firms from the industry. Jidousha Unten Daikougyou no Gyoumu no Tekiseika ni Kansuru Houritsu [Law to Optimize the Driving Agent Business], Law no. 57 of 2001.
25. Osaka District Court, 992 Roudou Hanrei 23, July 1, 2009.
26. Sendai High Court, Heisei 20 (u) 192, Feb. 24, 2009.
27. Sendai District Court, Heisei 20 (wa) 268, Nov. 29, 2008.
28. Saitama District Court, Heisei 20 (wa) 347, June 5, 2008.
29. Sendai District Court, Heisei 17 (wa) 362, Jan. 23, 2006.
30. The courts have a hindsight bias here; they know how the evening ends. See Chris Guthrie, Jeffrey J. Rachlinski, and Andrew Wistrich, Inside the Judicial Mind, 86 Cornell Law Review 777, 799–805 (2001) (empirical study finding susceptibility of judges to hindsight comparable to that of other decision-makers).
31. Yoneatsu Osaki et al., Waga Kuni no Seijin Inshu Koudou oyobi Arukoorushou ni Kansuru Zenkoku Chousa [National Study of Alcoholism and Drinking among Japanese Adults, 40(5) Nihon Arukooru Yakubutsu Igakkai Zasshi [Japanese Journal of Alcohol Studies and Drug Dependence] 455, 458 (2005).
32. See Isao Shimizu and Toshio Kusaka, Shin Koutsuu Jiko Sousa no Kiso to Youten [Automobile Accident Investigation] 114 (2012). A dated but representative example appears as an attachment to Supreme Court, 277 Hanrei Times 129 (June 2, 1972). The same case held that the intoxication card does not violate the confrontation clause of Japan's Constitution.
33. Shigehiro Tomimatsu, Shin Jidousha Jiko Kyoujutsu Chousho Kisai Youkou [New Edition: Guidelines for Taking Automobile Accident Affidavits] 238 (2010).
34. Shouichi Kimura, Shin Koutsuu Jiken Kyoujutsu Chousho [New Edition: Auto Accident Affidavits and Investigations] 186 (4th ed. 2016).
35. Shouichi Kimura, Shin Koutsuu Jiken Kyoujutsu Chousho [New Edition: Auto Accident Affidavits and Investigations] 188 (4th ed. 2016).
36. Isao Shimizu and Toshio Kusaka, Shin Koutsuu Jiko Sousa no Kiso to Youten [Automobile Accident Investigation] 114 (2012).
37. Supreme Court, 272 Hanrei Times 298, Dec. 23, 1971.
38. See Mitsuo Okano, Koutsuu Jihan to Keiji Sekinin [Criminal Liability and Traffic Crimes] 37 (2007)
39. Isao Shimizu and Toshio Kusaka, Shin Koutsuu Jiko Sousa no Kiso to Youten [Automobile Accident Investigation] 121 (2012).
40. Koutsu Jiko Sougou Bunseki Sentaa, Heisei 28nen Koutsu Toukei [2016 Transportation Statistics] 60 (2017).
41. See Lisa Katayama, 2-Channel Gives Japan's Famously Quiet People a Mighty Voice, Wired, Apr. 19, 2007, available at https://www.wired.com/2007/04/2-channel-gives-japans-famously-quiet-people-a-mighty-voice/.
42. Kobe District Court, Heisei 29 (gyou u) 36, Mar. 27, 2018.
43. See, e.g., Tokyo District Court, Heisei 24 (wa) 6704, Mar. 11, 2016 (three-stop pub crawl leads to sexual assault by superior); Fukuoka High Court, Heisei 25 (u) 122, June 26, 2015 (seven-stop pub crawl leads to drunk driving with eight-month prison sentence).
44. In 2013 the provision was removed from the Penal Code and placed into a stand-alone statute regarding all acts of injury or death caused by a vehicle (including negligent driving, driving while ill, driving without a license, driving through a red light, and so on). Penalties were set at imprisonment of not more than twelve years for injury and not more than fifteen years for death. Jidousha no Unten ni yori Hito o Shishou saseru Koui tou no Shobatsu ni kansuru Houritsu [Act on Punishment of Acts Inflicting Injury or Death by Driving a Vehicle], Law no. 86 of 2013. The crime remains dangerous driving causing death or injury, but the language differs slightly: "A person who drives a vehicle in a state in which the person is likely to be unable to drive safely under the influence of alcohol or drugs, and thereby comes to have difficulty in driving safely under the influence of such alcohol or drugs [shall be punished upon injury or death]" (art. 3(1)). The Japanese Federation of Bar Associations opposed the legislation, citing

difficulties in interpretation, the lack of need for a new provision, and the potential for discrimination against people with illnesses such as epilepsy, who were prohibited from driving until 2002. See Nihon Bengoshi Rengoukai [Japan Federation of Bar Associations], "Jidousha no Unten ni yori Hito o Shishou saseru Koui tou no Shobatsu ni kansuru Houritsu An" ni Kansuru Ikensho [Opinion regarding "Plan for Act on Punishment of Acts Inflicting Injury or Death by Driving a Vehicle"], May 9, 2013, available at https://www.nichibenren.or.jp/library/ja/opinion/report/data/2013/opinion_130509_2.pdf. Courts in fact subsequently found liability under the statute for drivers with epilepsy (Tokyo High Court, 2391 Hanrei Jihou 56, Feb. 22, 2018; Kobe District Court, 2372 Hanrei Jihou 137, Mar. 29, 2017) as well as diabetes (Osaka High Court, 2365 Hanrei Jihou 102, Mar. 16. 2017).

45. Some U.S. states are considerably harsher, notably California, where prosecutors can charge not only vehicular manslaughter but second-degree "Watson Murder" if a drunk driver kills a person under certain circumstances. See People v. Watson, 30 Cal. 3d 290 (1981); see also Mark S. Levin, People v. Watson: Drunk Driving Homicide-Murder or Enhanced Manslaughter?, 71 California Law Review 1298 (1983).
46. See, e.g., People v. Schaefer, 473 Mich. 418, 703 NW2d 774 (2005); Daniel J. Levin and Travis M. Reeds eds., Michigan Drunk Driving Law and Practice 98–99 (5th ed. 2016). The lack of a causation requirement does not violate due process. See, e.g., Baker v. State, 377 So. 2d 17 (Fla. 1979).
47. See, e.g., Emma E. Cook, Reconstructing Adult Masculinities: Part-time Work in Contemporary Japan 35 (2016).
48. Tokyo District Court, 2014 (wa) 13397, June 2, 2016.
49. See, e.g., Hiroshima High Court, Heisei 19 (u) 236, May 27, 2008.
50. Kouji Kawamoto, Watashi wa Inshu Unten de Keimusho ni Hairimashita [I Went to Prison for Drunk Driving] 15–6 (2009).
51. Fukuoka District Court, 1268 Hanrei Times 330, Jan. 8, 2008.
52. Fukuoka High Court, 1323 Hanrei Times 65, May 15, 2009.
53. See J. Mark Ramseyer, Predicting Court Outcomes through Political Preferences: The Japanese Supreme Court and the Chaos of 1993, 58 Duke Law Journal 1557, 1578 (2009).
54. See, e.g., Mutsuo Tahara et al., eds., Shin Chuushaku Minji Saiseihou [New Annotated Civil Rehabilitation Law] (2006).
55. Supreme Court, 2152 Hanrei Jihou 15, Oct. 31, 2011.
56. Mutsuo Tahara, Kobetsu Iken ga Katarumono [Commentary on Opinions] 402–3 (2014).
57. Takeyoshi Imai, Inshu Unten Taisaku Rippou no Igi to Kadai [The Significance and Problems of the Drunk Driving Legislation], 1342 Jurisuto [The Jurist] 128 (2007); Shigetomi Higaki, Douro Koutsuu Hou no Ichibu o Kaisei Suru Houritsu (Heisei 19nen Houritsu Dai 90gou) ni Tsuite [Regarding the Law to Revise the Road Traffic Law (Law no. 90 of 2007)], 1342 Jurisuto [The Jurist] 141 (2007).
58. See, e.g., Yamasaki Hirotarou Fukuoka Shichou "Inshu Unten wa Sodachi ni Choukai Menshoku" to no Houshin o Shimesu [Fukuoka Mayor Yamasaki Hirotarou Reveals Plans for "Quick Disciplinary Dismissal for Drunk Driving"], Jiji Press, Aug. 29, 2006, available at http://headlines.yahoo.co.jp/hl?a=20060828-00000162-jij-soci.
59. One study finds that the impact of lowering the alcohol limit from 0.05 to 0.03 following the Inoue crash resulted in a 64 percent reduction in alcohol-related crashes for teenagers, a 50 percent reduction for male adults, and a 52 percent reduction for female adults. E. Desapriya et al., Impact of Lowering the Legal Blood Alcohol Concentration Limit to 0.03 on Male, Female and Teenage Drivers Involved in Alcohol-Related Crashes in Japan, 14(3) International Journal of Injury Control and Safety Promotion 181 (2007). The reductions occurred even as the overall accident rate remained constant. But studies from 2011 and 2013 find that the decrease in drunk driving was the result of media coverage and publicity campaigns surrounding the 1999 (Inoue) and 2006 (Imabayashi) cases, not increased penalties or enforcement. Shinji Nakahara, Kota Katanoda and Masao Ichikawa, Onset of a Declining Trend in Fatal Motor Vehicle Crashes Involving Drunk-Driving in Japan, 23(3) Journal of Epidemiology 195 (2013); Shinji Nakahara and Masao Ichikawa, Effects of High-Profile Collisions on Drunk-Driving Penalties and Alcohol-Related Crashes in Japan, 17 Injury Prevention 182 (2011).

60. Sendai District Court, Heisei 17 (wa) 362, Jan. 23, 2006.
61. Sendai District Court, Heisei 19 (wa) 234, Oct. 31, 2007.
62. Tokyo District Court Hachiouji Branch, 1164 Hanrei Times 188, May 8, 2003.
63. Tokyo District Court Hachiouji Branch, 1118 Hanrei Times 299, Oct. 29, 2002.
64. Yamagata District Court, 1241 Hanrei Times 152, Nov. 24, 2006.
65. Osaka District Court, 1059 Hanrei Times 165, Nov. 21, 2000.
66. Tsu District Court, Heisei 16 (wa) 393, Oct. 3, 2006.
67. Saitama District Court, Heisei 21 (wa) 1465, Feb. 14, 2011.
68. Donald Richie, The Japan Journals 1947–2004 279 (2004).
69. Saitama District Court, Heisei 21 (wa) 1465, Feb. 14, 2010, *aff'd*, Tokyo High Court, 23 (u) 521, Nov. 17, 2011, *aff'd*, Supreme Court, 1394 Hanrei Times 139, Apr. 15, 2013. They lost a civil suit on similar grounds. Tokyo District Court, Heisei 23 (wa) 4829, Mar. 27, 2012.
70. Sapporo High Court, 2006 (ne) 209, Jan. 26, 2007.
71. Kyoto District Court, Heisei 26 (gyou u) 36, Apr. 14, 2016.

Chapter 5

1. Joseph Sanders et al., Distributing Responsibility for Wrongdoing inside Corporate Hierarchies: Public Judgments in Three Societies, 21(4) Law & Social Inquiry 815 (1996).
2. V. Lee Hamilton and Joseph Sanders, Everyday Justice: Responsibility and the Individual in Japan and the United States 181 (1992).
3. Richard E. Nisbett, The Geography of Thought: How Asians and Westerners Think Differently … and Why 114 (2003).
4. See, e.g., Jones v. U.S., 308 F.2d 307 (D.C. Cir. 1962).
5. Supreme Court, 229 Hanrei Times 252, Nov. 7, 1968.
6. Yokohama District Court, 284 Hanrei Jihou 31, Nov. 27, 1961.
7. Supreme Court, 229 Hanrei Times 252, Nov. 7, 1968. The opinion contains only a statement of law. The facts of the case, as well as the defendant's brief, come from Preface note to Supreme Court, 541 Hanrei Jihou 83, Nov. 7, 1968. See also Nagoya District Court, 332 Hanrei Jihou 5, May 29, 1961 (similar case of stripping a drunk person resulting in death and guilty verdict).
8. Tokyo High Court, 617 Hanrei Times 172, Dec. 10, 1985.
9. Tokyo High Court, Heisei 22 (u) 2053, Apr. 18, 2011.
10. See Taniguchi Kouichi, Sunakku to Sou De Nai Mono [Snacks and Non-Snacks], Nippon.com, July 5, 2018, available at https://www.nippon.com/ja/column/g00556/.
11. Houen ga Danzai Shita Gaaruzu Baa "Dorinku Bakku" Shisutemu no "Aku": Joshi Kousei wa Naze Shinda no ka? [The "Evil" behind the Court-Convicted Girls Bar's Drink Back System: Why Did a High School Girl Die?], Sankei West, Aug. 10, 2013, available at http://www.sankei.com/west/news/130810/wst1308100072-n1.html.
12. Osaka District Court, Heisei 24 (wa) 1748, July 31, 2013.
13. John Owen Haley, Authority without Power: Law and the Japanese Paradox 129 (1991) ("by almost any standard, criminal justice in Japan is extraordinarily lenient").
14. Daniel H. Foote, The Benevolent Paternalism of Japanese Justice, 80 California Law Review 317, 318 (1992).
15. Osaka District Court, Heisei 31 (wa) 7371, Feb. 26, 2019.
16. See, e.g., 21sai Hosuto "Kongetsu wa Shinu Ki de!" Teki-ra Ikkinomi de Shibou [21-Year Old Host Dies after Chug Drinking, with Notes That Say "This Month It's All Out to the Death!," Sankei West, Oct. 6, 2015, available at https://www.sankei.com/west/news/151006/wst1510060005-n1.html.
17. See Hosuto Ikki Nomi Shibou wa Rousai [Host Club Chug Drinking Death Covered by Workers' Compensation], May 29, 2019, available at https://www.nikkei.com/article/DGXMZO45419380Z20C19A5AC8Z00/.
18. See, e.g., Osaka District Court, Heisei 29 (gyou u) 1, Sept. 30, 2018; Osaka District Court, Heisei 25 (gyou u) 39, May 30, 2016.
19. Ikki Nomi Shibou, Ryoushin ga Teiso [Parents Sue after Chugging Death], Nihon Keizai Shinbun, July 23, 2015, available at http://www.nikkei.com/article/DGXLZO89628810-T20C15A7CC1000/.

20. See, e.g., Ikkinomi Shibou, Ryoushin ga Teiso: Toudaisei Saakuru no 21nin o [Parents Sue 21 Tokyo University Club Students over Chug Drinking Death], Nihon Keizai Shinbun, July 23, 2015, available at https://www.nikkei.com/article/DGXLZO89628810T20C15A7CC1000/.
21. Saitama District Court, Heisei 28 (wa) 1756, Oct. 26, 2017; Tokyo District Court, 1791 Hanrei Jihou 152, Mar. 27, 2002; Tokyo District Court, 1562 Hanrei Jihou 141, Dec. 16, 1994.
22. Tokyo District Court, Shouwa 51 (wa) 10399, Mar. 25, 1980.
23. See, e.g., Ikkinomishi Izoku ga Kindaisei o Kokuso "Kaihouyakura 119ban sezu" [Chug Drinking Death at Kinki University Results in Suit by Family: "Caregivers Failed to Call Emergency Number"], Mainichi Shinbun, Feb. 4, 2019, available at https://mainichi.jp/articles/20190203/k00/00m/040/192000c; Ikkinomi Joutaika 3nenmae ni mo Hoka no Gakusei ga Kyuukyuu Hansou Kindaisei Inshu Shibou [Kinki University Drinking Death: The Habitualization of Chug Drinking, Three Years Prior Another Student Rushed to Aid], Mainichi Shinbun, Feb. 7, 2019, available at https://mainichi.jp/articles/20190207/k00/00m/040/258000c.
24. Brent McDonald and Kate Sylvester, Learning to Get Drunk: The Importance of Drinking in Japanese University Sports Clubs, 49(3/4) International Review of the Sociology of Sport 331 (2014).
25. Miyazaki District Court, 578 Hanrei Times 88, Oct. 30, 1985.
26. See, e.g., Kumamoto Daigaku Igakubu Kousai Gyakuten Shouso Made no Ikisatsu [History of Kumamoto University School of Medicine Case until High Court Reversal], Asuku, available at https://www.ask.or.jp/article/alcohol.
27. See Ishi wa Dono Kurai Osake o Nomuno? Ishi 4000nin ni Kiita Inshu no Hindo ni Tsuite [How Much Do Doctors Drink? A Survey of 4,000 Doctors regarding Drinking Patterns], Medudent, Feb. 27, 2017, available at https://ishicome.medpeer.jp/entry/859 (reporting results of 2014 survey).
28. See, e.g., Igakubu no Nomikai wa Tanoshii? [Are Medical Department Drinking Parties Fun?], Igakusei no Kaishaku (popular blog for aspiring medical students), Dec. 15, 2018, available at https://www.medudent.com/entry/med-alcohol.
29. Fukuoka High Court, 1254 Hanrei Times 203, Nov. 14, 2006.
30. See, e.g., Tokyo District Court, Heisei 23 (gou) 293, Feb. 1, 2013 (judo instructor convicted of sexual assault after "ikki" games at barbecue restaurant with students).
31. Kofu District Court, 2123 Hanrei Jihou 108, June 30, 2011.
32. Masami Ito, The Scourge of Binge Drinking on Youth, Japan Times, Apr. 2, 2016, available at http://www.japantimes.co.jp/life/2016/04/02/lifestyle/scourge-binge-drinking-youth/#.WYe2OK2ZPUJ (quoting Susumu Asano).
33. Osaka District Court, Heisei 17 (wa) 9954, July 27, 2007.
34. See, e.g., Shakotobashi to wa [What Is Storage Skipping?], MOTA [Motor: Move On, Travel Around], May 18, 2018, available at https://autoc-one.jp/knowhow/5002074/.
35. Douro Koutsuu Jitsumu Kenkyuukai, Jimu Shiryou Douro Koutsuuhou Kaisetsu [Commentary on the Road Traffic Law] 682 (12th ed. 2002).
36. Osaka District Court, 1321 Hanrei Times 188, May 18, 2009.
37. Matsuyama District Court, 1113 Hanrei Times 231, Oct. 29, 2001.
38. Tokyo District Court, Heisei 14 (wa) 19806, Feb. 25, 2003.
39. See Mark D. West, Law in Everyday Japan: Sex, Sumo, Suicide, and Statutes 215–66 (2005).
40. See, e.g., K. Annabelle Smith, Why Japan Is Obsessed with Kentucky Fried Chicken on Christmas, Smithsonian Magazine, Dec. 14, 2012, available at http://www.smithsonianmag.com/arts-culture/why-japan-is-obsessed-with-kentucky-fried-chicken-on-christmas-1-161666960/.
41. Kobe District Court, 1338 Hanrei Times 220, Sept. 14, 2010.
42. Osaka High Court, 2121 Hanrei Jihou 134, Feb. 23, 2011. Many cases of this sort are straightforward. See, e.g., Tokyo District Court, Heisei 27 (wa) 4469, Mar. 24, 2015 (seventy-year-old with history of alcoholism and cancer falls off a cliff behind a "Danger: Do Not Enter" sign; tests show blood alcohol levels consistent with drinking "seven to ten beers, seven *gou* to one *shou* of sake, or a bottle of whisky"; court finds for insurer).
43. Supreme Court, 1400 Hanrei Times 106, Apr. 16, 2013.

Chapter 6

1. Hiroshima High Court, Heisei 19 (u) 236, May 27, 2008.
2. Sapporo District Court, Heisei 28 (wa) 13, Sept. 28, 2016.
3. Yuji Shiroshita, Current Trends and Issues in Japanese Sentencing, 22(4) Federal Sentencing Reporter 243 (2010).
4. Daniel H. Foote, The Benevolent Paternalism of Japanese Justice, 80 California Law Review 317 (1992).
5. Supreme Court, 195 Hanrei Times 114, July 13, 1966.
6. Kunihiko Endou, Ryoukei Handan Katei no Souron Kentou (2) [A General Study of the Process of Criminal Sentencing], 1185 Hanrei Times 24, 36, Oct. 1, 2005.
7. See, e.g., David T. Johnson, The Japanese Way of Justice: Prosecuting Crime in Japan 241–42 (2002).
8. One Japanese judge finds the U.S. Sentencing Guidelines "unbelievable" in their removal of discretion from the judiciary. Kunihiko Endou, Ryoukei Handan Katei no Souron Kentou (4) [A General Study of the Process of Criminal Sentencing], 1187 Hanrei Times 36, 43, Nov. 1, 2005.
9. Kunio Harada, Ryoukei Handan no Jissai [The Practice of Sentencing in Japan] 3 (3rd ed. 2008).
10. Yuuichi Okada, Ryoukei—Saiban no Tachiba kara [Sentencing: A Judicial Perspective] in Makoto Mitsui et al. ed., 2 Shin Keiji Tetsuzuki [New Criminal Procedure] 481, 484 (2002).
11. Yuji Shiroshita, Current Trends and Issues in Japanese Sentencing, 2294 Federal Sentencing Reporter 243 (2010).
12. See, e.g., David T. Johnson, The Japanese Way of Justice: Prosecuting Crime in Japan 66 (2002); Jirou Nomura, Nihon no Saibankan [Japanese Judges] 37 (1994).
13. "Kei Omosugi" Chiken ga Irei no Kousou, Kousai ga Kei Karaku [In Rare Case, Prosecutors Say "Sentence Too Heavy"; High Court to Lower], Nihon Keizai Shinbun, Oct. 5, 2017, available at https://www.nikkei.com/article/DGXMZO21940880V01C17A0CC1000/.
14. See James Q. Whitman, Equality in Criminal Law: The Two Divergent Western Roads, 1(1) Journal of Legal Analysis 119, 144 (2009).
15. See, e.g., Akira Sugeno, Keiryou ni kansuru Shinri Tetsuzuki no Henka [Changes in Trial and Process Related to Sentencing], in Nihon Bengoshi Rengoukai Saibain'in Honbu [Japan Federation of Bar Associations Lay Judge Department] ed., Saiban'in Saiban to Ryoukei [Sentencing in Lay Judge Litigation] 8 (2012); Chikara Shinozuka, Touben mo Aichiken Bengoshikai no Ryoukei Deetabeesu e no Sannyuu o [Introducing the Tokyo and Aichi Prefectural Bar Associations' Sentencing Database], 10(6) Libra 26 (2010). One study shows considerable variation in sentencing decisions even among judges who sit on the same court, even with the database. See Kenji Takeuchi, Fukuoka no Deetabeesu ni Kizuku Ryoukei no Jitta Chousa [An Examination of the Fukuoka Sentencing Database], 30 Keiji Bengo [Criminal Defense] 31 (2002).
16. See, e.g., Ministry of Justice, Saiban'in Seido ni Kansuru Kentoukai Dai 11kai Haifu Shiryou 3: Saiban'in Saiban no Jisshi Joukyou ni Tsuite [Handout 3, Current Situation of Lay Judge Trials, 11th Meeting of Committee to Examine the Lay Judge System], July 13, 2012, available at http://www.moj.go.jp/keiji1/keiji08_00014.html.
17. See, e.g., Ministry of Justice, Saiban'in Seido ni Kansuru Kentoukai Dai 6kai Haifu Shiryou 4: Kyuukei Bunpu [Handout 4, Distribution of Prosecutor Requests, 6th Meeting of Committee to Examine the Lay Judge System], June 8, 2001, available at http://www.moj.go.jp/keiji1/keiji12_00035.html; see also Yuji Shiroshita, Current Trends and Issues in Japanese Sentencing, 2294 Federal Sentencing Reporter 243 (2010) (calculating a 79 percent ratio).
18. See, e.g., Saiban'in Seido 10nen [Ten Years of the Lay Judge System], Sankei News, May 15, 2019, available at https://www.sankei.com/affairs/news/190515/afr1905150016-n1.html.
19. Supreme Court, 1410 Hanrei Times 82 July 24, 2014. The decision was controversial, as it seemed to some to undermine the goals of having a citizen-led panel. See, e.g., Ippan Shimin ga "Keiryou" Kimeru "Saiban'in Saiban" ni Mondai Ari? [Is There a Problem with "Lay-Judge Trials" in Which Ordinary Citizens Decide Sentencing?], Bengoshi Dotto Komu News, Aug. 2, 2014, available at https://www.bengo4.com/saiban/1135/1269/n_1834/. See also Osaka

High Court, 2370 Hanrei Jihou 90, Mar. 9, 2017 (overturning lay-judge-panel death penalty sentence for homeless, unemployed defendant who had auditory hallucinations and who killed two strangers).

20. Housei Shingikai, Kaisei Keihou Souan, May 29, 1974. See Tadahiro Tanizawa, Sentencing Standards in Japan, UNAFEI Report for 1978 and Resource Material Series No. 16 (1979).
21. Supreme Court, 2(11) Keishuu 1275, Oct. 6, 1948.
22. Toshitarou Naka and Toshmaro Koujou, Ryoukei no Jisshouteki Kenkyuu [Research on Sentencing], 15(1) Shihou Kenkyuu Houkokusho [Judicial Research Report] (1965).
23. Kensuke Itou and Touru Kojima, Ryoukei to Sekinin: Yobou ni Kansuru Ankeeto [Survey regarding Prevention in Criminal Sentencing and Responsibility], 165 Housei Ronshuu [Journal of Law and Politics] 57 (1996).
24. See, e.g., Touru Kojima, Ryoukei no Suuryouteki Jisshou Kenkyuu no Kadai [Empirical Research and Issues on Sentencing], 174 Housei Ronshuu [Journal of Law and Politics] 1 (1998) 175 Housei Ronshuu [Journal of Law and Politics] 1 (1998), 176 Housei Ronshuu [Journal of Law and Politics] 1 (1998). The factors that prosecutors use to determine their requested sentences (the accompanying documents contain both negative and positive factors) are virtually identical. Norio Munakata, Kensatsukan kara Mita Joujou to Ryoukei [A Prosecutor's View of Sentencing], 29(6) Jiyuu to Seigi [Liberty and Justice] 41 (1978).
25. Masayuki Kawaai, Hikokunin no Hansei Taido nado to Ryoukei [The Role of Defendants' Remorse in Sentencing], 1268 Hanrei Times 43 (2008).
26. Masayuki Kawaai, Hikokunin no Hansei Taido nado to Ryoukei [The Role of Defendants' Remorse in Sentencing], 1268 Hanrei Times 43 (2008).
27. Tsuguo Fujimaki, Koutsuu Jiko to Shazai [Automobile Accidents and Apologies], 53(7) Jiyuu to Seigi [Liberty and Justice] 11, 13 (2002). That sentiment is also generally consistent with the social psychology literature that suggests that people in Japan are more likely to prefer mitigating accounts, such as apologies or excuses, than Americans, who prefer assertive accounts such as justifications. Ritsu Itoi, Ken-Ichi Ohbuchi, and Mitsuteru Fukuno, A Cross-Cultural Study of Preference of Accounts: Relationship Closeness, Harm Severity, and Motives of Account Making, 26(10) Journal of Applied Social Psychology, 913 (1996); see also Mitsuteru Fukuno and Ken-ichi Ohbuchi, How Effective Are Different Accounts of Harm-Doing in Softening Victims' Reactions? A Scenario Investigation of the Effects of Severity, Relationship, and Culture, 1 Asian Journal of Social Psychology 167 (1998); V. Lee Hamilton and Joseph Sanders, Everyday Justice: Responsibility and the Individual in Japan and the United States 181 (1992).
28. See William Ian Miller, Faking It, 83–90 (2003).
29. See, e.g., Tokyo High Court, 1062 Hanrei Jihou 30, Oct. 29, 1982.
30. Norio Munakata, Kensatukan kara Mita Joujou to Ryoukei [A Prosecutor's View of Sentencing], 29(6) Jiyuu to Seigi [Liberty and Justice] 41 (1978).
31. David T. Johnson, The Japanese Way of Justice: Prosecuting Crime in Japan 209 (2002).
32. Kunio Harada, Ryoukei Handan no Jissai [The Practice of Sentencing in Japan] 369 (3rd ed. 2008).
33. Some judges seem to strain to find any redeeming factor in the defendant that can help them bring his sentence to the usual proportion of the prosecutor's request. In a 2010 case of arson while under the influence, for instance, the court issued a three-year sentence when prosecutors had requested four based in part on the fact that the defendant showed remorse in the following minimalist manner: He said "sorry" (*sumimasen deshita*) upon his arrest and elaborated a bit more in the courtroom with "I would like to apologize to everyone" (*minasan ni moushiwakenai koto o shite, sumimasen*). Oita District Court, Heisei 21 (wa) 107, Aug. 2, 2010.
34. Osaka District Court, Heisei 22 (wa) 113, July 2, 2010.
35. Kanazawa District Court, Heisei 27 (wa) 18, Nov. 27, 2015.
36. Nagoya District Court, Heisei 28 (wa) 333, Mar. 8, 2017.
37. See, e.g., Nagoya District Court, Heisei 27 (wa) 161, May 11, 2017 (also Pokemon Go on smartphone); Sapporo High Court, 1100 Hanrei Jihou 111, Dec. 8, 2015 (smartphone plus intoxication).
38. See, e.g., Osaka District Court, Heisei 28 (wa) 1981, Sept. 1, 2016 (drugs, citing family, oath, lack of criminal history).

39. See, e.g., Yokohama District Court, Heisei 26 (wa) 1872, June 9, 2016 (running a red light, citing lack of priors and remorse).
40. See, e.g., Yokohama District Court, Heisei 27 (wa) 313, June 23, 2015 (wrong pedals, citing payment to victim, lack of priors, promise of support of family).
41. Jidousha no Unten ni yori Hito o Shishou saseru Koui tou no Shobatsu ni kansuru Houritsu [Act on Punishment of Acts Inflicting Injury or Death by Driving a Vehicle], Law no. 86 of 2013.
42. Some particular kinds of cases are more patterned. In capital punishment cases, for instance, there are strong correlations between the number of people a defendant kills and whether he will be put to death: The chances of receiving the death penalty for a defendant who has killed one person are 4 percent; two people, 54 percent; three people, 76 percent. J. Mark Ramseyer, Who Hangs Whom for What? The Death Penalty in Japan, 4 Journal of Legal Analysis 365 (2012). But in death penalty cases, Supreme Court precedent requires that courts look at the body count, and there are no such rigid factors in the alcohol-related cases here. Japan v. Shonen N, Supreme Court, 37(6) Keishuu 609, July 8, 1983 (imposition of the death penalty requires an examination of the defendant's motivations, the heinous nature of the crime, the number of victims, the pain felt by the victims' families, the influence on society, and the defendant's age, criminal history, and actions after the crime).
43. Tokyo District Court, 1119 Hanrei Times 272, Nov. 20, 2002.
44. Tokyo District Court, 2015 Hanrei Jihou 158, July 16, 2008.
45. Sendai District Court, Heisei 17 (wa) 362, Jan. 23, 2006.
46. Sendai High Court, Heisei 23 (u) 122, Nov. 15, 2011.
47. Some courts state that they are relying not only on family members but on society itself to rehabilitate the defendant. See, e.g., Tokyo District Court, Heisei 14 (kei wa) 187, Mar. 28, 2002.
48. See, e.g., John O. Haley, Apology and Pardon: Learning from Japan, in Amitai Etzioni ed., Civic Repentance 117 (1999); David T. Johnson, The Japanese Way of Justice: Prosecuting Crime in Japan 179–213 (2002).
49. Ikumi Inoue, Juunenme no Uttae [Ten-Year Lawsuit] 110–15 (2009).
50. Kunio Harada, Ryoukei Handan no Jissai [The Practice of Sentencing in Japan] 37 (3rd ed. 2008); Masaaki Yoneyama, Hikokunin no Zokusei to Ryoukei [Attributes of the Defendant and Sentencing], in Ousaka Keiji Kitsumu Kenkyuukai ed., 3 Ryoukei Jitsumu Taikei [A Treatise on Sentencing Law and Practice] 79, 129 (2011).
51. Amy Beth Borovoy, The Too-Good Wife: Alcohol, Codependency, and the Politics of Nurturance in Postwar Japan 58–59 (2005).
52. Tokyo District Court, 1039 Roudou Hanrei 90, May 10, 2011.
53. See, e.g., Osaka District Court, 2006 (wa) 1261, Aug. 15, 2006; Tokyo District Court, Heisei 13 (wa) 2983, Feb. 26, 2002.
54. Nara District Court, Heisei 22 (wa) 142, Dec. 13, 2010.
55. See Naomi Sugawara, Arukooru Izon to DV ga Haikei ni aru Boukou Jiken [Alcoholism and Domestic Violence as Background in a Case of Violence] in Makoto Ibusuki ed., Chiryouteki Shihou no Jisseki [The Practice of Therapeutic Justice] 173 (2018).
56. Kobe District Court, Heisei 15 (wa) 96, Apr. 15, 2003.
57. Kagoshima District Court, Heisei 21 (wa) 247, Dec. 17, 2009.
58. Fukuoka District Court Kokura Branch, Heisei 21 (wa) 163, June 2, 2009.
59. See, e.g., Osaka District Court, 1790 Hanrei Jihou 159, July 8, 2002.
60. See, e.g., Miyazaki District Court, Heisei 24 (wa) 140, Mar. 26, 2014.
61. Osaka District Court, Heisei 20 (wa) 1224, Aug. 21, 2009.
62. Osaka District Court, Heisei 18 (wa) 3913, Sept. 12, 2006.
63. Tokyo High Court, 182 Hanrei Jihou 153, Apr. 22, 2002.
64. Utsunomiya District Court, Heisei 15 (wa) 233, July 23, 2003.
65. Yokohama District Court, Heisei 13 (wa) 2107, Nov. 7, 2001.
66. Amy Beth Borovoy, The Too-Good Wife: Alcohol, Codependency, and the Politics of Nurturance in Postwar Japan 58–59 (2005).
67. Amy Beth Borovoy, The Too-Good Wife: Alcohol, Codependency, and the Politics of Nurturance in Postwar Japan 59 (2005) (quoting Stephen Richard Smith, Drinking and Sobriety in Japan, Ph.D. Dissertation, Columbia University (1988)).

68. Amy Beth Borovoy, The Too-Good Wife: Alcohol, Codependency, and the Politics of Nurturance in Postwar Japan 50 (2005).
69. Utsunomiya District Court, Heisei 21 (wa) 2, Mar. 3, 2009.
70. Fukuoka District Court Kokura Branch, Heisei 21 (wa) 163, June 2, 2009.
71. Kyoto District Court, Heisei 26 (wa) 859, Mar. 27, 2015.
72. See Kyoto District Court, Heisei 25 (wa) 1317, Sept. 19, 2014.
73. See, e.g., Kyoto District Court, Heisei 25 (2a) 1428, Sept. 19, 2014; Osaka District Court, Heisei 22 (wa) 113, July 2, 2010.
74. Aomori District Court, Heisei 18 (wa) 123, Sept. 25, 2006.
75. Takamatsu District Court, Heisei 23 (wa) 314, Jan. 19, 2012.
76. See Hannah Maslen and Julian V. Roberts, Remorse and Sentencing: An Analysis of Sentencing Guidelines and Sentencing Practice, in Andrew Ashworth and Julian V. Roberts eds., Sentencing Guidelines: Exploring the English Mode 122–39 (2013).
77. United States Sentencing Guidelines section 3E1.1. See also Scott E. Sundby, The Capital Jury and Absolution: The Intersection of Trial Strategy, Remorse, and the Death Penalty, 83 Cornell Law Review 1557 (1998) (role of remorse in death-penalty cases).
78. See, e.g., Lolly Bowean and Steve Schmadeke, Judge Scolds Cop Accused of Fatal DUI Crash, Chicago Tribune, Dec. 23, 2009, available at https://www.chicagotribune.com/news/ct-xpm-2009-12-23-0912220475-story.html.
79. See, e.g., Jennifer Earl, Judge Throws Drunk Driver's Mom in Jail for Laughing at Victim's Family in Court, CBS News, Feb. 28, 2017, available at https://www.cbsnews.com/news/judge-throws-drunk-drivers-mom-in-jail-for-laughing-at-victims-family-in-court/.

Chapter 7

1. The high-profile cases amplified an existing trend toward social recognition. See, e.g., Tokyo District Court, Heisei 14 (kei wa) 187, Mar, 28, 2002 ("lately, the cries from society against injuries and deaths from drunk driving have increased").
2. See John Owen Haley, The Spirit of Japanese Law 157 (1998).
3. See, e.g., Graham v. Florida, 130 S. Ct. 2011 (2010); Roper v. Simmons, 543 U.S. 551 (2005).
4. Fukuoka District Court, 1268 Hanrei Times 330, Jan. 8, 2008.
5. Fukuoka High Court, 1323 Hanrei Times 65, May 15, 2009. When considering the impact that a crime has on society, an Osaka judge writes that the factor must be noted, but that one can't place too much emphasis on factors such as the celebrity of the defendant or the publicity of gossip magazines, as those factors do not address the severity of the crime. Kazuo Mizushima, Hanzai no Shakaiteki Eikyou to Ryoukei [The Influence of a Crime on Society in Sentencing], 1206 Hanrei Times 28 (2006).
6. Fukushima District Court, Heisei 6 (gyou u) 2, Feb. 16, 1998, *aff'd*, Sendai High Court, Heisei 10 (gyou u) 6, Mar. 30, 2003.
7. Urawa District Court, Heisei 9 (gyou u) 4, June 9, 1997, *aff'd*, Tokyo High Court, Heisei 9 (gyou u) 85, Feb. 19, 1997, *aff'd*, Supreme Court, Heisei 10 (gyou tsu) 74, July 16, 1998.
8. Yokohama District Court, 672 Hanrei Times 139, Mar. 9, 1988.
9. Tokyo High Court, Heisei 8 (gyou ko) 19, Jan. 30, 1997.
10. See, e.g., Tokyo High Court, 289 Hanrei Times 387, Sept. 27, 1972; Tokyo High Court, Shouwa 50 (u) 1092, Dec. 23, 1976.
11. Keiko Kato, Necktie-Alcoholics: Cultural Forces and Japanese Alcoholism, Master's Thesis, Washington State University (2000), available at https://research.libraries.wsu.edu/xmlui/handle/2376/38.
12. Miseinensha Inshu Kinshihou [Law Prohibiting Minors from Drinking], Law no. 20 of 1922.
13. Takahiro Aoki, Kindai Nihon no Kinshu Undou to Kinshuhouan kara mita Girei no naka no Sake [Ritual Sake as Seen in Prohibition Movements and the Prohibition Bill in Modern Japan], 205 (3) Kokuritsu Rekishi Minzoku Hakubutsukan Kenkyuu Houkoku [Bulletin of the Natural Museum of Japanese History] 7 (2017), available at https://www.rekihaku.ac.jp/outline/publication/ronbun/ronbun9/pdf/205001.pdf.
14. Susumu Higuchi et al., Japan: Alcohol Today, 102 Addiction 1849, 1853 (2007); see also Susumu Higuchi et al., Young People's Drinking Behavior in Japan, International Center for

Alcohol Policies Symposium on Young People's Drinking, 2004, available at http://www.icap.org/LinkClick.aspx?fileticket=tMW8of1JAgU%3D&tabid=199 (reporting that 70 percent drink).

15. In 2011, 63.5 percent of U.S. high school seniors had consumed alcohol in the past year, and 2.1 percent reported daily use. Lloyd D. Johnston et al., Monitoring the Future Study, University of Michigan (2011), available at http://monitoringthefuture.org/pubs/monographs/mtf-overview2011.pdf.
16. Utsunomiya Family Court, Heisei 15 (shou i) 1, Sept. 30, 2004.
17. The minimum income level reportedly can be lowered based on other factors that reflect income stability. See Purachina Kaado [Platinum Card], Heikin Nenshuu, www.heikinnenshu.jp/tokushu/pratinum.html; Amekkusu Purachina no Nenshuu wa? [What Is the Minimum Annual Income for an American Express Platinum Card?], Money Press, June 21, 2019, www.mone-press.info/amex-platinum-annual-income-/.
18. Kyoto District Court, 2199 Hanrei Jihou 52, May 23, 2013.
19. Kokka Koumuin Hou, Law No. 120 of 1947, art. 82; Chihou Koumuin Hou, Law No. 261 of 1950, art. 29.
20. Zadankai [Roundtable], Joujou to Keiryou [Circumstances and Sentencing], 29(6) Jiyuu to Seigi [Freedom and Justice] 49, 59–60 (1978) (statement of Inoue Kenjirou).
21. See, e.g., Ministry of Internal Affairs and Communications, Choukai Shobun Shasuu Oyobi Bungen Shobun Shasuu ni Tsuite [Regarding the Number of Disciplinary Actions and Partial Actions], available at http://www.soumu.go.jp/main_content/000608363.pdf.
22. See, e.g., Sendai District Court, Roudou Hanrei 12, Dec. 24, 2008.
23. Jinjiin [National Personnel Authority], Choukai Shobun no Shishin ni Tsuite [Guidelines for Disciplinary Action], Mar. 31, 2000, as amended Feb. 27, 2015, available at http://www.jinji.go.jp/kisoku/tsuuchi/12_choukai/1202000_H12shokushoku68.htm.
24. See, e.g., Eric C. Sibbitt, Recent Development: Regulating Gambling in the Shadow of the Law: Form and Substance in the Regulation of Japan's Pachinko Industry, 38 Harvard International Law Journal. 568 (1997).
25. Katsuhiro Oono, Keisatsukan no Inshu Joutai ni kansuru Kenkyuu [Police Drinking Patterns], 30(3) Arukooru Kenkyuu to Yakubutsu Izon [Alcohol Studies and Drug Dependence] 97 (1995).
26. Fukuoka District Court, 732 Roudou Hanrei 58, Dec. 24, 1997.
27. Supreme Court, 357 Hanrei Times 142, Dec. 20, 1977.
28. Onomimono [Beverages], Japan Airlines, https://www.jal.co.jp/inter/service/economy/meal/beverages.html (Japanese); Beverages, Japan Airlines, http://www.jal.co.jp/en/inter/service/economy/meal/beverages.html (English).
29. Tokyo District Court, 2196 Hanrei Jihou 132, Mar. 26, 2013.
30. Tokyo High Court, 2196 Hanrei Jihou 129, July 13, 2013.
31. See, e.g., Fukuoka High Court Naha Branch, 2015 (u) 55, Aug. 16, 2016 (defendant consumes five drinks, sleeps seven hours in his car, has an accident, and is found guilty of DUI); Sapporo High Court, 1100 Hanrei Jihou 111, Dec. 8, 2015 (defendant consumes roughly ten drinks over the course of seven and a half hours, court dismisses argument that he was "fatigued, still had symptoms of a hangover, and was waking up, so his level of intoxication just before driving was low").
32. Tokyo High Court, Heisei 24 (u) 248, May 14, 2012.
33. Tokyo High Court, 1325 Hanrei Times 60, Dec. 17, 2009; Tokyo District Court, Heisei 21 (gou wa) 199, Aug. 6, 2009; Osaka District Court, Heisei 17 (wa) 3529, Mar. 24, 2008; Yokohama District Court, 1691 Hanrei Jihou 158, Oct. 6, 1999; Nagasaki District Court, 4 (3) Keiji Hanrei Geppou 530, Mar. 10, 1962.
34. Kobe District Court, Heisei 20 (gyou u) 25, Nov. 26, 2008, *aff'd*, Osaka High Court, Heisei 21 (gyou u) 4, Apr. 24, 2009.
35. See, e.g., Takamatsu High Court, Heisei 27 (gyou ko) 15, Mar. 25, 2016.
36. See, e.g., Ministry of Education, Choukai Shobun ni Kansuru Shobun Kijun no Naiyou [Contents of Regulations concerning Discipline], Apr. 1, 2018, available at http://www.mext.go.jp/component/a_menu/education/detail/__icsFiles/afieldfile/2018/12/25/1411825_10.pdf; Tottori District Court, Heisei 28 (gyou u) 4, Jan. 20, 2017.

37. See Jinjiin, Choukai Shobun no Shishin ni Tsuite [Concerning Guidelines of Disciplinary Action], Sept. 7, 2018 revision, available at https://www.jinji.go.jp/kisoku/tsuuchi/12_choukai/1202000_H12shokushoku68.html.
38. Kochi District Court, 1029 Roudou Hanrei 13, Sept. 21, 2010.
39. Takamatsu High Court, 1352 Hanrei Times 13, May 10, 2011.
40. Sendai District Court, Heisei 22 (gyou u) 22, Oct. 27, 2011.
41. See also Nara District Court, 2009 (u) 20, Jan. 13, 2011 (dismissal of middle school principal appropriate when he was arrested for drunk driving after returning from golf outing; court noted that (a) taking alcohol from one's home to the course was an acknowledgment of the possibility of drunk driving and (b) he used a vacation day to golf on the anniversary of the school's founding).
42. See Mark D. West, Law in Everyday Japan: Sex, Sumo, Suicide, and Statutes 9–56 (2005).
43. See Petition to Nagano District Court Civil Division, Nagano Chuo Law Firm, http://nclo.gr.jp/cms/wp-content/uploads/2011/05/20110511121312.pdf.
44. See television news screenshots posted at Aabe blog entry, May 29, 2013, https://ameblo.jp/aabe/entry-11540579133.html.
45. Nagano District Court, 2205 Hanrei Jihou 129, Nov. 30, 2012.
46. Tokyo High Court, 2205 Hanrei Jihou 125, May 29, 2013.
47. Nishin mo "Shobun Omosugi" Inshu Yokujitsu no Shukiobi Unten de Menshoku [Again on Appeal, Court Finds Termination after Next-Day Drunk Driving Penalty "Too Heavy"], Nihon Keizai Shinbun, May 29, 2013, available at https://www.nikkei.com/article/DGXNASDG29048_Z20C13A5CR8000/.
48. Kyoto District Court, 1374 Hanrei Times 148, Feb. 23, 2012.
49. See Amy Beth Borovoy, The Too-Good Wife: Alcohol, Codependency, and the Politics of Nurturance in Postwar Japan (2005).
50. Mark D. West, Lovesick Japan: Sex, Marriage, Romance, Law 180–86 (2011).
51. Supreme Court, 6(2) Minshuu 110, Feb. 19, 1952.
52. Saikousai Jimusoukyoku, Shihou Toukei Nenpou, Kaji Hen [Annual Report of Judicial Statistics, Family Cases] 36–7 (2019).
53. Yopparai Otto [Drunk Husband], Yomiuri Hatsugen Komachi, Jan. 10, 2014, available at http://komachi.yomiuri.co.jp/t/2014/0110/637580.htm.
54. Otto no Sakeguse to Watashi e no Kanjou ni Tsuite Nayndemasu [I'm Worried about My Husband's Drinking and His Feelings toward Me], Yomiuri Hatsugen Komachi, Jan. 17, 2019, available at https://komachi.yomiuri.co.jp/t/2019/0117/832883.htm.
55. Sonna ni Dame Shufu Desuka? [Am I Such a Bad Wife?], Yomiuri Hatsugen Komachi, Dec. 12, 2014, available at http://komachi.yomiuri.co.jp/t/2014/1212/692895.htm.
56. See, e.g., Tokyo District Court, 105 Hanrei Times 215, Sept. 26, 2000 ("it is truly unfortunate that these litigants, an older married couple, desire a divorce").
57. See, e.g., Nagoya District Court, 1409 Hanrei Jihou 97, Sept. 20, 1991.
58. Tokyo High Court, 1060 Hanrei Times 240, Jan. 18, 2001.
59. For instance, Shiga Naoya's short story "Han's Crime" puts the following words into the testimony of a witness to homicide: "he doesn't gamble or chase after women or drink" (*tobaku mo onna asobi mo inshu mo*). Naoya Shiga, Gendai Nihon Bungaku Taikei [Modern Japanese Literature] 220, 221 (Vol. 34, 1968).
60. Tokyo District Court, Heisei 14 (ta) 752, Dec. 25, 2003.
61. Tokyo District Court, Heisei 13 (ta) 776, Mar. 15, 2004.
62. Tokyo District Court, Heisei 14 (ta) 613, Nov. 11, 2005.
63. Keiou Puraza Hoteru no Kekkonshiki Hiyou, Mitsumori Kingaku [Keio Plaza Hotel: Estimated Wedding Costs], Minna no Uedeingu [Weddings for Everyone], available at https://www.mwed.jp/hall/10288/cost/. Conrad Tokyo and Grand Hyatt Tokyo figures available on same site at https://www.mwed.jp/hall/11289/cost/1044577/ and https://www.mwed.jp/hall/11281/cost/.
64. "Kekkonshiki no Hiyou" Mitsumori, Souba kara Okane no Setsuyaku Pointo Matome ["Wedding Expense" Estimates and Tips on How to Pay a Below-Market Price], July 3, 2019, Minna no Uedeingu [Weddings for Everyone] available at https://www.mwed.jp/articles/7017/.

65. Keiou Puraza Hoteru no Kekkonshiki Hiyou, Mitsumori Kingaku [Keio Plaza Hotel: Estimated Wedding Costs], Minna no Uedeingu [Weddings for Everyone], available at https://www.mwed.jp/hall/10288/cost/.
66. Tokyo District Court, Heisei 13 (ta) 316, Nov. 11, 2002. See also Tokyo District Court, Heisei 15 (ta) 860, Apr. 28, 2004 (husband's drinking combined with violence and psychological abuse are sufficient for divorce).
67. One court cited a drunk-driving conviction as evidence of "grave reason," but the case contained the additional element of domestic violence. Tokyo District Court, Heisei 16 (ta) 7, June 24, 2004.
68. Sometimes plaintiffs do not challenge such statements even in relevant litigation. For instance, a politician brought a successful defamation suit against a publisher after its tabloid published photographs of him with his mistress. The accompanying article said that he missed a meeting because he was "sloppily drunk" (*berobero ni youtteita*). The plaintiff did not challenge the statement, and it is not clear if he did not because he actually was drunk or if he did not think that the statement defamed him. Hiroshima District Court, 1203 Hanrei Times 356, Dec. 21, 2004.
69. A litany of cases defines more precisely how these provisions operate, but two basic principles guide. First, there is a truth defense, but only for matters of public concern. Supreme Court, 20(5) Minshuu 1118, June 23, 1966. There is no truth defense for matters of private concern. Second, if the subject matter of the defamatory statement is of public concern, the truth defense is met if defendants can show that they have a reasonable belief, even if mistaken, that the statements were true. Supreme Court, 23 Keishuu 7, June 25, 1969. Private behavior can be of public concern depending on the "character of a person's social activity and their level of influence on society through such activity." Supreme Court, 1000 Hanrei Jihou 25, Apr. 16, 1981.
70. Supreme Court, 1845 Hanrei Jihou 26, 32, Oct. 16, 2003.
71. Fujito v. Yomiuri Shinbun, Supreme Court, 20(5) Minshuu 1118, June 23, 1966. I discuss the law more extensively in Mark D. West, Secrets, Sex, and Spectacle: The Rules of Scandal in Japan and the United States 70–113 (2006).
72. Josei 90% "Yopparatta Dansei wa Suki de wa nai" to Kaitou [90 percent of Women Answer "I Don't Like Drunk Men], Mainabi News, May 5, 2015, available at http://news.mynavi.jp/news/2015/05/05/055/.
73. Josei ga Yurusanai "Yopparai" Rankingu! [Women Rank Unforgivable Drunks], Mainabi Woman, Jan. 13, 2017, available at https://woman.mynavi.jp/article/170113-35/.
74. Konna Onna wa Kirawareru? Miteite Minikui "Josei no Yopparaikata" 4sen [This Kind of Woman Is Disliked? This Is Ugly: Four Kinds of Drunk Women], Mainabi Woman, Aug. 3, 2016, available at https://woman.mynavi.jp/article/160803-50/.
75. Konna Yopparai Onna wa Iyada! Dansei 100nin ga Souguu Shita Donbiki "Deisui Onna" [This Kind of Drunk Woman Is the Worst! Turnoff "Dead Drunk Women" Encountered by 100 Men], Kurashinisita, Aug. 5, 2006, available at https://kurashinista.jp/column/detail/2275.
76. Honki ni Suru Baka o Miru "Yopparai Onna" no Omowaseburina Taido 9 Pataan [Nine Patterns of "Drunk Women" That Make Them Look Stupid], Sugoren, Mar. 11, 2016, available at http://www.sugoren.com/report/1409986253986/.
77. Dansei ga Kawaii to Omou Yopparai Josei and Donbiki Saseru Onna 10sen [The 10 Behaviors of Drunk Women That Men Find Cute and That Turn Them Off], Blair, Jan. 21, 2017, available at https://blair.jp/170121-yopparai-onna.
78. Tokyo District Court, Heisei 17 (wa) 12818, July 28, 2006.
79. Nine years later Hirosue played a character in a film who became dead drunk, or at least intoxicated enough to pass out in a taxi after drinking too much wine. Owatta Hito [Life in Overtime] (2015).
80. Masatomo Yamasaki, "Gekkan Pen" Jiken Umoreteita Shinjitsu [The Truth behind the Gekkan Pen Incident] 81–2 (2001).
81. Tokyo District Court, Heisei 15 (wa) 25953, Jan. 23, 2006.
82. See, e.g., Osaka High Court, 2004 Hanrei Jihou 83, Dec. 26, 2007.

Chapter 8

1. Kirchoff v. Abbey, 2011 U.S. Dist. LEXIS 114838 (D. Md. Oct. 5, 2011).
2. Sugina v. McDonald, 2012 U.S. Dist. LEXIS 34430 (E.D. Ca. 2012).
3. Heisei 26 (wa) 3420, Osaka District Court, Mar. 28, 2016.
4. Heisei 22 (wa) 16472, Tokyo District Court, June 29, 2011.
5. See, e.g., Michel Piccaya's Watch the Gap photograph, Stock Photo ID 322686173, available at https://www.shutterstock.com/image-photo/tokyo-japan-january-1-watch-gap-322686173.
6. See Fumikiri, Hoomu Sharyou no Anzen Taisaku [Crossing, Platform, and Train Safety Measures], JR-West, available at http://www.westjr.co.jp/safety/action/measures/; see also Hoomu no Benchi, Heikou kara Chokkaku e, Suikaku to Tenraku Boushi [Platform Benches Shifted from Parallel to Perpendicular to Keep Drunk Passengers from Falling], Tokyo Shinbun, Apr. 3, 2019, available at https://www.tokyo-np.co.jp/article/national/list/201904/CK2019040302000286.html.
7. See Kokudou Koutsuushou, Dai 7kai Eki Hoomu ni Okeru Anzensei Koujou no Tame no Kentoukai Shiryou 1, Eki Hoomu kara no Tenraku ni Kansuru Joukyou [Status of Station Platform Falls, Exhibit 1, Seventh Meeting of the Committee to Investigate the Improvement of Station Platform Safety], July 25, 2017, available at http://www.mlit.go.jp/common/001195206.pdf.
8. See Kenji Kawamoto, Yopparai Tengoku (Drunkards' Heaven), photography series, available at https://www.lensculture.com/articles/kenji-kawamoto-yopparai-tengoku-drunkards-heaven.
9. Full-height barriers are nearly 100 percent effective at preventing such incidents, and less expensive half-height barriers eliminate death-by-fall accidents and suicides by 76 percent. Michiko Ueda, Yasuyuki Sawada, and Tetsuya Matsubayashi, The Effectiveness of Installing Physical Barriers for Preventing Railway Suicides and Accidents: Evidence from Japan, 178 Journal of Affective Disorders 1 (June 2015).
10. Such incidents are legally defined as accidents resulting in human injury or death by train or train car operation. See Tetsudou Jiko tou Houkoku Kisoku [Rules regarding Announcements of Railroad Incidents], Unyushou [Transport Ministry], Regulation 8 of 1987.
11. See, e.g., Mamoru Sakamoto, Shashou Maruura Joumu Techou [Undercover Conductor's Handbook] 147 (1998).
12. Yuuichi Satou, Tetsudou Jishin Jiko De-ta Bukku 2002–2009 [Data Book on Railway Accidents] (2011); see also Tetsudou Jinshin Jiko Mappu [Railway Accident Map], available at http://kishadan.com/map/railway-human-accidents/ (interactive map of accidents since 2005 created by Satou).
13. Kokodokoutsuushou, Testsukidou Yusou no Anzen ni Kakawaru Jouhou [Information regarding the Safety of Rail Transportation] 11, n.8 (July 2018), available at http://www.mlit.go.jp/common/001246059.pdf.
14. Masao Ichikawa, Haruhiko Inada, and Minae Kumeji, Reconsidering the Effects of Blue-Light Installation for Prevention of Railway Suicides, 152–54 Journal of Affective Disorders 183 (2014).
15. See, e.g., Yuuichi Satou, Hatsu Koukai "Tetsudou Jisatsu" ga Ooi Rosen Rankingu [First Time Made Public: Ranking of Rail Lines Based on "Railroad Suicide," Touyou Keizai, June 1, 2016, available at http://toyokeizai.net/articles/-/120456; Yuuichi Satou, Tetsdou no Jinji Jiko, Kantou de Zouka, Nenkan 600ken de Mainichi Hitori Ijou ga Jisatsu [Railway Human Accidents Increase in the Kanto Region, over 600 per Year, More Than One Person per Day Commits Suicide], Business Journal, Dec. 13, 2013, available at http://biz-journal.jp/2013/12/post_3598.html.
16. See, e.g., Alisa Freedman, Tokyo in Transit: Japanese Culture on the Rails and Road 108 (2011).
17. Emma G. Fitzsimmons, Yet Another Worrisome Statistic: More People Are Going on the Tracks, New York Times, Sept. 17, 2018, available at https://www.nytimes.com/2018/09/17/nyregion/nyc-subway-tracks-delays.html. Statistics for London's sprawling Tube also pale in comparison to the Japanese figures, with 644 attempts in the entire decade between 2000 and 2010, and roughly 70 in each of fiscal years 2018 and 2019. Tom Batchelor, Suicide Attempts on Tube Fall for First Time in Five Years as TfL Staff Interventions Double,

Independent, Mar. 1, 2019, available at https://www.independent.co.uk/news/uk/home-news/suicide-tube-london-underground-tfl-samaritans-a8801566.html.

18. See "Tetsudou Jisatsu:" Izoku Keiken Katari Ikinaosu ["Railroad Suicide": Reviving the Survivor Narrative], Tokyo Shinbun, Jan. 20, 2019 (evening edition), available at https://www.tokyo-np.co.jp/article/national/list/201901/CK2019012002000116.html.
19. Yuuichi Satou, Tetsudou Jishin Jiko De-ta Bukku 2002-2009 [Data Book on Railway Accidents] 74, 92 (2011); see also Naoki Morimoto, Misetchi no Sekinin: Tetsudougawa no Shuchou Shihou mo Tsuinin [Responsibility Not Established: Court Sides with Railway], Kobe Shinbun, Oct. 2, 2016, available at https://www.kobe-np.co.jp/rentoku/rensai/09/201610/0009549257.shtml# (media coverage in series on platform doors).
20. Osaka District Court, Heisei 22 (wa) 6406, Jan. 11, 2012.
21. Daniel H. Foote, Namonai Kaomonai Shihou [Nameless, Faceless Justice] (2007).
22. J. Mark Ramseyer, Second-Best Justice: The Virtues of Japanese Private Law 9 (2015).

INDEX

For the benefit of digital users, indexed terms that span two pages (e.g., 52–53) may, on occasion, appear on only one of those pages.